School of American Research
Advanced Seminar Series

DOUGLAS W. SCHWARTZ, GENERAL EDITOR

SCHOOL OF AMERICAN RESEARCH
ADVANCED SEMINAR SERIES

Reconstructing Prehistoric Pueblo Societies
EDITED BY WILLIAM LONGACRE

New Perspectives on the Pueblos
EDITED BY ALFONSO ORTIZ

Structure and Process in Latin America
EDITED BY ARNOLD STRICKON AND SIDNEY M. GREENFIELD

The Classic Maya Collapse
EDITED BY T. PATRICK CULBERT

Methods and Theories of Anthropological Genetics
EDITED BY M. H. CRAWFORD AND P. L. WORKMAN

Sixteenth-Century Mexico
EDITED BY MUNRO S. EDMONSON

Sixteenth-Century Mexico

SIXTEENTH-CENTURY MEXICO

The Work of Sahagún

EDITED BY

MUNRO S. EDMONSON

A SCHOOL OF AMERICAN RESEARCH BOOK

UNIVERSITY OF NEW MEXICO PRESS · Albuquerque

To Father Ángel María Garibay Kintana (*1892–1967*) and Doctor Howard Francis Cline (*1915–71*), whose forceful presence in all discussions of the things of New Spain not even time can stay.

Acknowledgments

The editor wishes to acknowledge his personal appreciation and that of the participants in the seminar that led to this volume for the initiative, hospitality, and support of the staff of the School of American Research, and particularly its director, Dr. Douglas W. Schwartz. Without them there would have been no seminar and no report on it. Specific gratitude is also due to Dr. Miguel León-Portilla, whose participation and assistance at every stage of the project have been unstinting and enthusiastic, and constitute also a *sine qua non*. I am grateful to Miss Jane M. Dabdoub for her help in translating the Spanish papers of the seminar for English publication, and to my wife, Barbara, and my daughter, Sallie, for substantial assistance with proofreading and the composition of the index. Finally, I am deeply indebted to a fine group of colleagues for transforming an exigent task into a personally and professionally rewarding experience.

Munro S. Edmonson

Foreword

The Aztecs have been called the Romans of the New World. Whether they or the Inca best deserve this title is difficult to determine. It is true that a knowledge of their political system, religious beliefs, economic base, and cultural history is central to any understanding of the dynamics that shaped the Western Hemisphere in the early sixteenth century.

An opportunity to study Aztec culture more extensively than perhaps any other "aboriginal" society came through the genius and enduring labors of one man—Fray Bernardino de Sahagún. At the age of thirty, this Franciscan priest came to the New World from Spain; he spent his entire life in missionary work in and around Mexico City. But his was a special kind of church-related activity, based on the assumption that only through detailed understanding of Aztec culture and religion could effective conversion to the Christian faith take place. Assisted by a group of Aztecs trained to write their language in Latin letters, and by artists and copy assistants who were able to interpret and expand on Aztec pictures, Sahagún produced his *General History of the Things of New Spain*. It was written in Nahuatl, the Aztec language, and in Spanish.

Over a span of thirty-five years, the School of American Research and the University of Utah have worked with the translators and interpreters of Sahagún's work, Arthur J. O. Anderson and Charles Dibble, in order to publish the twelve volumes of Sahagún's *General History*. It was only fitting, therefore, that the school, as part of its Advanced Seminar Program in anthropology, bring together, under the astute chairmanship of Munro Edmonson, a group of scholars conversant with various aspects of Aztec studies. The purpose of the seminar was to take stock of what is now known of both Sahagún and the Aztec of the sixteenth century.

This volume, part of which will be published in Spanish by the Instituto de Investigaciones Sociales of the Universidad Nacional Autónoma de México, puts into contemporary perspective for scholars and individuals interested in the late prehistoric power of Central Mexico, the history, science, literature, and general culture of the Aztec, and the man, who, over four hundred years ago, made it possible for them to come to life today—Sahagún.

Douglas W. Schwartz

School of American Research

Contents

Contents

Figures

Tables

Plates

Introduction

MUNRO S. EDMONSON
Tulane University

Bernardino de Sahagún (c. 1499–1590) occupies a unique position in the history of Mexico and in the history of History. The Franciscan friar's lifelong dedication to the study of the Aztecs, their language and their thought, is almost without parallel in his own or any other time, and his *General History of the Things of New Spain* is a towering monument to the man and his times. It is altogether fitting that scholarly interest in his life and work continues to grow and expand, and it is a measure of his remarkable achievement that even a considerable group of contemporary scholars has been able to make only the most preliminary advances into the morass of riddles he left behind him.

Because of the substantial expansion of scholarly interest, it seems opportune to review the state of our knowledge of Sahagún and his work, and it was with this goal in mind that a small working seminar was formed under the auspices of the School of American Research in Santa Fe. The present volume is the report of that seminar, which met in Santa

Fe November 13–16, 1972. It is the hope of the participants that the report may be of immediate utility for the many scholars whose work touches the world of Sahagún, and further that it may facilitate the solution of a number of pressing problems confronting scholarship in this area.

Our report will deal first with the biography of Sahagún and the historiography of his work. We shall then treat interpretative and substantive questions: What more can we learn from Sahagún? Finally we shall consider the programmatic perspectives of this field of study, including problems of documentation and bibliography, to which we hope the appended bibliography may be a contribution.

We know distressingly little of the life of Sahagún, and most of that little cannot be separated from the evidence of his work itself. (See the García Icazbalceta biography [1954:327–87] drawn from Mendieta and other early sources, and the modern essays by Nicolau D'Olwer [1952, 1973].) Can we hope to know more? He was born in Sahagún in Leon (Mendieta 1945:1:663). The date of his birth (c. 1499) is known only approximately; it is arrived at by backdating from his own remark that he was over seventy in 1569–70 (Sahagún 1956:1:107; 1942:30, fol. 2v). His surname is said to have been Ribeira (Chavero 1877:7; 1948:7). He arrived in Mexico in 1529. Although many scholars have searched in Sahagún and elsewhere in Spain for records of his first thirty years, none have been found, and the archives of the Franciscan order have not been available to investigation. Further search may yet provide the documentation of his entering the order; perhaps the *probanza* certifying his descent, the *libro de profesión* recording his vows, the register of students at the University of Salamanca where he was educated (now lost), the lists of departures for the Indies. Without such documentation, even informed guesses—such as speculation that he may have come from a converso Jewish family—have no utility for appraising the preparation he brought to his work in the New World.

We are on solider ground when we examine the background of the Franciscan order, which was certainly the most important influence on Sahagún's life both before and after his arrival in Mexico. The utopian aims of the order are well documented (Phelan 1956) and surely go a long way towards explaining the distinctive character of the Franciscan missionary endeavor in New Spain. To what extent did Sahagún really participate in this ideology? The question recurs continually throughout his life and work, and we shall have occasion to return to it.

EARLY WORK, *1529–47*

From 1529 to 1547, Sahagún's missionary work was primarily linguistic. The question of his involvement in the purposes of his order and the closely related question of his growing awareness of Aztec culture could probably be greatly illuminated by the examination of his biblical translations and psalmody of this period. The 1540 "Sermonario" and "Santoral" in the Newberry Library at Chicago (Sahagún 1540a; 1540b) show more of Sahagún's own hand than any other documents we possess. The hard pressed scholarship of former generations has quite naturally opted for the more urgent and exotic problems of his later works, but the value of a close examination of these earlier documents could be very great indeed. In Chapter 2 of this book, "Sahagún in His Times," Arthur J. O. Anderson takes up the question of Sahagún's orientation to his work in broad perspective and suggests some answers to it.

Other possible documentation for this period may also exist in the *registros* of the Franciscan order, in viceregal correspondence, or in Sahagún's other projects, such as his translation for the courts. To understand the context of Sahagún's work it is particularly important to understand its relation (and his relation) to the work of other notable figures of his order who also contributed mightily to the comprehension of Mexican culture: Fray Andrés de Olmos, Fray Alonso de Molina and Fray Toribio de Benavente Motolinía. One wonders, in fact, whether a close study would reveal the nature and extent of Sahagún's reading and its relation to his work. The history of the College of Tlaltelolco from 1536 on would surely place in relevant context Sahagún's own orientation on the eve of the genesis of his celebrated *General History*. The archives of the school may yet exist, and there may well be other documentation. In short, the study of the Franciscan missionary effort in sixteenth-century Mexico is only just under way, and it promises many rewards.

A particularly important perspective on the life and work of Sahagún is provided by the parallel experiences and achievements of Fray Andrés de Olmos. Chapter 3, "The Ethnographic Works of Andrés de Olmos, by S. Jeffrey K. Wilkerson, not only documents this point but also sheds

3

a great deal of light on the process of formation of Sahagún's work. (Dr. Wilkerson was not present at the seminar in Santa Fe but his paper touches upon many of the important issues considered there, and its timeliness and relevance justify its inclusion in this volume.)

THE TLALTELOLCO DRAFTS, 1547–62

The *General History of the Things of New Spain* took shape between 1547 (the date of Book 6 on "Rhetoric and Moral Philosophy") and 1562. It was an enormous and highly complex enterprise, and it raises a host of questions. It seems doubtful that it was initially envisioned as a single work. In a measure, in fact, each of its books has its own history, and the textual exegesis to which the whole must eventually be subjected should parallel in intricacy the problems of the historical interpretation of the Old Testament. It is at this point, perhaps, that the question of Sahagún's purpose becomes most urgent—and most opaque.

The composition of the Nahuatl text of what became Book 6 dates to 1547. At the same time and for a number of years afterward other materials were being collected, copied, and arranged by Sahagún himself and by a number of Indian assistants; we cannot rule out the possibility that such work may have begun even earlier. This activity must have resulted in preliminary drafts and outlines of the later work, but we have no direct means of dating these. The order of composition is important for the light it could throw on the evolving conception of the final work, but it is also material to the question of how the work was done and to the interpretation we can put on it.

Perhaps the most startling innovation in Sahagún's mode of procedure was his rigorous and systematic use of informants. The result is the inclusion in the work of a wide range of materials corresponding to different interests and purposes, collected in different ways, and expressed in different styles. Parts of the text are made up of preconquest Nahuatl rhetoric—formal orations directly recorded from the still extant oral tradition. Other parts are clearly shaped by more or less explicit questionnaires designed to elicit specific information. Some passages are just as clearly spontaneous elaborations by informants, clarifying particular

4

points. Yet others reflect an explicit concern with collecting and preserving Nahuatl vocabulary. And finally there are passages of commentary and interpretation added by Sahagún himself.

Particularly interesting are the most traditional of these materials, the *huehuetlatolli* (speeches of the elders), which are already included in Book 6 by 1547. These fascinating texts are examined by Thelma D. Sullivan in Chapter 4, "The Rhetorical Orations, or *Huehuetlatolli,* Collected by Sahagún." It is worth emphasizing that these texts are very close to the pre-Spanish past. Informants who were Sahagún's own age or older in 1547 would have been fully adult participants in Aztec society when Cortés arrived, and the old men of 1547 would already have been middle-aged in 1521. It is clear, too, that Sahagún sought out older informants with these facts in mind.

The *huehuetlatolli* are not the only passages of the corpus that reveal a strongly aboriginal cast. A close structural, stylistic, and linguistic analysis of the whole text would be of enormous value in helping to order and interpret these materials and to place them in relation to the passages collected by other means and for other purposes. At the same time such a detailed examination of the text would be enormously facilitated by the collection and critical publication of the texts themselves—a serious problem to which we shall return.

It is clear that as early as 1547 Sahagún had initiated the systematic collection of an encyclopedic range of information on Aztec culture and society. Chapter 5 of this volume presents an illuminating study by Alfredo López Austin of the manner in which these materials were assembled: "The Research Methods of Fray Bernardino de Sahagún: the Questionnaires." Sahagún used a variety of informants, seeking out older people for traditional religious lore, females for herbal and medical information, *calpixqui* (mayordomos) or *tonalpouhque* (diviners) for esoteric data. It is noteworthy that his access to the priestly class was limited and that it was principally with the *pochteca* (merchant) class that his contacts were extensive and sustained.

After collecting substantial information over a period of years among the merchants in Tlaltelolco, Sahagún made a special trip to Tepepulco, a nonmerchant town, around 1558–61, to check the materials. The long period of what we have called the "formation" of the *General History* raises important questions about the sources and reliability of the information the *History* contains. Sahagún and his informants aged, and the intent of the whole enterprise may well have changed too, at least in some respects. The problem of reliability of the Nahuatl texts is furthermore compounded by the simultaneous employment of the artists who produced a parallel artistic text. The different ages and preparation of the artists and of the linguistic and ethnographic informants, and the varying dates of composition present tantalizing interpretative problems relating both to the trustworthiness of Sahagún's information and the developing intent of his work.

By the end of the "formative" period of Sahagún's great work, we have as evidence of nearly fifteen years of sustained and highly organized effort the manuscripts of working papers: the "Primeros Memoriales" (1560?) and the "Memoriales Complementarios" (1561?). These texts, together with Book 6 and as yet unidentified sections of the Nahuatl text and the illustrations, constitute our primary evidence as to Sahagún's motives, methods, and sources up to about 1562. These materials are all in Nahuatl or in pictures, and they may well include the largest amount of pre-Columbian matter of the later work in both media. We urgently need a careful study of the texts and pictures with particular reference to the chronology of their composition and their implications for Sahagún's intent. (It is a matter of some interest that one of the warmest discussions of our seminar concerned the distribution and significance of Sahagún's use of "etc." in his later Spanish text of the *History*, and what bearing it had on the Nahuatl text.)

Chapter 6, Donald Robertson's paper on "The Treatment of Architecture in the Florentine Codex of Sahagún," provides an illustrative introduction to the task of chronological analysis and raises questions of central importance to the aims of the pictures in particular and the *General History* as a whole. Not only are the pictures made by different hands and in different styles, but a comparison of parallel pictures and texts reveals a range of differing relationships between them. It is conceivable, in fact, that some of the pictures may be primary, a kind of continuation of the Aztec tradition of writing in pictures, with the Nahuatl text standing as an exegesis or commentary; in other cases the texts may have come first, the pictures being added in illustration or clarification. The question is an important one.

THE MADRID CODICES, *1562-75*

Around 1562, in any case, Sahagún's work entered a new phase, one of collation and organization on the one hand and of translation on the other. The first resulted in the manuscript of Tlaltelolco (1561–65?), only fragments of which survive, and the second in the "Three Column Memoriales" (1564?). This was followed by the annotated "Memoriales con Escolios" (the dating of which is particularly disputed over a range from 1557 to 1569), the "Memoriales in Spanish" (1568?), and the "Breve Compendio" (1570?). Spanish prologues and appendices were added late (1565–71?). In short, although the period from about 1562 to about 1575 probably involved continuing fieldwork, it was primarily a time of analysis, organization, and composition, and close analysis of the various working drafts, revisions, and sketches should make possible a much more accurate view than we now have of how the *General History of the Things of New Spain* took the shape it did.

We know that Sahagún worked with different classes of Indian assistants. Some were employed as informants, some as scribes or artists, and some (particularly the *trilingües*) as translators. And all of them affected the work. How many hands were laid on this body of materials and where? It will be some time before we are in a position to assess the total work from this aspect. The corpus of Sahagún's work is so scattered, so voluminous, and so inaccessible to scholarship that a massive effort of organization and publication is a necessary prelude to tight conclusions on any of the details. But in a broad sense our central problem is still to understand what Sahagún had in mind.

The General History of the Things of New Spain is, in a sense, not a single work, but three. It is a Nahuatl encyclopedia; it is a picture manuscript; and it is a Spanish ethnography. Why did it take this form? What considerations led Sahagún to compose the work in Nahuatl? Why were the pictures drawn? And why was it translated into Spanish?

A host of subsidiary questions must be confronted before scholarship can answer these fundamental queries. A strategic body of data in this connection is made up of what Sahagún himself tells us, not only in his explanatory and sometimes historical prologues, but also inadvertently in his marginal notes, in his editorial or other alterations from draft, in what

7

he omitted as well as what he included, in the style or even in the errors or interpretative distortions of his translation, in the organization of the work and the internal structure of the constituent books and chapters.

On present evidence the suggestion is reasonable that as late as 1564–65 the linguistic purposes of Sahagún's collection of texts were, if not primary, at least salient. Such purposes are of course congruent with his missionary commitment and with the earlier selection of Nahuatl as the primary vehicle for the evangelization of Mexico. The comprehensive range of the subjects covered may well have been a conscious response to the formally expressed interest of the Spanish crown in the description of its newly acquired lands and peoples. The encyclopedic organization of the materials may also reflect earlier medieval models of the treatment of natural history, ultimately descended from Pliny. But the suggestion is also strong that the traditions of the Franciscan order, shaped in the New World into increasingly specific policies and practices directed toward a utopian church, framed Sahagún's thought and directed his interests toward preservation of Aztec culture for its own sake—not merely as a linguistic instrument of catechization, but also as a basis for a new Christian Mexico. There remains, of course, the tantalizing perspective of Sahagún as a Renaissance scholar, pushing beyond the known into the new world of Indian Mexico and attracted by the beauties of Aztec literature and the mysteries of Aztec thought. Inevitably he must have been profoundly influenced by the culture he was prompted to reshape.

The Nahuatl text of the *General History* could serve Indian nativism as well as the Spanish missionary effort. The same is true of the pictorial manuscript. The purposes of the Spanish version are more obscure, at least up to about 1575, when the question of Sahagún's intentions came under the scrutiny of the Inquisition and the crown. The earlier Spanish translations merit special study for the light they might shed on the central questions of the intent of the work.

THE FLORENTINE CODEX, 1575–85

The production of the smooth Spanish translation is a very different matter: it was a response to crisis, and the crisis itself sheds a great deal of light both on Sahagún's motives and on the motives attributed to him by his contemporaries. It seems clear that the crown, nervous over the Indian rebellions in Peru, became alarmed at an enterprise that it suspected of providing too substantial an encouragement to the autonomy of Aztec tradition. A Spanish version of the work was suddenly necessary in order to defend not only Sahagún but the whole thrust of the Franciscan missionary effort from the Inquisition. The Spanish version was produced in relative haste in 1575–77 and was sent to Spain with Fray Rodrigo de Sequera as its advocate. At about the same time, but for Sahagún's own purposes, the Tolosa manuscript was prepared (1575–80?).

The suppression of the Spanish version over a period of 300 years makes it clear that the ambiguities of Sahagún's achievement were appreciated by his fellows, and generated real controversy. Small wonder that they are often obscure to us today. But the crisis itself throws into high relief the specificity of the utopian program of the Franciscan order in Mexico and the central importance of that program to Sahagún's thought (see Baudot 1969). And it is clearly against this missionary background that we must assess Sahagún as an ethnographer, linguist, folklorist, Renaissance humanist, historian, and indigenist.

LAST YEARS, *1585–90*

Despite the crisis, Sahagún continued his life work. Chapter 7 of our report, Georges Baudot's essay on "The Last Years of Fray Bernardino Sahagún, 1585–90," provides important new information on this period from recently discovered documents. While continuing his active participation in the life of his order and in the controversy surrounding it, Sahagún also continued his scholarly work of editing and revising the *General History*, leaving us at his death in 1590 with nearly fifty years' accumulation of texts, illustrations, and translation that were destined to be scattered over two continents—to the dismay of subsequent scholarship.

No one manuscript can claim to be the definitive version of Sahagún's masterpiece. Hence we confront the urgent necessity of locating and compiling the relevant sources, cataloguing and arranging them, and making them available to the expanding circle of interested scholars. The task is beyond the capacities of a small working seminar. It requires team effort over a period of time. But we can make a beginning. Our concrete suggestions are:

(1) To initiate steps to create centers of relevant documentation, concentrating source materials through exchange among collections and aiming to establish centers in two or three strategic research libraries.

(2) To produce a descriptive catalogue of what is known to exist in the world's manuscript collections relevant to Sahagún and his work.

(3) To make the materials accessible to scholarship through a program of publication of the basic groups, and particularly:
   (a) a critical edition of the Spanish text of the *General History of the Things of New Spain*
   (b) a complete edition of the Madrid Codices
   (c) a facsimile edition of the Florentine Codex
   (d) an annotated translation of the "Primeros Memoriales"

(4) To produce a general bibliography of relevant published sources.

(5) To facilitate informational exchange among interested scholars.

It is particularly important that ways be found to make the Madrid and Florentine codices available to serious scholars. The Florentine Codex is now totally inaccessible, and the danger of deterioration or damage to the Madrid Codices may make them so at any time. Complete sets of color transparencies or other photographic reproductions that could be made available to qualified persons or organizations are an urgent necessity.

As an initial guide to the core manuscripts, we offer an outline, even though it mainly reflects what we *don't* know of the manuscript history of Sahagún's opus. Except for the first and last dates (1547 and 1585), all the dating remains in some measure insecure. The notes on publication are abbreviated to indicate only the general publication status of the various manuscripts; more detailed citations will be found in the bibliography under Sahagún, together with references to Sahagún's other works.

It is apparent that Sahagún's *General History* is a work of formidable magnitude and difficulty, and that we badly need background studies on the man, his times, and his work in order to interpret it. At the same

10

TABLE 1
PRINCIPAL
MANUSCRIPTS OF SAHAGÚN'S
GENERAL HISTORY
(After Jiménez Moreno 1938; Nicolau D'Olwer 1952, 1973)

From	Date	Manuscript	Whereabouts	Published Version
Tlaltelolco (1542–58)	1547	Book 6 (Nah.)	(Florentine Codex)	1950–69:6
Tepepulco (1558–61)	1560?	"Primeros Memoriales" (Nah.)	(Madrid Codices)	1905–8:6
Tlaltelolco (1561–65)	1561?	"Memoriales Complementarios" (Nah.)	(Madrid Codices)	1905–8:6
	1563?	"Memoriales con Escolios" (Nah., Sp.)	(Madrid Codices)	1905–8:6, 7
	1564?	"Memoriales en Tres Columnas" (Nah., Sp.)	(Madrid Codices)	1905–8:7, 8
	1565?	Madrid Codices (Sp.)	Academy, Madrid	1905–8
Tenochtitlan (1565–90)	1566?	Book 4 (Sp.)	National Library, Mexico	None
	1567?	Prologues and Appendices (Sp.)	(Florentine (Codex)	1938
	1568?	"Memoriales en Español" (Sp.)	Academy, Madrid	1905–8:7
	1570?	"Breve Compendio"	Vatican Library, Rome	1942
	1577?	Florentine Codex (Nah., Sp., Illustrations)	Laurentian Library, Florence	Without Sp.: 1950–69
	1580?	MS of Tolosa (Sp.)	Academy, Madrid	None
		a) Panes copy (1793)	National Library, Mexico	1938
		b) Bauza copy (1820)	Public Library New York	1831–48
	1585	"Arte Adivinatoria" (Sp.)	National Library, Mexico	None
	1585	"Calendario" (Nah., Sp., Lat.)	National Library, Mexico	1918
	1585	"Libro de la Conquista" (Nah., Sp.)	Laietana Library, Barcelona?	Without Sp.: 1950–69: 12
	1585	"Vocabulario Trilingüe" (Nah., Sp., Lat.)	Newberry Library, Chicago?	None

time we shall continue to study it for what it can tell us of the great American civilization it describes. What can we hope to learn further from Sahagún? How much is our comprehension of Aztec society and culture likely to be improved by further exploration of this, our finest source? The increasing number of scholars working in this field has already made possible greater specialization and corresponding enrichment of detail. This is apparent, for example, in improved and more sensitive translations from the Nahuatl, including by now: Anderson and Dibble (Sahagún 1950–69), Baudot (1972), Brinton (1890), Castillo (1969), Garibay (1940b, 1953–54, 1958), Lehmann (1927), León-Portilla (1959), López Austin (1971a, 1971b, 1972), Schultze Jena (1957), Seler (1927), Sullivan (1963, 1965), and von Gall (1940).

SAHAGÚN'S MEXICO

A peculiar problem is posed by the stylistic features of the more traditional texts, and particularly by what Garibay baptized *disfrasismo:* the coupling of two images to suggest a third meaning. It is becoming clear that the poetic features of Nahuatl style are even more complex than Garibay believed, including not only couplet parallelism as a general feature and Garabay's binomial *disfrasismo* as an embellishment, but also a polynomial repetition with both semantic and poetic force. Clearly there can be no rules about the "proper" translation of texts that communicate at several levels, and neither a literal nor an interpretative translation can be satisfactory for all purposes.

In traditional texts, but also in others, the problems of translation are compounded by both historical and religious obscurity. We cannot write rules either for the interpretation of proper names: the names of the gods, of the great cities, of persons. One may still argue over the etymologies of Huitzilopochtli, Teotihuacan, or Nacxitl. It is startling that we can trace so few linguistic borrowings into Nahuatl. Is this partly due to our comparative ignorance of Otomi, Mixtec, and Zapotec?

The Otomanguean background of central and southern Mexican history clearly needs more scholarly attention than it has received, and not merely for antiquarian or linguistic reasons. We have found ourselves surprised, at a working seminar on Sahagún, to be spending considerable time in discussion of what we don't know about Mixtec and Zapotec society. And the relation between them and the Aztec society depicted by Sahagún is an important and totally neglected question.

What then of Aztec society itself? Even apart from Sahagún we have rich documentation of its local operation from group land titles, state land titles (tribute rolls) and individual land titles. After the middle of the sixteenth century, these are supplemented by wills. From Sahagún and from these adjunct sources, the evidence is beginning to clarify some basic issues about the nature of Aztec society, and particularly about one of its fundamental features, the calpulli. In Chapter 8, "The Sahagún Texts as a Source of Sociological Information," Edward E. Calnek discusses this direction of research and some of the initial problems encountered.

Sahagún's own presentation of the Aztec kinship system is both curious and revealing: curious because of what it omits and revealing because of the structure of what it includes. It is congruent with the interpretation that the calpulli, like other bilateral kinship structures, is a protean form not clearly bounded in either genealogical or social space. Sahagún's description underlines the point that "relatives" in the ascending generations can be comparatively clearly defined, while those in one's own and later generations (apart from direct lineal descendants) cannot. Whether collateral kin are counted as relatives or not depends on individual choices conditioned by a number of nonkinship considerations: residence, rank, occupation, politics, and religion. To argue over whether the calpulli is primarly a political or an economic or a kinship structure is fruitless: its indeterminacy is a definitional feature governed by the descent rule, and Sahagún has described it very well.

An important body of materials on Aztec society in general is assembled in Sahagún's Books 9 and 10. These are treated by Leonhard Schultze Jena in his "Structure of Ancient Aztec Society in Family, Class and Occupation" (1952), and might have been the subject of another chapter in our report by Prof. Dr. Günter Zimmermann of the University of Hamburg. Dr. Zimmermann's untimely death at almost the very moment of our seminar has robbed us of this contribution and of a brilliant colleague. What he might have contributed is hinted at by a hitherto unpublished review of Schultze Jena's work which has been edited for posthumous publication by Dr. Peter Tschohl of the University of Cologne.

The enormous range of Sahagún's materials on Aztec sciences and lore presents us with problems of both scope and detail. Alfredo López Austin illustrates many of these in Chapter 9, "Sahagún's Work and the Medicine of the Ancient Nahuas: Research Possibilities." A particularly interesting question arises in the area of science: Is the guiding scheme of Sahagún's organization (and in the questionnaires) European natural history or Aztecan ethno-science? A study of the various taxonomies presented would be of extraordinary value in answering this question, and perhaps also in what it could tell us of the structure of knowledge in ancient Mexico.

But if Aztec science generates questions, Aztec philosophy and religion generate even more. Though we have some important contributions in both fields (e.g., Ricard 1947; León-Portilla 1963), we need a much more precise understanding of both native thought and missionary intentions in order to grasp the nuances of Sahagún's presentation. Chapter 10, Charles E. Dibble's paper on "The Nahuatlization of Christianity," confronts this central issue and points toward the necessary answers by focusing on the problems of expressing Spanish Catholicism in polytheistic Nahuatl. Much of the drama and ambiguity of Mexican history is contained in this confrontation, and one cannot interpret the conquest of Mexico without a clear view of it.

A number of additional questions arise from Sahagún's treatment of this confrontation. Is it logic, medieval scholasticism, missionary zeal, or Aztec philosophy that dictates the presentation of the gods in calendrical order and/or in the order of priestly rank? Why does Sahagún seemingly present the gods and ceremonies only to refute them, but then proceed to treat Aztecan astrology badly and ambiguously but as though it might be valid? Why is ethics his favorite topic, and what are the implications of his accepting attitude: Is he expressing Aztec nativism or Franciscanism? Why is a prayer for the king's death among the texts?

The world view of the Aztecs remains substantially problematic, and Sahagún's evidence is crucial for interpreting it. Our working seminar considered this evidence in relation to virtue and vice, the Aztecs' attitudes towards drinking and sex, the characterological rigidity and fatalism that colors Nahuatl humor, folklore, custom, and law—even the surviving and characteristically Mexican *albur*, the homosexually punning wordplay that Sahagún describes for the Aztecs and that is widespread in modern Mexico. Our discussion even included Aztecan defecation. It is extraordinarily curious that Sahagún has covered such an incredible range of materials and omitted such obviously central features of Aztec culture as general cosmology and the sequence of the creations. Why?

In the course of a week's discussion we discovered more questions than answers. But we were also able to focus on some questions of particular urgency. Miguel León-Portilla's paper on "The Problematics of Sahagún," Chapter 11, summarizes these, emphasizing the important steps that must be taken soon if even our present level of scholarship is to be maintained.

2

Sahagún in His Times

ARTHUR J. O. ANDERSON
San Diego, California

In compliance with the trends of our times we emphasize Fray Bernardino de Sahagún as the leading pioneer in American ethnography. So he is. In his own time, his importance among his ecclesiastical colleagues was unquestioned if not everywhere acclaimed. Opinions of his contemporaries as to the value of the body of information on ancient Mexican civilization which he was organizing were, at best, varied; at worst, so adversely was his interest in those studies regarded by both layman and priest that the three-hundred-year eclipse of his work both as a religious and as an ethnographer was more predictable than surprising. That the material survived in any form, let alone with its beauty and relative completeness, is miraculous.

So well known are the trends that went against the survival of his work that one unconsciously oversimplifies them. Besides Sahagún's bold methods and indigenist approach, unorthodox in his time, one could name such considerations as Spain's spirit of conquest, her imperial policies, what many today would term "racism," what was developing in the church's evangelical-hierarchical ebb and flow through and past the Council of Trent, and so on.

Despite the very considerable confusion still preventing the compilation of a definitive Sahagún bibliography, we can see that he unquestionably wrote more to promote the religious purposes of his order as he saw them than because of secular (or ethnographic) interests. To begin with what Sahagún says in the prologue to Book 1 of the *General History of the Things of New Spain* and continues to repeat, the purpose of his compilation in its various forms was to further the conversion of the natives. Consequently, it is natural that a good third of the work is devoted to "divine things," as Nicolau D'Olwer calls them (1952:68)— the native religious life to be extirpated—and much of the rest to the recording of what in Sahagún's concept and that of his colleagues was good and should be perpetuated.

Or one can try to consider his total literary output. Volumes 11–13 of the *Handbook of Middle American Indians* may eventually attempt to deal with this problem. According to one of the most unsophisticated lists of his writings, that of Mendieta (1870:663), which equates the "Once libros de marca de pliego" with the *General History*, if one puts them on the secular side, the religious titles outnumber this work four to one as they include the "Sermones" (Sahagún 1540a; 1540b), the "Postilla" (Sahagún 1579a), the "Modo y plática que los doce primeros padres tuvieron . . ." (Sahagún 1564a), and the "Cantares" (Sahagún 1583). Nicolau D'Olwer's Sahagún chronology (1952:200–201), if one arbitrarily and probably wrongly includes the "Breve compendio" (Sahagún 1570), the "Calendario mexicano, latino y castellano" (Sahagún 1585b), and the "Arte adivinatoria" (Sahagún 1585a) on the secular side with the *General History* in its various developments and transformations, sets against the preceding four titles nine which perhaps are acceptable as separate and distinct: "Sermones," "Postilla," "Cantares" (or "Psalmodia cristiana"), "Evangelios y epístolas" (Sahagún 1858), "Coloquios y doctrina cristiana" (Sahagún 1949), "Ejercicios cotidianos" (Sahagún 1574a), "Vida de San Bernardino" (Sahagún 1574b), "Manual del cristiano" (Sahagún 1578), "Apéndice a la postilla o doctrina cristiana" (Sahagún 1579b). The balance is weighted on the religious side, especially when one considers that the purpose of writing the first four works was to promote religious, not secular, ends.

The exclusively religion-based aspects of the Aztec culture occupy, as has been suggested, about one-third of the *General History*. In this series, Book 1 devotes more than half its length to the appendix refuting the worship of the gods described in it; Book 4's appendix, the exposé of the 260-day calendar and of (presumably) Motolinía's naïveté in believing it harmless, is nearly a tenth as long as the description of the calendar. There are also the prologues, various exclamations of the author and addresses to the reader, interpolations, and, ending Book 5, a "last word," much of which one can regard as castigations of idolatry and warnings to Sahagún's colleagues. But besides the appendix to Book 4 just mentioned, there are other indications of how seriously, especially in his last years, Sahagún took calendar and feast day matters in the "Calendario mexicano, latino y castellano" and in the "Arte adivinatoria," and, besides the appendix to Book 1, there is the "Breve compendio," preceded by its naturally slanted summary of ancient Mexican religious beliefs and practices. Georges Baudot has further developed points like these in Chapter 7.

In connection with the accounts and appraisals of the pre-Hispanic religious life, it is curious that beliefs which might well have been expected most deeply to intrigue Sahagún receive scant mention or none. Ometecutli and Omeciuatl are not even mentioned among the gods in the first book of the *General History*, nor in the third, on the origin of the gods. In the sixth they are quite fittingly invoked several times directly by midwives in the so-called baptism, and obliquely in rulers' admonitory discourses; in the tenth they are mentioned once, not inappropriately, though hardly described, in connection with the Tolteca, in the last chapter. It is Tezcatlipoca whom the texts mention in a way which recalls one or another of Ometecutli's attributes (cf. Sahagún 1942:29–30). As Miguel León-Portilla pointed out in the November 16, 1972 session of the School of American Research's "Seminario sobre Sahagún," he gives us no "Legend of the Suns"; there is no true cosmic sense, no understanding of the general cosmic scene; there is little more than a hint at the superimposed heavens. Ideas developed in the subsequent interchange, to which Georges Baudot and Alfredo López Austin contributed, may well provide the explanation: inade-

19

quately informed informants (perhaps from among the *pochteca*, who appear to have been the standbys most often questioned) or a deliberate neglect of any ancient belief which might contribute to an indigenous "bible" to combat Christian theology, or both. As to the "popular and household gods" (Sahagún 1942:30ff.), though the record is consistently better, its completeness (in depth and breadth) is yet to be thoroughly discussed. On the other hand, to return to León-Portilla's comments, the omens and superstitions, as well as other beliefs and practices, were handled with quite sensitive understanding.

Besides the supernaturals to be inveighed against, there are the old holy places and the use of Aztec holy names for Christian saints or God. Hence, for example, an explanation in the prologue to Book 11 (Florentine Codex) of why God is not *teotl* (because of the term's associations).[1] Or we have passages in the "Calendario mexicano, latino y castellano" (Sahagún 1585b) and in an interpolation in Spanish only in Book 11 of the *General History*, following Chapter 12 (Sahagún 1577), casting such doubts upon the shrine at Tepeyacac (as well as those at Tlaxcala and Huexotzinco) as to account in great measure for what has been referred to as the Franciscan conspiracy of silence as to the apparition and miracles of our Lady of Guadalupe and the achievement of Juan Diego as related in *Nican mopohua* (Valeriano 1961). For the speedy mass conversions of the period before midcentury had proved to be mostly illusory; increasing depression and exasperation color Sahagún's Spanish-only interpolations in the *General History* (notably Book 11) and the whole of his "Calendario mexicano, latino y castellano." If a more leisurely winning of souls—through substitution for and appropriation of locations, names, and days already hallowed among a heathen population—had long go succeeded in parts of Europe, New World conditions were not comparable, and, moreover, social, political, and economic ideals of the Franciscan order conflicted with imperial policy as formed by the government in Spain and as interpreted by the laity in the colonies. Further, events in the 1570s and 1580s considerably saddened his last years, of which Nicolau D'Olwer (1952) and Baudot (see Chapter 7) tell us most feelingly.

Speaking of the "sixty-one years that [Sahagún] lived in this land," Mendieta (1870:664) tells us that "he particularly spent the major part of them supporting and improving . . . the College of the Holy Cross,

. . . where he worked without a day's rest up to his death in teaching and indoctrination of the sons of Indian leaders. . . ." The account is a very broad sketch, mentioning only two key dates, 1529 and 1590, so that here one is far from certain of one's proportions. From Sahagún's own account in Book 10, in the interpolation of the Spanish text following Chapter 27 (Sahagún 1577), where a better idea of chronology and the time element is possible, intermittent rather than continuous lecturing at the college is indicated, though since the account leaves off in 1576 his contributions from then to 1590 could indeed have been continuous. But there is no indication of any lapse in his deep interest in the college and its work in evangelization, as he gives us a smattering of information about the college's origin and considerable detail about the students in general, their indoctrination, their help to the evangelizing fathers, and about the expulsions, the experiments that failed as well as those which succeeded, and so on.

His interest continued unabated until he died, for, as Mendieta tells us (1870:664), ". . . he had his children, the Indians he cared for in the college, brought to him, and taking leave of them, he was taken to Mexico, where, having devoutly received all the sacraments at the Convent of St. Francis of that city, he died like one blessed in the Lord, and is buried there." That he was dear to the Indian leaders and their followers, a proportion of whom must have been alumni of the College of the Holy Cross, is obvious in Chimalpahín's interpolation in the rather full account of the year 1590: ". . . our beloved father, Fray Bernardino de Sahagún, a priest of St. Francis, died. He was in Tlatelolco and was buried here within [the Convent of] St. Francis. All the rulers came. . . ." (Chimalpahín 1889:311; Nicolau D'Olwer 1952:131–32).[2]

His attentions were not given exclusively to saving his Indian charges. The "Libro de entradas y profesiones de los novicios" of San Francisco de México (Anon. 1562–84) preserves a series of professions made between February 11 and November 29, 1562, each one followed by a comment, sometimes two, in Sahagún's hand. Most of what he wrote is legible.

For instance, on November 3 Pedro Cavallero professed that:

> On the third of the month of November 1562, I, Pedro Cavallero, resident of the port of St. Mary, assert that I am the legitimate son of Alonso Cavallero and Juana de Carmona, deceased, and likewise

say that I am not bound to any woman whatever by the words of matrimony, and that in my lineage none have had any penance imposed by the Inquisition nor have been burned; and that I am sound in body and have not had any contagious disease nor have I been denounced nor accused by a judge, nor do I have any debts whatever. Because this is the truth, I have signed it with my name.

Pedro Cavallero

after which Sahagún wrote: "The aforesigned took the habit for the choir on the day, month, and year cited above, in the afternoon after compline between six and seven," and followed it by his well-known, unique signature.

Sahagún's remarks show that he watched, guided, criticized, and if necessary took part in the expulsion of these young Spanish candidates for the novitiate:

On March 12, of Melchor Nuñez de la Cerda: "The aforementioned took the habit for the choir the very day, year, and month above at the hour of compline" (signature), followed by "The aforementioned deceived us in that he had many debts and said he didn't, and we threw him out so he would go pay them."

On March 31, of Pedro de Serezeda: "The aforementioned took the habit for the choir the first day of April of the year cited above; he says he is twenty-five years of age" (signature), followed by: "He became a lay brother on May 20 of the same year."

On May 25, of Juan Lorenzo: "The aforementioned took the habit on May 27, 1562; he took it for the choir" (signature), followed by: "We threw him out as frivolous."

There are thirteen in all, following the same pattern. Neither Sahagún's predecessors nor his successors commented in any way. Sahagún's other nine comments are as follows:

On Hernando de la Cadena (who professed on February 11): "The aforementioned took the habit on the twelfth of the month stated above, at mealtime. He says he is thirty-three" (signature).

On Pedro Camacho (February 12): "He who is named above took the habit on the thirteenth of the month of February 1562; he took it as a lay brother; he is twenty-two years of age" (signature).

On Alonso Alvarez (March 3): "On the sixth of March of the year stated above, at mealtime, the aforementioned took the habit; he says he is sixteen" (signature).

On Juan de León (March 29): "The aforementioned took the habit for the choir on March 28 at mealtime in Our Lord's passion (*domjna in passione*)" (signature).

On Cristóbal Fernández (March 31): "The aforementioned is for the choir; he says he is twenty; he took the habit the first day of April of the year stated above" (signature).

On Francisco de Luzio (April 17): "The habit was given to the aforementioned the same day at five in the afternoon for the choir; he is seventeen years old more or less" (signature), followed by: "We threw him out as a troublemaker [*discolo*] September 29, 1562."

On Pasqual de Sangal (April 17): "The habit was given to the aforementioned the same day at five in the afternoon; he is for a lay brother; he is thirty years old" (signature), followed by: "The aforementioned entered somewhat ill and the illness got worse; a month and a half after he took the habit we sent him to be cured and to return when he was well; he was not lacking through any other defect at all."

On Cristóbal Sánchez (September 25): "This Cristóbal Sánchez took the habit for the choir September 25, 1562; it was given to him at six in the afternoon" (signature), followed by: "The aforesaid couldn't last five days, nor was the warning of many fathers sufficient to hold him two more days; he left as an unstable and badly brought up man with little judgment."

On Andrés Méndez (November 29): "This one was thrown out for being dissolute and badly brought up." Followed by: "The aforementioned then two days after he took the habit fell ill with erysipelas and ate meat throughout the period of fasting; he was in the infirmary and his cell as a patient, sleeping in a blanket and not going to matins; he did not set a good example at the time of his illness; he did not test himself nor did we test him in all that time; it seems to me that he didn't take the vow seriously . . ." (signature); the last six or seven words are illegible.

Date discrepancies are between the date of professing and of Sahagún's comment.

Nicolau D'Olwer's chronology (1952:200) places Sahagún in Tlatelolco in 1561–62. If so, he must have moved from the convent in

Tlatelolco to that of St. Francis in Mexico (as guardian?) very early in 1562, and for that year only.

Along the broadest of lines, Mendieta's account of Sahagún divides his life into two parts. The first is based on the statement, "He shortly learned the Mexican language and knew it well, for no other to the present has equaled him in arriving at its secrets, and no one has been so occupied in writing in it," and from there leads through his interest (". . . in rendering the whole Mexican language into its parts . . . in its distinctiveness and nature . . . seeing that it was already becoming corrupted through mixture with ours . . .") to his purpose ("in this employment of the Mexican language, uprooting idolatry, preaching, confessing, indoctrinating the Indians and writing for their benefit, this man of God spent sixty-one years . . ."). The second part centered about him as particularly devoted, as we have seen, to the College of the Holy Cross, "supremely zealous in matters of faith, desiring and endeavoring with all his strength that it be very truly impressed upon the new converts" (Mendieta 1870:664).

The general impression given by all our data is that of a Sahagún of unquenchable energy, continuously active despite a growing infirmity which made it impossible for him to write legibly, wholly devoted to the propagation of the faith among the natives along the lines hoped for by the Franciscan order in the New World and its fitting maintenance by native and Spaniard alike. A sequence of circumstances eventually led to the production of the *General History* through development of standardized questionnaires answered by older informants in picture writing explained to and recorded by the trilingual students (López Austin 1969c) with subsequent revisions using essentially the informants' own words. The scheme of development and the eventual result, neither of which could have been originally foreseen, are what make it unique. Durán (1951) used informants and refers to picture writing; Landa (1941) used informants. That Sahagún's product was not like theirs, nor even like his own "Arte adivinatoria," nor like the introduction to the "Breve compendio," nor like his appendices to Books 1 and 4 of the *General History*, is, from the perspective of our times and ideals, remarkable. For, according to what he tells us of himself in the *General History* and what we gather from other sources, in becoming an indigenist and an ethnologist he worked not only against the prevail-

24

ing trends of his time but against what was a part of his own training, ambition, and personality.

NOTES

1. In the *Arte,* which appeared in 1645, however, Horacio Carochi (1892) did not object to use of the phrase *in teotl Dios,* and neither he nor, in the eighteenth century, Francisco Xavier Clavigero (n.d.) hesitated to use such a term as *tloque nauaque.*

2. Chimalpahín's Nahuatl text reads: "*Yn ipan yc 5 mani de febrero, yhcuac momiquilli in totlaçotatzin Fray Bernardino de Sahagun, S. Francsico teopixqui, Tlatilulco moetzticatca: auh nican callihtic S. Francisco motocatzinco, mochintin huallaque yn tlahtoque Tlatilulco quimotequillico*"; Nicolau D'Olwer draws attention to the erroneous date and location (omitted in my translation).

3

The Ethnographic Works of Andrés De Olmos, Precursor and Contemporary of Sahagún[1]

S. J E F F R E Y K. W I L K E R S O N
Florida State Museum

If the works of the great Franciscan missionary-scholars of the six-teenth century are to be put into perspective, an effort must be made to understand their contributions, methodology, and mutual influences on each other. The time-space framework over which ideas and inter-pretations traveled must be examined and evaluated against the then cathartic philosophical climate of the Old World and the syncretic intellectualism of the New.

The mendicant orders represented the response of one of the oldest Mediterranean institutions, the Latin church, to changing social factors in late medieval Europe. Even within their own cultural traditions, such institutions embody contradictions. The environment of cultural hetero-geneity and the truncation of indigenous society in New Spain could only make more difficult the task of the orders which had been charged to activate, extend, enforce, and guard the church. These purposes were at times approached with the curiosity typical of the Renaissance, and resulted in centers of structured acculturation such as Santa Cruz de Tlatelolco. From such cultural contact came diverse humanistic treatises, some of which were the harbingers of social science. Within a century, this behavioral approach was for the most part suppressed by reverberations of the European Counter-Reformation, but not before some of the first modern ethnographies had been produced.

These documents constitute ample and largely reliable sources for studies of acculturation, syncretism, and pre-Columbian customs and institutions. Their value is not solely historic but also anthropological and, in some cases, methodological. During the Franciscan literary florescence of the middle of the sixteenth century two individuals in particular are noteworthy for their concern for methodology and content: Fray Andrés de Olmos and Fray Bernardino de Sahagún. The extensive writings of the latter have received increasing attention in this century as a basic source. That the earlier and less profuse treatises of Andrés de Olmos have received little attention is due in no small part to their anonymity and scattered locations.

If we are to consider the nature of the intellectual relationship of the two Franciscans we must first reestablish the scope and order of the works of Andrés de Olmos. This is no simple task, as many of his writings were considered lost in his own lifetime. In fact, in his later years he was asked to write a summary of his earlier extensive works. Apparently a number of these manuscripts had been sent back to Spain by way of clerical travelers and were lost in the Iberian peninsula. It also seems that, although a number of works were topically and conceptually unrelated, even those which were sequential may never have been together in finished form in the author's hands.

The life of Olmos reflects not only contact with other major Franciscans and Dominicans of the time, but also considerable missionary effort marked by extensive travel and linguistic achievement. Olmos's life is summarized by Mendieta (1870), Ricard (1947), and Meade (1950). He was born in Oña, not far from Burgos, in Castilla la Vieja about the year 1491. At the age of twenty he entered the Franciscan monastery at Valladolid under the direction of Fray Juan de Zumárraga.

Apparently he became a confidant of Zumárraga and assisted him in the investigation of heresies. In 1528 Zumárraga was appointed bishop of Mexico and left for New Spain, taking Olmos with him.

The following year Olmos began the first of many trips; he was sent to Guatemala to search for Toribio de Benavente (Motolinía) who was thought to be lost. He returned with Motolinía in July 1530. Sometime between his return and 1532 he founded the Custodia del Salvador de Tampico in the province of Pánuco. By 1533 he was back in Mexico City writing to Charles V. In the same year he was ordered to investigate antiquities by the president of the Second Audiencia, Sebastián Ramírez de Fuenleal, and the Custodian of the Franciscans in New Spain, Fray Martín de Valencia. This may have been the major stimulus for his ethnographic writings.

Between 1533 and 1539 he was probably a lecturer at the college of Santa Cruz de Tlatelolco. By sometime in 1539, however, he was placed in charge of the small monastery of San Andrés de Hueytlalpan in the northern Sierra de Puebla. At that time the small town was the cabecera for a large area stretching into the coastal lowlands of Veracruz and including speakers of Nahuatl, Huastec, and Totonac. The following year he wrote to Zumárraga, by then head of the Inquisition, about the idolatrous behavior of the Totonac cacique of Matlatlán. He indicated that he had confiscated and had in his possession certain pictorial material.

In 1543 he was named guardian in Tecamachalco in the Valley of Mexico, and he visited Tlalmanalco and the monastery at Cuernavaca. The next year he made a trip toward "La Florida," converting a group of Indians, probably from Tamaulipas, and bringing them back to a site near Tampico. In 1546 he met with Bartolomé de las Casas and by 1547 he was back in the Hueytlalpan district, finishing his surviving Nahuatl grammar (Olmos 1875) at Papantla.

Between 1552 and 1554 he finished his "Treatise on the Seven Principal Sins" (Olmos 1552) in Papantla and wrote to the viceroy requesting permission to reestablish a monastery and town at Tampico. In 1554 the request was approved and Tampico was established. In 1556 and 1557 he wrote to Charles V soliciting permission to populate the area between Tampico and the Mississippi. His later years are largely undocumented, but he appears to have pursued missionary activities in the Tampico area. He died there in 1570 or 1571 at the age of seventy-nine or eighty and is probably buried near Tampico Alto, Veracruz.

Like Sahagún, he had a long life and a career fully within the six-teenth-century Franciscan tradition, but unlike Sahagún he traveled widely and spent considerable time in the ecclesiastical hinterlands. Ethnographic or linguistic scholarship was not his life's work; rather it was a tool for implementing the Franciscan goals, which he seemed to see in immediate and imperative terms.

The works of Olmos can be divided into three general groups: homi-letic, linguistic, and ethnographic. These are not distinct groupings, but rather merging categories which reflect the author's overriding mission-ary purpose. Examples have survived of the first type (e.g., "Treatise on the Seven Principal Sins") and of the second (e.g., *Arte de la lengua mexi-cana*). The third category is more problematical and complex, as most of these works appear not to have been signed by the author and seem to have become separated early in their histories. It is, however, this cate-gory that we must examine most closely if we are to obtain some ap-proximation of the methodological and ethnohistorical contributions of Olmos. To this end we must consider a series of documents, some un-published or unknown until recently, which have usually been thought to be anonymous. The first, and most essential is the Codex Tudela, a page of which is shown in Plate 1.

CODEX TUDELA

The Codex Tudela, also known as the Codex of the Museo de las Américas, is first and foremost an ethnographic document. It was not composed as an account of personal experience like Bernal Díaz's *True History* (1964), or for political purposes like Hernán Cortés's *Letters* (1963), or for assessment reasons like the *Relaciones Geográficas* (Paso y Troncoso 1905–6), nor for that matter as a reservoir of esoteric and genealogical knowledge like the preconquest codices. There is no signa-ture on or in the manuscript, no indication of political opinions, ecclesi-astical or secular, and no non-European information presented without an explicit attempt at explanation. Data are presented in an orderly fashion, although folios were reshuffled with time.

As an ethnography the Codex Tudela is notable on several counts.

Methodologically it embodies a sophistication seen only in one other surviving document of the mid-sixteenth century, the Florentine Codex. It is an attempt to derive and organize data on the pre-Cortesian and early colonial Indians of central Mexico by direct use of indigenous sources from several locales. To this end indigenous paintings are used as the basis of explanation to the reader and were undoubtedly used as the basis for interviewing the informants who provided the data for the Spanish text.

The material in the Codex Tudela appeared shortly after the completion of the codex in other sixteenth-century works such as the Codex Magliabecchiano (Anon. 1904) and the *Chronicle of New Spain* of Cervantes de Salazar (1914). This same material has later ramifications in "Costumbres . . . de la Nueva España" (Gómez de Orozco 1945), the Codex Ríos (1900) and Veytia's *Ancient History of Mexico* (1944). It also represents a source for Zurita's *History of New Spain* (1909), Mendieta's *Ecclesiastical History* (1870), and Torquemada's *Indian Monarchy* (1943-44).

The pictorial aspect of the document provides a complete picture of indigenous ritual life. While it is executed in several styles, the most radical departure being a series of full-page figures in a European or European-influenced hand, there is a consistency of intent. Colors are vivid and generally well applied. The poses and proportions of the individuals depicted are often stereotyped in such a way as to indicate pre-Hispanic artistic traditions.

The text follows the illustrations closely and systematically, sometimes as if the author was following an outline. Although the main concern is ritual, a wide range of other material is presented, from foodstuffs to secular games. There is no question that although some illustrations are incomplete and some passages very brief, the work was conceived as a single unit and executed by one person. It represents the labor of a man whose broad concern for alien peoples and attention to detail were fully in keeping with the intellectual curiosity generated by the developing European Renaissance.

The Codex Tudela covers various topics and presents numerous problems of ordering and interpretation. For purposes of consideration here, the ordering in Table 2, based upon the contents of each folio, is used for interpretation. This grouping is not purely heuristic, as it rests on various unifying factors ranging from artistic expression to strict compliance to topic. The general divisions include: (A) "European" figures, (B) the eighteenth-month calendar, (C) movable feasts and daily ritual life, and (D) the tonalamatl and divination.

TABLE 2
INTERNAL DIVISIONS OF THE CODEX TUDELA

	Front cover	1r–1v
A	"European" figures & maguey plant	2r–9v
B	Eighteen-month calendar	10r–28v
C	Movable feasts & daily ritual life	
	(in reconstructed order)	
	1. Fifty-two-year cycle	77v–85r
	2. Mantas	85v–88v
	3. Xochipilli	29r–30v
		48r
	4. Ometochtli	
	a. Local names & feasts	31r–39v
		41r–41v
		44r–45v
		40r–40v
		47r–47v
	b. Ritual pulque process (Mayuel?)	68r–69v
		63r–63v
		65r–65v
		70r–71v
	5. Quetzalcoatl	42r–42v
		49r–49v
	6. Mictlantecutli	
	a. God of death	56r–56v
		46r–46v
		51r–52v
		64r–64v
		76r–77r
		67r–67v
		53r?–53v
	b. Death & election of a great lord	55r–55v
		54r–54v
		50r–50v
		72r–72v
	c. Death of individuals in other social groups	57r–60v
	7. Tezcatlipoca	62r–62v
	8. Yopes	
	a. Social sanctions	74r–75v
	b. Thieves (Mexica? Yopes? adulterers?)	61r–61v

TABLE 2, cont'd

D Tonalamatl & Divination	
1. Count of the days	90r– 96r
2. Rulers of the east + 130 figures	97r–103v
3. Rulers of the north + 130 figures	104r–110v
4. Rulers of the west + 130 figures	111r–117v
5. Rulers of the south + 130 figures	118r–124r
6. Divination format	124v–125r
	125v
	127v
Back cover	128r
	129v

A. "European" Figures

The first section is a series of full-page figures representing Indians of various regions in indigenous attire with corresponding accoutrements. The unity of depiction seems to indicate one artist, although the subjects vary geographically from Guatemala to the extreme northeastern portion of New Spain at the time, the Huasteca. Given the lack of aboriginal technique in proportions and execution, and the conceptual similarity of these depictions to figures of known origin, we may conclude that these illustrations were drawn by a European; consequently they are referred to as the "European" figures.

The problem of ordering in the manuscript begins in this first section. The reconstruction of the original order—that is, the original order in the Tudela, not in its probable precursor—was based on the examination of figures occupying opposite sides of the same folio and on a comparison (to be discussed in another publication) with the order in the first eight folios of "Costumbres . . . de la Nueva España." As has been pointed out by Robertson (1959:132), this latter document, published by Gómez de Orozco (1945), is a later copy of a portion of the Tudela Codex and closely preserves the present ordering as a whole.

Between the production of the unillustrated "Costumbres" copy and the purchase of the document by the Museo de las Américas in Madrid, reported by Tudela (1949) and Ballesteros-Gaibrois (1948), the initial folios had apparently become unbound and disordered. It is quite possi-

33

ble that they were in this condition even before the "Costumbres" copy was made, as the sixteenth-century pagination of the manuscript, which is consistent throughout the remainder, only appears on one folio of this initial section. Much of the shuffling appears to be recent, however, for the section described by Ballesteros (1948:65–66) maintains a different order from that of the later photographic copies which were used as the basis for this interpretation. In Ballesteros the section began with the illustration of the maguey plant, whereas in the later copies (and the "Costumbres" ordering) the plant ended the series.

Regardless of when the folios were rearranged, the reconstituted order emphasizes an interesting fact that will have some bearing on the establishment of authorship. The figures are grouped according to ethnic affinity and labeled as such rather than simply presented haphazardly under a vague title such as "Indians of New Spain." It is obvious that the author understood and could recognize distinct cultural groups and that his illustrations attempted to indicate distinctions of dress (note the gloss: "costume of an Indian from Mexico," folio 2r). The range of groups presented is also important for the overall interpretation: from Guatemala and Acapulco on the Mar del Sur, to Michoacán, then inland to Mexico, and (here using the "Costumbres" copy) Veracruz, Pánuco, and the Chichimec realm on the Mar del Norte. As can be observed (see Fig. 1), these places fall directly along the lines of early sixteenth-century communication in New Spain. Considering the unity of observation and depiction in the series, unless the figures were added later or come from another source (which we will later see is probably not so), we may consider that one criterion for the identity of the author is that he was present in all these regions.

The maguey plant included in this section may or may not represent herbal curiosity on the part of the artist but stylistically it belongs here. In a sense it is quite different from the other topics, but other sections of the text bear out its importance and from that standpoint justify its inclusion in the work as a whole. We will refer to this in later discussion. The method of portrayal is very similar to the full-page illustrations of plants, for example in folios 19 and 27 of the *Badianus Manuscript* (Emmart 1940), that date from approximately the same period (1552). In both there is a cross-section impression, and plant roots are shown with no indication of a ground line.

34

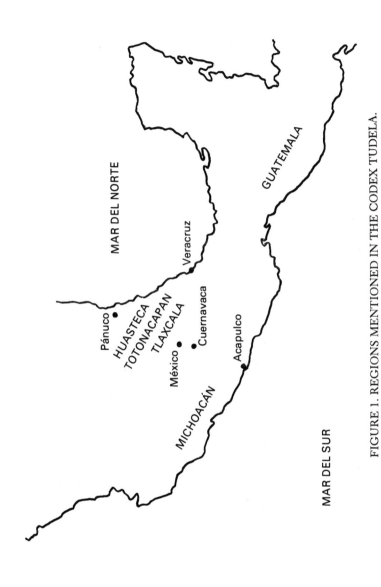

FIGURE 1. REGIONS MENTIONED IN THE CODEX TUDELA.

B. *The Eighteen-Month Calendar*

The second major section is the eighteen-month calendar. That this unit has not suffered rearrangement is indicated by the various dates for the feasts and the "early" pagination. In terms of content this portion of the document follows a strict format. The placement of the figures on the recto sides of successive folios in spite of various text lengths suggests that the drawings were completed first and the description added later. In almost every case the text indicates the name of the feast, its duration, the name of the god to whom it is dedicated, the ritual itself, and the date in the Julian calendar. This forms the core of the presentation. Once these conditions were fulfilled the author would apparently add whatever else he knew about the feast. Thus, we find many references to social classes, material culture, dances, dress, food, specific places, and individual persons.

This general information as well as the standard presentation enables us better to come to grips with the intent of the author, both as to scope and as to subject matter. The systematic nature of his approach is immediately apparent, as is his ability to understand the material in depth, unlike many other writers of the sixteenth century (see for example the treatment of the calendrics in Cervantes de Salazar's *Chronicle* or Mendieta's *History*). Certainly, alien gods are referred to as demons, but considering the integration of Catholicism with the Spanish state and the often narrow fervor of the early missionaries, the intellectual tolerance displayed in the Tudela manuscript is readily observable. There is no apologetic or directly demeaning presentation. Although the author is certainly not totally objective, the intent was to present the data in an organized fashion, to record what was meaningful to people of a different culture.

The dates cited for each month present specific problems as to affiliation and adequate time placement. With the exception of the initial month all the dates that were first set down were so corrected that six months have three dates and eleven have two. Table 3 presents the differing dates.

In the Codex Tudela the year (the 365-day rather than the 260-day year) begins on February 1. This is the only date not changed by subse-

TABLE 3
EIGHTEEN-MONTH CALENDAR DATES*

Month	Tudela 1	Tudela 2	Tudela 3	Maglia.	Motolinía	Cervantes de Salazar
1	Feb 1 47				Jan 1 20	Mar 1 20
2	Mar 20 21	Feb 2 39	Feb 21 20	Mar 21 20	Jan 21 20	Mar 21 20
3	Apr 10 20	Mar 13 20		Apr 10 ?	Feb 10 20	Apr 10 20
4	Apr 30 21	Apr 12 29			Mar 2 20	Apr 30 20
5	May 20 21	Apr 11 28	Apr 22 20		Mar 21 ?	May 20 20
6	Jun 10 19	May 9 20	May 12 21		? 41	Jun 9 20
7	Jun 29 10	May 29 20	Jun 2 19		May 1 20	Jun 29 20
8	Jul 9 20	Jun 18 21	Jun 21 20		May 21 20	Jul 19 20
9	Jul 29 20	Jul 9 23	Jul 11 21		Jun 10 20	Aug 8 20
10	Aug 18 20	Aug 1 20			Jun 30 20	Aug 28 20
11	Sep 7 20	Aug 21 20			Jul 20 20	
12	Sep 27 20	Sep 10 20			Aug 9 20	
13	Oct 17 20	Sep 30 20			Aug 29 20	
14	Nov 6 20	Oct 20 21			Sep 18 20	
15	Nov 26 20	Nov 10 20			Oct 8 20	
16	Dec 16 20	Nov 30 20			Oct 28 20	
17	Jan 5 20	Dec 20 21			Nov 17 20	
18	Jan 25 7	Jan 10 21		Feb 4 25?	Dec 7 25	

* Dates in italics are those also found in "Costumbres."

quent corrections. The final set of dates, which are those we find copied in the "Costumbres" version, produces months generally 20 days long. One month, the seventh, has 19 days but is corrected by the preceding month, which has 21. The 5 "null" days are not located together in this interpretation; in fact they are not mentioned at all in the text. It appears that 2 are annexed to the last month, giving a 22-day length, while the other 3 are annexed to the ninth, fourteenth, and seventeenth months.

Certain comparisons with related material should be mentioned here. Motolinía's interpretation of the year, which was used along with the information of Andrés de Olmos in Book 2 of Mendieta's work, sets the beginning date at March 1. Although Motolinía states this in the text (1941:39), his tabular presentation of the data has the initial month beginning on January 1. Other than the discrepancy in the initial dates, the only difference between his data and those of Olmos is that he adds the five days to the last month, making it twenty-five days long. Cervantes de Salazar's *Chronicle*, probably based in part on the same source as the Codex Tudela, has the year beginning on March 1. He presents, however, only ten months, each twenty days long, before running out of enthusiasm for the topic. Of his ten dated months the second through the seventh correspond to (or at times are one day different from) the same months as identified by the first set of dates in the Tudela Codex (see Table 3). It is quite possible that he arrived at the beginning date of March 1 by noticing that the second month began on the twentieth and that the text only mentions lengths of twenty days, which would make the first of February erroneous.

The various sets of dates in the Tudela manuscript suggest the possibility that the last set, the only one recorded in "Costumbres," was added later by another hand. There is some indication that this may have occurred, as two distinct dates are recorded within the text. The description of the second month originally included the citation March 1 (which is the same as the principal gloss). This is crossed out in favor of two other dates. The description of the eleventh month contains the date September 7 (with a later correction), which would correspond only to the first series of dates. Unless the author made the corrections himself, ignoring the text, this means that the corrected dates were probably calculated by a different person. Although that appears to be the most likely explanation, it is also possible that the author (possibly following his conceptual format) placed the first set of days near the figures representing each month as guidelines, and only upon review, perhaps much later, noticed the discrepancies in that set of dates. Whoever made the correction had a mid-sixteenth-century script, as did the author or scribe of the text.

Another manuscript, "Historia de los mexicanos por sus Pinturas," has the new year beginning in March (Anon. 1941:234). This compatibility of data in Motolinía's *History*, Cervantes de Salazar's *Chronicle*, "Pinturas," and the first set of dates in the Codex Tudela (discounting the first month of that series), all of which came from the same sources or region, would tend to support the present interpretation.

The Codex Magliabecchiano only preserves three dates, for the second, third, and eighteenth months respectively. The first two are in accord with the first set of days in the Codex Tudela and again appear to support the March 1 interpretation. The last date allows for twenty-five dates and as such would probably include the five "null days" at the end of the year as does Motolinía. Adding these facts to the previous data it would seem that the correct date for the new year in the region described is March 1, and there is some indication that the five extra days were added to the end of the eighteen months rather than spread out among them.

C. Daily Ritual Life

The third major section is a conglomerate of related topics, perhaps best labeled "Daily Ritual Life." For the most part these are movable feasts, sometimes involving major deities such as Quetzalcoatl and Mictlantecutli or relatively minor yet significant rituals such as sweat baths and divination. The last two divisions of this section are in their original order, in contrast to the remaining portion of the section. One is the fifty-two-year cycle with the corresponding glyphs, and the other is a selection of mantas (ceremonial or tribute blankets) used in religious rites.

The problem of original order in this section must be considered simultaneously with the contents if the interpretation is to be meaningful. The obviously jumbled condition of these folios, some without glosses or complete figures, makes reconstruction difficult. As "Costumbres" and, to some extent, the Codex Magliabecchiano follow the same pattern of disorder, it appears that this was the condition of the manuscript from early in its history. The Codex Magliabecchiano begins with the year and manta sections rather than at the end of Section C like the Codex Tudela. When we discuss the affiliations of the Tudela manuscript we shall see that there is reason to believe that these two sequences should precede the remainder of the section rather than follow it. This would also give greater continuity between this section in general and the following section, in which the author's emphasis is on the divinatory nature of the tonalamatl.

Considering the orderly presentation of the material in Section B, we should have expected similar order in this following section also. A close examination of the present contents shows that although they are in some cases extremely out of order, certain major themes can be ascertained. Some of these definitely indicate a sequential nature within the unit itself (see Table 2).

Tudela de la Orden (1948:553–54), in his announcement of the manuscript, briefly described the divisions of the section which we have designated C. His parts 2–4 correspond to our C:

part 2:
   a) Other Feasts Distinct from the Monthly Feasts of the First Part
   b) Gods of the Drunkards
   c) Sacrifices
   d) Rites
   e) Burials and Funerals
   f) Miscellaneous Customs
part 3: Years
part 4: Blankets

Parts 3 and 4 are obvious units, but the others are somewhat more problematic. The entire section (except the "years" and "mantas") might be entitled "Movable Feasts and Their Deities." The "Gods of the Drunkards" portion represents a meaningful unit to some extent. Since movable feasts are generally related to particular deities it seems likely that the descriptions would cluster around them. The following are the divisions that result when such an approach is taken:

   I. Fifty-two-year cycle
   II. Mantas

III. Xochipilli
IV. Ometochtli
V. Quetzalcoatl
VI. Mictlantecutli
VII. Tezcatlipoca
VIII. Yopes

Leaving aside for the moment the two initial divisions, the first movable feast presented is that of Xochipilli. In the Codex Tudela only the first feast associated with this deity (Chiconxochitl) is given. The second is represented only by an incomplete glyph (folio 30r). The Codex Magliabecchiano (folios 47v, 48r), however, does present text with this portion. It is also possible that the folio (48r) dealing with the patolli game belongs to this division as there is some indication in the Codex Magliabecchiano (folios 59v, 60r) that Xochipilli or a variant, Macuilxochitl, was associated with luck in this game.

The folios dealing with Ometochtli or variants of the pulque god constitute the largest single division in this portion. The uniform nature of the figures in this division, the stereotyped poses, standard proportions, similarity of coloring, and many common accoutrements such as shield devices, indicate certain affinities to the common gloss "God of Drunkards." This general unity, far more apparent in these folios than in other divisions, suggests that the pictures illustrate one cult in various places. The place signs which appear with many of the figures lend credence to this interpretation. Caso (1936:27) interpreted the corresponding section in the Codex Magliabecchiano as a cult of drunkenness with local names, as did Spence before him (1923:288). Sahagún also considers the pulque gods in the Florentine Codex (Book 4, chapters 4 and 5) and presents some figures similar to those of the Tudela Codex (folio 40, Book 1). The Madrid Codices also contain illustrations of pulque gods (Sahagún: 1964: plates IX-15, XII-22, XIII-23), some of them the same deities seen in the Tudela manuscript (see Table 8 for place sign identification).

The second subdivision of the Ometochtli unit deals with the ritual production of pulque. The relationship of this drink (sometimes referred to as *vino* in the Tudela and Magliabecchiano codices) to Ometochtli has been cited repeatedly. The material on pulque thus complements the rest of the unit. Gibson (1964: 150) has pointed out the increase in pulque production that corresponded to the fragmentation of indigenous social organization, and Cuevas (1922:28) has documented the Franciscan concern for the pattern. This tends to indicate that, regardless of the preconquest importance of pulque, the emphasis it received in the period when the data for the Tudela Codex were gathered would warrant its inclusion. The importance of pulque may also account for the maguey plant mentioned above.

Quite possibly this section is about Mayuel, goddess of pulque. The Magliabecchiano presentation of this deity includes a maguey plant. Her depiction in *Codex Borbonicus* (Hamy 1899:8) involves symbols, notably the olla with a cord support and the "cups," which are included in the pulque production sequence in the Tudela Codex. Pactecatl (Hamy 1899:11) also includes symbols similar to the pulque-Mayuel series in the Tudela Codex. Conceivably, the pulque sequence should be divided among the various pulque gods with these particular attributes, or perhaps the section was meant to follow the depiction of the related deities and present material relevant to all of them.

The next unit is that of Quetzalcoatl and consists of only one folio. Cervantes de Salazar (1914:51) mentions Quetzalcoatl as being associated with movable feasts; he gives as much attention to this deity as to others who have much longer texts in the Tudela version. This may mean that Cervantes de Salazar purposely gave equal weight to varying quantities of data or that there was more text available in the version he had at his disposal.

A second folio showing a figure with Quetzalcoatl accoutrements (a half conch shell and headdress) is labeled Pactecoatl. According to Spence (1923:293) this is Patecatl, one of the pulque gods, and consequently it has been placed in that section of the reconstruction. The Magliabecchiano Codex has two folios (61r and 62r) devoted to Quetzalcoatl.

The next unit is concerned with Mictlantecutli and the social aspects of death. There appear to be three parts in all. The first deals with the deity himself. He is presented pictorially as a monster figure, including the only full front-view depiction in the document. Cervantes de Salazar (1914:51) considers this feast to be of the same general nature—"Extravagant Celebrations"—as those of Xochipilli, Ometochtli, and Quetzalcoatl. The folios presenting the rites appropriate to this deity are readily linked into a sequence. It appears that Mictlantecutli had specific

42

rites in addition to the ceremonies common at burial. Folio 64v of the Codex Magliabecchiano indicates that the friars used the concept of Mictlan to indicate where the unfaithful would go, in spite of the fact that the concept is not really parallel to that of Hell.

The second and third sections on Mictlantecutli deal with the death and burial of individuals from distinct social classes. The second section is concerned with the death and election of a "great lord." The implication is that this is not just any important noble but rather a governor or very prominent leader. Particular mention is made in this section (folios 55r, 55v) of Moctezuma and his death as a captive of the Spaniards in Tenochtitlan. The implication is that the rituals described are commensurate with such a death and the elevation of another to fill the office. This sequence is five folios in length.

The third and last subdivision of the unit deals with the death of other individuals in various social classes. This includes nobles, minor nobility, merchants, and common men. The corresponding figures illustrate the required or normal artifacts interred with the corpse in each case. Sacrifice is also appropriate in some cases. This portion completes the view of Mictlantecutli, first as a deity with rites of worship much like those of other gods and then in the capacity occasioned by a death.

The next unit is only one folio in the Codex Tudela and is concerned with Tezcatlipoca. Unless the gloss is erroneous, this deity is somehow associated with the *temazcal* or sweat bath (folios 62r, 62v). It seems more likely that this should be Tlazolteotl, but neither the Magliabecchiano nor the Tudela Codex gives any indication except for the poorly drawn figure over the entranceway to the sweat bath. The text indicates the author's concern over the fact that both sexes are bathing together.

The last unit (8) deals with Yopes; this topic also occurs in the European Figures and Manta sections (folio 3r, Codex Magliabecchiano). Here the presentation in two folios shows the negotiations for marriage and the punishment of adulterers. According to Barlow (1949:map), the Yopes were found occupying the area along what was to become the road from Mexico City to Acapulco and constituted an independent seigniory at the time of the conquest. The text makes reference to Yopetuzco. A letter from the early 1530s in the *Epistolario de la Nueva España* (Paso y Troncoso 1939–42:2:item 88) indicates that the Yopes were not completely pacified and were then a matter of concern for the Spaniards.

Another folio in the reconstruction, labeled only "punishment of thieves" ("*castigo de ladrones*") is placed in this unit without certain identification. Should the gloss be erroneous, this folio (61) could easily represent the punishment of adulterers among the Mexica. In this case it would probably have been included by the author to illustrate the difference between the way the Yopes punished adulterers and the way other groups—the groups that provided most of the information in the documents—did. It is also possible, since the entire section is organized around movable feasts associated with principal deities, that this folio may have been meant to illustrate some aspect of Iztlacoliuhqui, who was concerned with social sins. Both the Codex Telleriano-Remensis (folio 17r) and the *Codex Borbonicus* (Hamy 1899:12) show death by stoning in association with Iztlacoliuhqui.

In general the author seems to consider the movable feasts to have less religious impact than the fixed feasts. Consequently, he makes many references to very common aspects of life—marriage, punishment, sweat baths—which do not come up in discussion of the more esoteric monthly feasts. Certainly most aspects of life in a theocratic culture have ritual overtones, but the emphasis is much less complex and strict. The author seems to conceptualize the next major section, the tonalamatl, within a divinatory framework; there are constant references to fortune and fate. Thus the contents of the Codex Tudela appear to form a progression from formal to informal and from that which is most complex to divination, which would be available to anyone (note the deerskin for divination depicted at the end of the section). This is very much in accord with the scholastic divine-to-secular conceptualization characteristic of the Middle Ages and early Renaissance.

The division dealing with the fifty-two-year cycle and the mantas is discussed after the other units because in the present order of the manuscript it appears at the end, although (for reasons which will be explained later) it seems most logical for it to precede the above-mentioned movable feasts and rites. The unit treating the years is just that: each year is presented in glyph form and in some cases a gloss accompanies it. The presentation is important also for the inclusion of three glosses that indicate the years 1553 and 1554. We shall consider these dates later in other contexts.

The manta section appears to be an effort to illustrate the articles so often mentioned for various ritual purposes. There are sixteen references to them alone in the surviving text of the Codex Tudela. The Magliabecchiano version preserves many more such glosses than does the Tudela, including several indicating mantas of the Yopes (folio 3r). These glosses, plus the inclusion of symbols that resemble place signs (folio 6v), and mentions of Tlaxcalan deities like Mixcoatl (folio 4v), tend to indicate that the unit as a whole presents examples of the robes from a wide geographical range. This unit is much like an appendix on religious material culture to complement the treatment of religion in the text as a whole.

There are more mantas in the Codex Magliabecchiano than in the document we are treating. In the former they appear to fall into two groups that follow each other. The first is composed of those with complex or conglomerate designs. These have glosses which tend to illustrate their diversity as well as their religious affiliation. There are several, for example, which are glossed "five roses." These would seem to refer to Macuilxochitl, a variant of Xochipilli. The second, and smaller, group, presents mantas whose designs are portions of the previous conglomerate depictions. Some of these are glossed. This group as a whole gives the impression of attempting to explain the first by dismounting the iconography into individual and theoretically more comprehensible portrayals. Some of the designs in this second group are in the tribute portion of the Codex Mendoza (notably the half conch shell: folios 31r, 34r, 37r, 52r). Perhaps the simpler designs are really symbols for the more complex ones and were used much like abbreviations. This may also be the case in the Codex Mendoza (Clark 1938) where it would be very difficult to place a representation of an elaborate design in a space of a few millimeters square. From this standpoint some of these elements would be conventionalizations for manuscript writing.

D. The Tonalamatl and Divination

The last section has six divisions. The first has to do with the religious nature of the days and the ruling deities associated with them. The format of presentation here illustrates the same regularity and rigor of approach found in the section dealing with the eighteen-month calendar and in the preceding section. Each description of a week contains mention of its length, the appropriate deity, the bird symbol for the god, the manner of sacrifice to him, and the divinatory nature of the time period. There is also some indication that portions of the text may have been translated directly from informants.

Robertson (1959:128) also noted this possibility in his treatment of the Codex Tudela. It would seem to have the most application in the tonalamatl section and is primarily manifest in the recursive phrasing typical of formal indigenous speech in Mesoamerica. Thompson (1954: 170–71) has noted it among the Maya, and Garibay (1961:321; 1952:xv) observed it in Nahuatl and considered it typical of most primitive poetry. Its presence here may be due to the practice of taking notes in Nahuatl for later translation, a method which Sahagún also used. On phonetic grounds, Kubler and Gibson suggest the possibility of a native scribe for the Tovar Calendar (Kubler & Gibson 1951: 19).

The four divisions that follow present the rulers of each direction and the corresponding signs of the ruling deities and the days. The nature of the text dealing with these directional quarters will be discussed later when the broader relations of the document as a whole are treated.

The last section, only one folio in length, contains the representation of a deer pelt, with glosses and text explaining how it is interpreted. This is fully in keeping with the author's general conceptualization of the tonalamatl as a device for divination rather than a technique of formal religious time allotment. Thus the treatment of the supposedly lesser aspects of religion includes the nonformalized methods of dealing with fate and the supernatural and ends in a principal instrument or artifact of divination, the deerskin.

This last section contains within it several specific indications of continuity with the foregoing sections. It should be remembered that the "Costumbres" copy does not contain this section at all. There is an internal reference to the eighteen-month calendar on folio 96v. There is also the use of the diminutive -ico suffix (common among speakers from northern Spain) in sections C and D.

Place names mentioned in the text are presented in Table 4. They are concentrated in the south of the Valley of Mexico, in the region stretching from Mexico to Chalco. These will be considered more fully when we discuss relations and authorship.

One of the most important aspects of the document as a whole is the continuity of its methodology. This continuity cannot be emphasized too heavily. It is the basis for reestablishing Section C in the order discussed as well as for certain other inferences. The method exemplifies the humanistic approach to collecting source data by categories, underscoring the fact that it was not produced for reasons of casual, personal, or political curiosity. Although the Codex Tudela is an incomplete copy, it manifests both a systematic format and a pragmatic vocabulary and style. The author not only grasped what he saw in an alien culture but was also able to express it comprehensibly in a fashion intellectually consistent with humanism.

The incompleteness of the Codex Tudela is illustrated by unfinished figures and occasional textual differences with the Codex Magliabecchiano. Note the lack of completion and misconception of the banners held above the shields by figures in the eighteen-month calendar, and also the inclusion of a pulque god on folio 85r of the Codex Magliabecchiano where the Tudela Codex (folio 71r) has none.

Several criteria for determining the identity of the author emerge from considering the contents of the volume. In brief form they are:

1) The nearly equal precision of detail, indicating the ability to distinguish specific ethnic groups, suggests that he visited the geographical regions which are illustrated in figures or referred to in the text.

2) The thorough comprehension of indigenous culture indicates that he was equipped to communicate and observe. This implies that he was in a position, economic or social, to have contact with Indians over sufficient time to achieve knowledge of the culture and that he knew native languages.

3) The organized format of presentation indicates that he was intellectually aware of humanism and thus concerned with education or well educated himself, or both.

RELATIONSHIP WITH CONTEMPORANEOUS MANUSCRIPTS AND AUTHORSHIP

Anonymous manuscripts most often remain anonymous, particularly those whose origin is remote in time. A consideration of authorship must take into account primarily the relationships expressed by the nature of the contents themselves. We have observed on the basis of a brief ex-

TABLE 4
PLACES AND REGIONS MENTIONED
IN THE CODEX TUDELA†

In Text	Probably	A	B	C	D	Total	Franciscan	Dominican	Augustinian	Secular	Cabecera	Visita	Valley of Mexico	"Pinturas"
Tepuztlan	Tepoztlán			1		1	?					?	X	+
Tezcuco	Texcoco		1		1	2	X				X		X	+
Amequemac	Amecameca		1			1	X*				X		X	+
Chalco	Chalco Atenco		1			1	X				X		X	+
Tlalmanalco	Tlalmanalco		1			1	X				X		X	+
Chimalhuacaotzinco	Chimalhuacán Atenco		1			1		X			X		X	
Misquique	Mixquic		1			1			X		X		X	+
Cuitlahuac	Cuitláhuac		1			1	X*				X		X	
Mexicalzinco	Mexicalzingo		1			1	X				X		X	
Yztapalapa	Ixtapalapa		1	1		2				X	X		X	+
Cuyuacan	Coyoacán		3			3	X*				X		X	+
Xuchimilco	Xochimilco		1			1	X				X		X	+
Vchilobuzco	Huitzilpochco		1			1			X	X	X		X	+
Culhuacan	Culhuacán		1			1					X		X	
Macatlan	Barrio of Mexico		2			2	?					?	X	+

In Text	Name Probably	Tudela A	Tudela B	Tudela C	Tudela D	Total	Franciscan	Dominican	Augustinian	Secular	Cabecera	Visita	Valley of Mexico	"Pinturas"
Huexucingo	Huejotzingo		2			2	?				?			+
Tehutleco	?		1			1								
Çacatepeque	Zacatepec		1			1	X				X		X	+
Chapultepeque	Chapultepec		1	1		2	X				X		X	+
Cuernavaca	Cuernavaca			1		1	X				?			+
Tacuba	Tacuba			1	1	2	X				X	?	X	+
Cempoulla	Zempoala (Veracruz?)				1	1								+
Mexico	Mexico	1	10	6		17	?				X		X	+
Capulco	Acapulco	2				2	?				?			+
Panuco	Pánuco (Veracruz)	2				2	X				X			+
Guatimala	Guatemala	1				1	?							+
Mechuacan	Michoacán	2	2			4	?							+
Vera Cruz	Veracruz	2				2	?							+
Tascala	Tlaxcala		4			4	?							+
29	28	10	38	11	3	62	13	1	2	2	18		18	20

* Indicates towns which were initially Franciscan but changed to other orders after the first decades of the colonial period.

† Religious order affiliation is based primarily on Gibson (1964) and Vásquez Vásquez (1965).

amination of these contents that the Codex Tudela has some unusual qualities for the pre-Sahagún era of colonial writing, especially in its methodology. We also have postulated in a preliminary fashion certain attributes of the author.

Documentation does not permit a quantitative appraisal of all individuals who might fit the postulated criteria in the acceptable time period. It is useful, however, to relate the contents and style of the Codex Tudela to those of other manuscripts. The Tudela Codex has an appendixlike character. Many topics are dealt with systematically and in some cases briefly. It is also incomplete when its individual figures and text are compared with those of the Magliabecchiano Codex, although as a whole the Codex Tudela is more complete in terms of topics treated. Its unfinished air can probably be attributed to the copyist, whereas the presentation and content can be imputed to the author.

A well-known document presented in a similar style is "History of the Mexicans through Their Pictures," "Historia de los Mexicanos por sus Pinturas." It is incomplete in that all paintings are lacking. García Icazbalceta's short description of it in the introduction to the volume in which it is included as an appendix (García Icazbalceta 1941b:xxxiv) indicates that it is a Spanish copy of the folios complete with figures that Ramírez de Fuenleal brought from Mexico in 1547. Fuenleal died in the same year, and the original was lost.

Gómez de Orozco's suggestion (1945:37) that "Costumbres" forms a fourth part of the Codex Mendoza can be disregarded on the basis of the incompatability of text, methodology, and style indicated in the Tudela Codex, from which the less ample "Costumbres" was derived. Robertson (1959:95–97) has shown that the Mendoza Codex was copied from older documents with the exception of the third part, which was composed for the work ordered by the viceroy. The version of "Pinturas" utilized here is that of 1941. There is a new edition with commentaries by Garibay (1965).

The presentation of the material in the "Pinturas" text is structurally similar to that in the Codex Tudela. The text makes constant reference to the figures, which seem to have been used as the basis for each topical discussion, and the systematic presentation is also similar to that of the Tudela Codex. The manuscript has three major sections which could be described as (A) Origin Myths, (B) Migration Myth and Political History of the Mexica, and (C) Summaries: Beliefs, Laws, Rulers. Chapter divisions continue to the end of the second section, eight chapters falling in the first and twelve in the second. The last section has two subtitles, but there seem to be at least seven formal topical divisions (see Table 5).

TABLE 5
ORGANIZATION OF "HISTORIA DE LOS MEXICANOS POR SUS PINTURAS"*

Pages†	Section	Chapter	Heading
	(A) Origin Myths		
209–10		1	De la creación y principio del mundo y de los primeros dioses
210–11		2	De como fué creado el mondo y por quien
211–12		3	De la creación del sol . . .
212–14		4	De la manera que tienen de contar (y de los gigantes)
214		5	Del diluvio y caída del cielo y de su restauración
214–15		6	De lo que subcedío después de haber alzado el cielo y las estrellas
215–16		7	Como fué fecho el sol, y lo que después de hecho sucedío
216–18		8	De lo que subcedío después de haber fecho el sol y la luna
	(B) Migration Myth & Political History of the Mexica		
218		9	Del principio y venida de los mexicanos á esta Nueva España
218–19		10	De cómo partieron los de Culuacán, y qué pueblos vinieron con ellos . . .
219–23		11	Del camino que trujeron, y las partes do[nde] estuvieron . . .
223–24		12	(Settle in Chapultepec)
224		13	(In Chapultepec)
225		14	(Flight from Chapultepec)
225		15	(Burying heart of a sacrifice in Michoacán)
225		16	(Servitude to Culuacán)
226		17	(In servitude)
226		18	(Driven out by Culuacán)
226–27		19	(Founding of Mexico)
227–34		20	(Military expansion of Mexica)

TABLE 5 cont'd

Pages†	Section	Chapter	Heading
	(C)	Summaries: Beliefs, Laws, Rulers	
234		(21)	(Year begins in March)
234–35		(22)	(The heavens and their levels)
235		(23)	(Culuacán migration)
235–37		(24)	(Señores of Mexico and other cities)
237–39		(25)	(Laws)
239–40		(26)	De do[nde] procedieron los señores de Tochimilco
240		(27)	La manera que tienen en contar los meses y días

* Information in parentheses is indicated but not stated in text.
† Page numbers are from the García Icazbalceta edition of 1941b.

Translations of Headings:

1. About the creation and beginning of the world and about the first gods
2. About how the world was created and by whom
3. About the creation of the sun . . .
4. About the way they have to count (and about the giants)
5. About the flood and falling of the sky and its restoration
6. About what happened after having raised the sky and the stars
7. How the sun was made, and what happened afterwards
8. About what happened after having made the sun and the moon
9. About the beginning and coming of the Mexicans to this New Spain
10. About how those of Culuacán departed and which peoples followed with them . . .
11. About the route they took, and the places where they were . . .
26. About where the lords of Tochimilco come from
27. The way that they have to count the months and days

Beyond basic format there are numerous indications that the Tudela Codex was originally articulated to the end of "Pinturas." The last unit of the third and final section of the manuscript is entitled "The Way They Have of Counting the Months and Days." It appears to be a summary:

It should be noted that they have twenty days to a week or month. . . . Also, they have four-year periods because they do not count the years by more names [than that]. Also, in the celebrations when the high priests sacrificed they put on certain white robes rounded at the head and put white feathers on them, that is, on their heads, and wore a colored blouse open at the front, and sacrificed that way. (Anon. 1941:240)

This reads like a résumé of what is to come and like the contents of the first portion of the Tudela Codex, the eighteen-month calendar followed by the fifty-two-year cycle and the manta section.

There are other indications that calendrical material was to follow the myths and political history presented in "Pinturas." Chapter 2 contains the following:

> Then they made out the days and divided them into months, giving each month twenty days, so they had eighteen, with three hundred and sixty days in the year, as will be told below. (Anon. 1941:210)

The text of Chapter 4 mentions:

> . . . I shall tell the manner and order they have in counting about years, and it is this. It has already been told how they have three hundred and sixty days in each year, and eighteen months, each month with twenty days; and how they used up the five days so that their celebrations would come out even (*fijas*), we shall tell below in the chapters that refer to festivals and their celebration. (Anon. 1941:212)

This last passage is followed by a brief description of how to count the years up to fifty-two with reference to paintings. The explication of the taking of "new fire" from Ixtapalapa is very similar in wording to the fuller description found on folios 83v, 84r, and 77v in the Codex Tudela. It should also be noted that the description of the use of mantas cited from "Pinturas" is worded similarly to the references to mantas in folios 11v and 96v of the Codex Tudela.

There are other indications of a complementary nature. The place names found in the two sources are very similar. "Pinturas" contains more than a hundred; Codex Tudela has considerably fewer but the majority of them are also to be found in the former document (see Table 6 and Figure 2).

The history presented in "Pinturas" is that of the Valley of Mexico and in particular of the Mexica and other groups in the south of the valley (note the particular presentation of material concerning Xochimilco and Culhuacán in the last section of "Pinturas"). References throughout "Pinturas" indicate a specific knowledge of the city of Mexico and the immediate area. Thus we find reference to the fact that

53

TABLE 6
PLACES AND REGIONS MENTIONED IN "PINTURAS"
(original spelling retained)

Name	A	B	C	Total	Tudela
Agualcomac		1		1	
Apazco		2		2	
Atitlabaca		1		1	
Atlacubaya			1	1	
Atlitlaquia		1		1	
Atlixco			1	1	
Atotoniltengo		1			
Azcapuzalco		11	7	18	
Azcla (Aztla)		3		3	
Capiscla		1		1	
Capulco		1		1	+
Castilla		3		3	
Catitlan		1		1	
Cempoal (Ver.)		2		2	+
Cempual	1			1	
Chalco	3	5		8	+
Chapultepeque		11	1	12	+
Chicomuxtoque		2		2	
Chimalcoque		1		1	
Chimalpupucaci		1		1	
Chimaluacan			1	1	
Chulula	1	3		4	
Chivichilat		1		1	
Cimlpal (Chimalpa)		2		2	
Clautitlan		2		2	
Coatebeque		2		2	
Coatlixan		1		1	
Cotasta			1	1	
Cuaistruaca		2		2	
Cuatitlan		1		1	
Cuatlicamat		1		1	
Cuatlecaxctan		1		1	
Cuauximilco		1		1	
Cuernavaca		1		1	+
Cuetlastla		2		2	

Name	A	B	C	Total	Tudela
Cuitlalauaca (Cuitralauaca)	1	1	2	4	
Cuiuacan		2		2	
Culuacan		29	5	34	+
Cuyacan		1	1	2	+
Cuzcatlan	1			1	
Cuzco		1		1	
Ecatebeque		2		2	+
Ensicox		1		1	
Ezpana	1	1		2	
Eztapalapa		3		3	+
Guaimula		1		1	+
Guautitlan		1	2	3	
Guatlinchan			1	1	
Guaximalpan		2		2	
Guaxocingo	1	2		3	+
Guazacalco		1	1	2	
Honduras	1	1		2	
Istacalco		1		1	
Ixocan		1		1	
Malinalco		1	1	2	
Marinalco		1		1	
Matalcingo		2		2	
Matlavacala		1	1	2	
Mexico	4	58	15	77	+
Michuacan (Mechoacan)		8		8	+
Mixiucan		1		1	
Mizquique (Mezquique)		2	1	3	+
Nepopualco		1		1	
Nextiquipaque		1		1	
Nueva Espana		2		2	
Nueva Galicia		1		1	
Ocozaza		1		1	
Ocvila			1	1	
Panuco		2		2	+
Petlauca(n)			2	2	
Puchitlan		1		1	
Quanmixtlitlan		1		1	

TABLE 6, cont'd

Name	A	B	C	Total	Tudela
Quausticaca		1		1	
Saltoca		2		2	
Suchimulco (Sochimilco)		5	5	10	+
Suyocingo		1		1	
Tacuba		1		1	+
Tacuxcalco		11		11	
Tamanalco		1		1	
Tascala (Tazcala)	1	5		6	+
Tatilulco		9	1	10	
Taxcuco (Texcoco)		12	2	14	+
Tecuzquiac		1		1	
Temazcaltitlan		1		1	
Temestitan		2		2	
Tenayucan (Tenayuca)		3	3	6	
Tenustitan		2		2	
Tepepan		1		1	
Tepexaquilla		1		1	
Tezmuluco		1		1	
Tezquiaque		1		1	
Tizapan		2		2	
Tlachetongo		1		1	
Tlacuba			1	1	
Tlapalla	2			2	
Tlatilulco		2	7	9	
Tlaula		1		1	
Tlemaco		1		1	
Tlilac		1		1	
Tluchitongo		1		1	
Tula	6	14	3	23	
Tulancingo		1		1	
Tultitlan			1	1	
Uchilobusco		1		1	+
Vepeucan			1	1	
Veracruz		1		1	+
Vetetlan		1		1	
Visachichitlan		1		1	

Name	A	B	C	Total	Tudela
Vizachitla		1		1	
Xaltocan		1		1	
Xuctectitl			1	1	
Zacaquipa		1		1	
Zozola		1		1	
Zumpango		3		3	
114	23	298	70	391	21

FIGURE 2. TOWNS OF THE VALLEY OF MEXICO MENTIONED IN THE CODEX TUDELA.

Istacalco was an estancia of Mexico (Anon. 1941:277), that Temazcaltitlan was then the barrio of "Saint Peter and Saint Paul" (Ibid.), that Tizapan was "an estancia that now belongs to Culhuacán" (Ibid.: 226), that there were ten houses in Nextiquipaque that served Mexico (Ibid.), and that Rodrigo Gómez found one of the round sculptures used in sacrifice while another is still in situ below a baptismal fountain (Ibid.: 230–31). The same is true in the Codex Tudela, where the text indicates that a round sacrifice stone is in the plaza near the houses of Cortés (Anon. 1553: folio 12v), that Tepuztlan is a possession of the Marques del Valle (Ibid.:folio 31r), and that a large stone fell through a bridge near the houses of Pedro de Alvarado (Ibid.:folio 84r).[2] This type of reference illustrates the author's familiarity in depth with the region in which he is writing and, as we shall see, helps to date and place "Pinturas"—and indirectly the Codex Tudela.

It seems that "Pinturas" was written in the city of Mexico, not only because of constant references to places within it but also for specific statements such as ". . . like that of Chapultepec in this City of Mexico" (Anon. 1941:218) and ". . . afterwards this city of Mexico was founded . . ." (Anon. 1941:224).

The time of writing can also be determined by examining the various specific references. One of the last sections of the manuscript contains the following reference to the governors of Mexico and Tlatelolco:

> . . . in Mexico the governors were Matemutci and Juan Velázquez y Tapia, who was not a noble, the last two in the time of the Marquis, in Tatilulco was the governor don Juan, father of the one who is now . . . (Anon. 1941:237)

Using the data given in Chapter 2 of Sahagún's eighth book in his *General History* (Sahagún 1946:287) concerning the Lords of "Tlatiluco" we find that Don Juan Avelitoc, the third governor, was succeeded by his son, Don Juan Quauiconoc, who held the office for seven years. Turning to Barlow's interpretation (1948:110) of the Tlatelolco Codex we find that the sixth governor, Don Martín Tlacaltecatl, began his office in 1542. Counting backward using Sahagún's data we arrive at the approximate dates of 1533–40 for the governorship of Juan Quauiconoc. Gibson's (1964:168) time placement of Andrés de Tapia Motelchiuhtzin as in charge of Tenochtitlan would mean contemporaneity with Quauiconoc's father as is stated in the "Pinturas" text. Thus it appears that

"Pinturas" was written in Mexico (or perhaps Tlatelolco) between the years 1533 and 1540.[3]

Several matters must be considered in the interpretation of the Tudela manuscript. As "Pinturas" makes references to the paintings of the years and the chapters on the months, it appears that at least some of the data now found in the Codex Tudela had already been collected by the time of completion of "Pinturas"; certainly the sequence of presentation had been worked out, implying knowledge of the topical outline on the part of the author. Leaving aside for the moment the question of dates, let us consider the problem of authorship for the two documents.

There appears to have been some agreement at the end of the last century by García Icazbalceta and Paso y Troncoso that Fray Andrés de Olmos was a probable author of "Pinturas." García Icazbalceta's presentation of their shared position (García Icazbalceta 1941b:xxv–xxxvi) indicates that the principal reason for this opinion was that Fuenleal, who took the complete manuscript to Spain in 1547, had commissioned Olmos to do an investigation of antiquities.

More recently Garibay (1953–54:2:33) has convincingly stated that "Pinturas" should be attributed to this Franciscan friar. He considers that the degree of understanding and integration of Nahuatl terms with a Spanish description is typical of Olmos. He also considers "Costumbres" (Gómez de Orozco 1945), a later copy of part of the Codex Tudela, to be attributable to Olmos, although from his standpoint the document is of little value (Garibay 1953–54:2:31,34). We can test the Olmos authorship much more definitively than Garibay has done in his style-based interpretation (although Paso y Troncoso and García Icazbalceta also agree on Olmos as the author of "Pinturas" on nonstylistic grounds) by applying what can be ascertained about Andrés de Olmos to the facts contained in the contents of "Pinturas" and the Tudela Codex.

Mendieta (1870:75) indicates in his prologue to Book 2 that his work was based on the books of Olmos and Motolinía. He further states with regard to Olmos:

> And the aforesaid father did it this way: having seen all the pictures that the chiefs and nobles in these provinces had of their antiquities, and the oldest men having given him an answer to everything he wished to ask them, he made of it all a very full book . . . (Mendieta 1870:75).

Thus we find that Olmos wrote a large work on indigenous topics. Both "Pinturas" and "Costumbres" are interpreted by Garibay (1953–54: 2:30–31) as representatives of a preliminary stage in this larger undertaking.

Mendieta also gives a clue as to why the work was undertaken in the first place. He states in his prologue:

> in the year 1533, the president of the Royal Audiencia of Mexico being Don Sebastian Ramirez de Fuenleal . . . , and the custodian of the order of our Father St. Francis in this New Spain being the holy man Fray Martín de Valencia, the father Fray Andrés de Olmos of the aforesaid order was charged by both of them (he being the best Mexican speaker there then was in this land and a learned and discreet man) to bring out in a book the antiquities of these native Indians, especially of Mexico, Tezcuco, and Tlaxcala . . . (Mendieta 1870:75).

It was also Fuenleal who brought the copy of "Pinturas" to Madrid in 1547. The 1533–40 time placement of "Pinturas" corresponds, as Mendieta indicates, to the fact that Olmos was charged to do such a work in 1533.

Since Mendieta's second book was based on Olmos and Motolinía, it should contain information from the Tudela Codex if the latter was a part of the "very full book." As Mendieta worked from a summary (used before him by Zurita and afterwards by Torquemada) made in later life by Olmos himself, the deletion of Motolinía's contribution to that section of the *Ecclesiastical History* should leave Olmos's interpretation of the summary (see Table 7). These textual relationships have been worked out and are discussed in some detail in a forthcoming analysis of the Codex Tudela. The possibility of a Motolinía authorship for the Codex Tudela, raised by the late Howard Cline (personal correspondence 1969), is also examined.

Although it does not appear that Mendieta fully understood the calendar, the description he gives in Chapter 14, "On the Celebrations They Made to Their Gods and On Their Calendar," appears to represent the Codex Tudela, even to the point of giving the number of figures on certain pages and translating the Nahuatl term *cipactli*. Mendieta also refers in the latter part of the chapter to a calendar wheel which he saw more than forty years earlier in the convent of Tlaxcala. Since he finished

TABLE 7
RELATIONSHIP OF THE OLMOS WORKS TO
SOME OTHER SIXTEENTH-CENTURY SOURCES

Motolinía Historia 1540s Treatise Ch.	Motolinía Historia Ch.	Motolinía Memoriales 1540s Pt.	Motolinía Memoriales Ch.	Alcobiz Leyes 1543? Pt.	Olmos Pinturas 1539? Ch.	Olmos Tudela 1553? Pt.	Olmos Huehuetlatolli 1547?	Olmos Suma +1560	Zurita Historia 1585 Pp.	Mendieta Historia 1596 Book 2 Ch.	Torquemada Monarquía 1614 Book	Torquemada Ch.
					1?, 2?			S	50	1	6	41
					3?			S		2	6	42
								S		3	6	43
								S	67	4	6	44
								S?		5	6	45
								S	56, 63	6	6	45
1	12	1	30–31					S	150	7		
										8		
										9		
										10		
								S	167	11	6	46
					3?			S	160–61	12	6	47
					21?, 4?	B, C1?, D1?		S	226	13	6	47
					27?			S		14		
1?	5?	1?	16?			B		S		15		

TABLE 7, cont'd

Motolinía Historia 1540s Treatise	Ch.	Memoriales 1540s Pt.	Ch.	Alcobiz Leyes 1543? Pt.	O · Pinturas 1539? Ch.	L · Tudela 1553? Pt.	M · Huehuetlatolli 1547?	O S · Suma +1560	Zurita Historia 1585 Pp.	Mendieta Historia... 1596 Book 2 Ch.	Torquemada Monarquía 1614 Book	Ch.
1	6-7	1	17-21			B, C$_1$		S	147	16		
			16?							17		
								S	151-53	18		
										19	6	48
							H			20	13	36
							H			21	13	36
							H			22	13	36
		2	3							23	13	28
		2	4			C?, D$_6$?		S?		24		
		2	5	1	25?					25	13	5
		2	13	1	25?					26	14	2
		2	13	1	25?					27	14	13
		2	15	1	25?					28		
		2	16-17							29		
		2	18							30	14	10
										31	14	11

Motolinía Historia 1540s Treatise Ch.	Motolinía Memoriales 1540s Pt.	Ch.	Alcobiz Leyes 1543? Pt.	Pinturas 1539? Ch.	Tudela 1553? Pt.	Olmos Huehuetlatolli 1547?	Suma +1560	Zurita Historia 1585 Pp.	Mendieta Historia... 1596 Book 2 Ch.	Torquemada Monarquía 1614 Book	Ch.
				9?			S	46–47, 48, 50, 44?	32		
				10?			S	67?	33	2	12
				9–18?, 19			S	46–47?, 111	34		
				20			S		35		
				20			S		36		
					C₈		S		37		
	2	10					S?		38	11	30
	2	10, 12 / 16–17					S?		39	11	30
	2	11–12							40	13	45
	2	2							41	13	46
	2	1									

63

his *History* in 1596, this would have been before 1556. He arrived in the New World in 1554 and was sent to the monastery at Xochimilco before going to Tlaxcala (García Icazbalceta 1870:xviii). At precisely this time Motolinía was bishop of Tlaxcala. Perhaps this was the wheel which Motolinía included in his book (facsimile in Steck 1951: opposite 59). This would mean either that Mendieta was working from an unillustrated copy of Motolinía or that he did not remember sufficiently the material that he had seen earlier. He also mentions the five extra days of the eighteen-month calendar as following the months. This is in agreement with Motolinía's calendar wheel and Olmos's material in the Codex Magliabecchiano.

The details of Olmos's life also help to clarify some of the facts to be found in the Codex Tudela and "Pinturas." That Olmos was a Franciscan would explain why the Tudela Codex mentions only a few places that were not under Franciscan control during the early colonial period (see Table 4). The wide geographic range of the "European" figures of the first section of Tudela also comes into better focus when we note that Olmos visited all of the places represented; he was in Guatemala in 1529 and in the other areas at various times throughout the remainder of his life. His concern for the Huasteca and the northeast also accounts for the special reference to Pánuco in the "Pinturas" text (Anon. 1941: 233–34).[4]

Apparently Olmos was a lecturer at Santa Cruz de Tlatelolco between 1533 and 1539. Steck (1944:40) indicates that he taught there but does not give dates, while Meade (1950) dates his lectureship between 1533 and 1539. Navarro (1955:69) states that Olmos taught logic and philosophy and had a doctorate in canon and civil law. The location of Santa Cruz would afford him an excellent opportunity to obtain information from all over the Valley of Mexico, as most of the pupils of this college were Indians from the upper classes of that area (Gibson 1964:99). Sahagún's method while he was at the college in the 1560s was to interview and use students as assistants (Robertson 1959:169). This interview technique presents another methodological similarity between Olmos and Sahagún.

The college was notable at this time for its humanistic approach and influence (Gibson 1964; Robertson 1959:156). Olmos was associated with Bishop Zumárraga, who in turn was heavily influenced by the humanism of Erasmus, and who brought Olmos with him to New Spain in 1528 (Kubler 1948:11). Thus, many of the attributes postulated for the author of the Codex Tudela on the basis of its contents are manifest in Andrés de Olmos. He was well educated and taught in a humanistic institution, and he was fluent in the Nahuatl required for extensive contact with the Indians represented in the text. He may have been sufficiently versatile to write in both Totonac and Huastec as well, as Ricard's bibliography would show (1947:506). He also fulfills the requirements of having visited all the regions which are indicated in the text and having sufficient time to obtain detailed information. In 1539 he was put in charge of the monastery of Hueytlapan, in the upper reaches of the present state of Puebla not far from the state of Veracruz. It is quite possible that additional information was gathered on Nahuatl speakers after he left the College of Santa Cruz. The tonalamatl may be an example of this because of particular references which would not necessarily be indicative of the central highlands.[5]

The Ometochtli section, at least the portion dealing with the representation of the cult in various towns, may also have been added after he left Santa Cruz. In 1543 he was named guardian in Tecamachalco (Meade 1950:408). Gibson (1964:108–9) indicates that this was a *visita* of Tacuba. At least one of the place signs in this section of the Tudela Codex, that for Tototepec, indicates another *visita* of Tacuba (see Table 8). In the same year, 1543, he visited the Franciscan cabecera of Tlalmanalco and the monastery of Cuernavaca. Since the text concerned with the first representation of Ometochtli (folio 31r) specifically mentioned Tepoztlan as being four leagues from Cuernavaca toward Mexico, it is not unlikely that some of the information in this section was acquired at this time. Barlow's map of the tribute regions (1949) shows Tepoztlan as being in the province of Chalco, where many of the other places mentioned in the Codex Tudela are also located. Thus indications are that most of the information that ultimately went into the Codex Tudela was gathered in the 1530s, but some may have been collected during the early 1540s.

The mid-1540s to early 1550s appear to have been a time of finishing the segments of the larger work. *Huehuetlatolli,* or *Speeches of the Elders,* was compiled, according to Garibay (1953–54:1:438) between 1540 and 1545. The grammar of Nahuatl, *Arte de la lengua mexicana* (later

TABLE 8
TENTATIVE IDENTIFICATION OF PLACE SIGNS
IN THE CODEX TUDELA

Folio	Probable town	Peñafiel 1885	Peñafiel 1897	Matrícula de Tributos
23r	Coatepec	p. 77/VII–fig. 6	p. 60/p. 18–figs. 11, 12/p. 19–figs. 1, 2	lam. 34–fig. 9
86r	Azcaputzalco*	p. 67/V–fig. 9	p. 38/p. 13–figs. 11, 12/p. 14–figs. 1, 2, 3	lam. 5–fig. 1
88r	Tonatiucho*	p. 221/XXXII–fig. 10	p. 92–fig. 12	lam. 36–fig. 8
31r	Tepoztlan	pp. 194–95/XVIII–figs. 1, 2, 3	p. 206/p. 75–figs. 3, 4, 5	lam. 26–fig. 13
33r	Yauhtepec	p. 248/XXXVIII–fig. 3	p. 323/p. 106–figs. 9, 10, 11	lam. 26–fig. 14
34r	Tulantzinco	p. 224/XXXIII–fig. 9	p. 300/p. 94–figs. 9, 10	lam. 33–fig. 3
39r	Tototepec	p. 224/XXXIII–fig. 2		
43r	Etlan*	p. 113/XIII–fig. 7	p. 115/p. 37–fig. 7	lam. 46–fig. 2
56r	Huepochtla*	p. 118–19/XIV–fig. 1		
36r	Centzontepec*			
37r	Huapalcalco*			
41r	Xaltepec*			
44r	Coyohuacan*			
47r	Coatzinco*			
38r	Culhuacan†			

* questionable
† probable

published by Siméon, 1885) was apparently finished, and the "Speeches" were annexed to the document in 1547 (Garibay 1953–54:1:438). This was finished in Papantla in the district of Hueytlapan. (The most complete copy of the *Arte* is the bound manuscript in the Latin American Library of Tulane University. It includes the "Speeches" as exercises following the grammar, folios 21r–25r.)

1553 is the date recorded twice in the Codex Tudela and is probably accurate. This might make it the next to last segment of the "very full book," as "Hechicerías y Sortilegios" (Anon. 1966; Garibay 1966) dates from the following year. This document, written in Nahuatl with a Spanish prologue, warrants textual comparison with the Codex Tudela and "Pinturas." It may constitute notes taken from informants and awaiting translation to Spanish for inclusion in either of the above two works or for a separate portion of the larger work. The manuscript is now in the Biblioteca Nacional de México.

The early 1550s for Olmos were probably a time of pushing to finish up the work which he had begun so many years earlier, because in the same year (1553) he requested permission from the viceroy, Don Luis Velasco, to found a monastery at Pánuco where he had worked earlier (Meade 1950:414). After this time there are no known manuscripts in Nahuatl or treating Nahuatl speakers that can be attributed to Olmos, except perhaps for the "Summary." According to Meade (1950), however, he did complete some short works in Huastec.

The internal dates in the text of the Codex Tudela would tend to indicate that the manuscript was finished in the monastery at Hueytlapan or somewhere in its jurisdiction. Meade (1950) notes that the "Seven Sermons" (also known as the "Treatise on the Seven Principal Sins") were finished at Papantla in 1552. It appears that Olmos carried his information with him and wrote up a final, or at least semifinal, draft wherever he was. Robertson (1959:133) has interpreted the phrase *"en México"* to be indicative of a different social class for the informant or writer and thus not implying location outside the city. A comparison of the data with what is known of the life of Olmos shows that although much of the information was gathered when the author taught in Tlatelolco, some of it was probably gathered while he was guardian of Tecamachalco at a later date. There is also the possibility that some of the data came from Nahuatl-speaking informants to the east, notably the tonalamatl and manta sections. Even the region of Hueytlapan presented ample opportunities to obtain Nahuatl-speaking informants. (Barlow [1949:51, 59–63] states that some of the towns in the Hueytlapan region were subdued by the Acolhua.) This would be in keeping with his project of examining the antiquities of ". . . particularly Mexico and Tezcuco and Tlaxcala . . ." (Mendieta 1870:75). The location of the writer in no way affected the subject matter of the manuscript, which is principally the

Mexica, an emphasis which is underscored when the manuscript is articulated with "Pinturas."

RELATIONSHIP WITH SUBSEQUENT MANUSCRIPTS

This topic has been treated in some detail by Robertson (1959), who sees the Codex Magliabecchiano and a portion of Cervantes de Salazar's *Chronicle* as deriving from the Codex Tudela or from the same source. The comparison of text and figures suggests that there are several discernible "lines" of copies which result from this original source.

The source manuscript itself may not be necessarily a single document. Mendieta's description of the history of the "very full book" indicates that there were various copies:

> . . . three or four copies were brought out which were sent to Spain and the original he later gave to a certain priest who was also going to Spain, so that no copy of this book was left to him. . . . (Mendieta 1870:75)

These "copies" may or may not have been complete. "Pinturas," brought to Spain in 1547 by Fuenleal, one of the two people who charged Olmos to do the work, was probably one of these copies. The Tudela Codex could easily be another, although we know only that it was in Spain by 1739 and that the "Costumbres" copy was most likely made shortly before that date. This dating of "Costumbres" is on the basis of the manuscript's handwriting, which in general is much clearer than sixteenth-century hands. Comparing the photograph of folio 34r in the 1945 publication of the text to handwriting samples in Haggard (1941) and Millares Carlo (1929), it would seem best dated around the end of the seventeenth or beginning of the eighteenth century.

The Magliabecchiano Codex treats about two-thirds of the topics found in the Codex Tudela, but it is distinct in several ways. Figures like those in folios 82r, 85r, 87r, and the like are more complete or illustrate different interpretations. Folio 85r of the Magliabecchiano shows rope where the symbols appear to be insects in folio 70r of the Tudela. Franco (1961:202–3) considers some common representations in this sequence to be butterflies, thus giving some credibility to the latter interpretation. The text is also more complete on certain subjects, in the Ometochtli sequences for example (folios 50v, 51v, 52v, 62v, 63v of Codex Magliabecchiano). In some cases the texts are totally different (for example the data dealing with the Temazcal: folio 76v Maglia- becchiano and 62r Tudela), while in others the text is broken or modi- fied in different places (the Tepoztlan data for example, folios 48v, 49v in Magliabecchiano and folio 31r in Tudela).

The last section of the Codex Tudela, the tonalamatl, is lacking in the Codex Magliabecchiano. As has been suggested previously, it is quite possible that this section was completed with information obtained at a later date than the rest and in a different area. This possibility, plus the probable completion of "Pinturas" (with its reference to material included in the Codex Tudela) by about 1539, would tend to indicate that all the material in the Codex Magliabecchiano was available before the 1553 date of the more comprehensive Codex Tudela. Nuttal (1903: xvii) and Robertson (1959:128) indicate that the paper in the codex was in use between 1562 and 1601. The Codex Magliabecchiano is con- sequently later than the Codex Tudela. It would thus be plausible that the Codex Magliabecchiano originates from a *copy* made before the Codex Tudela, with its additional information. However, the fact that both documents are out of order in the movable feast section in a similar but not identical fashion may show that the document from which the Magliabecchiano Codex was copied was in turn copied from a manuscript between the original and the Tudela Codex. These folios would have been out of order as in the two mentioned codices but more complete in text and figures than the Codex Tudela. For purposes of the discussion this is called the "Y line" (see Figure 3).

The second major manuscript that seems to be derived from the same source and to date from the 1560s is a portion of Cervantes de Salazar's *Chronicle of New Spain*. This document only uses the infor- mation found in the Codex Tudela in a summary fashion, and not specifically. The description that Cervantes gives, however, tends to indicate that he had more textual information at his disposal than is enumerated in the Codex Tudela. This is particularly true for his sec- tions on Paxpataque and Quetzalcoatl (Cervantes de Salazar 1914:51), and may be the case for his treatment of burials (Chapter 31).

There is also the greater correspondence of the dates in the *Chronicle* with the first set of dates in the Codex Tudela. Since the corrected

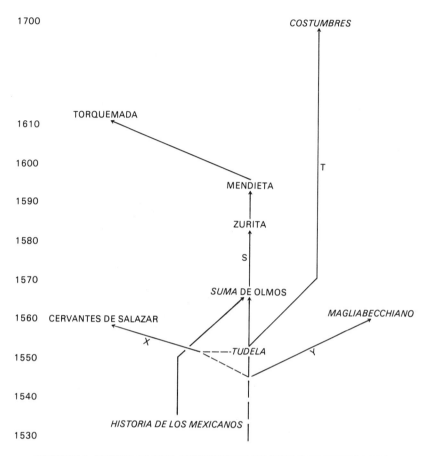

FIGURE 3. GENERAL RELATIONSHIPS OF THE CODEX TUDELA.

dates in the Codex Tudela were probably done at the same time as the 1554 date in the fifty-two-year cycle section, and Cervantes de Salazar did not arrive in Mexico City until 1551 and did not begin his work until 1560 (by which time Olmos considered his work lost), it would seem likely that he did not have the Tudela manuscript before him. The ordering of what data he does present, particularly the movable feasts, tends to indicate that his source was not in as disordered a condition as the Codex Tudela.[6]

The inclusion of tonalamatl information would deny any affiliation with the Codex Magliabecchiano. It would seem that his source was a manuscript which was at least textually more ample than the Codex

Tudela, and in its original order. This may have been the complete original itself or a copy, the "X" line (see Fig. 3).

Still another line carries the data found in the Codex Tudela. Apparently Olmos himself in later life wrote a résumé of the larger work which was in turn used by Alonso de Zurita in his *History of New Spain* and by Mendieta in the second book of his *Ecclesiastical History:*

> . . . he agreed to examine his notes and to make an epilogue or summary of what was contained in that book, as he did . . . and he told me in whose possession I would find this latter compilation in his own hand, and I had it and kept it in my possession . . . (Mendieta 1870:76).

Mendieta in turn was used as a source by Torquemada, as García Icazbalceta's introduction to the former work shows (1870:xxxvii–xlv). This line is called here the "summary (S) line" (see Fig. 3) but it has some implications for the Codex Tudela. In Chapter 24 Mendieta (1870:98) discusses the calendar, including material that is found in the Codex Tudela, and he mentions in reference to information coming from the "Summary" of Olmos ". . . this book of the calendar. . . ." This phrase could be interpreted to mean that the original work as a whole contained one book expressly devoted to calendrical material. This in turn would mean that the Codex Tudela represents an incomplete copy of that book, as would also the Codex Magliabecchiano, while Cervantes's source text may have been the original or a complete copy.

There are thus four lines of texts containing the calendrical material present in the Codex Tudela, all of which originate in the various copies of the calendrical book. The Tudela Codex is not the original, and most likely not the basis of any presently known documents except for the "Costumbres" copy (T line) of about 1700 (see Fig. 3).

IMPLICATIONS

The Codex Tudela, in conjunction with the "Historia de los Mexicanos por sus Pinturas," represents a major portion of the missing "very full book" of Fray Andrés de Olmos. As such it constitutes a very important early source for ethnographic data from New Spain in the first half of the sixteenth century. Likewise the *Arte de la lengua mexicana*, with the annexed "Speeches of the Elders" and "Hechicerías y

Sortilegios" appears to relate, topically if not structurally, to the Tudela–Pinturas ethnography and the lost larger work. The manuscript published by de Jonghe in 1902 may also fall in this group. (Plate 2 shows the opening of Chapter 8 from the *Arte*.)

Although it now appears that even if the entire original work of Olmos were to be recovered intact it would be no longer (or necessarily more useful anthropologically) than Sahagún's Florentine Codex, its value remains considerable for several reasons. The first is the early date of the information provided by Olmos.

As has been discussed, most if not all of the material for the Codex Tudela and "Pinturas" dates to the second decade of the Spanish presence in Mexico. The data were obtained during the time of incipient institutional consolidation following violent contact between cultures. The work of Olmos thus precedes most of the work of Sahagún, and it may, in fact, precede and influence Sahagún's Book 6, which probably dates to the middle of the sixteenth century. The early date and loss also serve to make it a useful independent check on data provided by other chroniclers, since, with the exception of the "Suma," Olmos's work apparently never circulated as a single unit for a prolonged time.

The scope of Olmos's work is also significant. It was meant to be comprehensive, and, even if only the Codex Tudela and "Pinturas" are considered, to a large degree it achieved that goal. Legends, origin myths, and lineage histories are presented, followed by laws, ethnicity, the solar calendar, major movable feasts, cults, the year count, artifacts, religious calendar (tonalamatl), and divination. Internal references in the documents suggest that, at least by the time the surviving copies were produced, the diverse parts were viewed as a single work, or as intended to be such. If we take into consideration the "Speeches" and "Hechicerías," the scope broadens still further. It is both ambitious and factual, leading to perhaps its most important aspect, methodology.

The methodology used by Olmos for eliciting information is clearly stated in the opening lines of "Pinturas":

(1) From the characters and writings they make use of and (2) from the recounting of the elders and (3) from those who were priests and religious leaders in the time of their infidelity and (4) from the talk of the lords and leaders to whom the law had been taught and

who were kept in the temples so they could learn it, (5) having assembled before me and (6) having brought their books and pictures which, according to what they demonstrated, were old and many of them dyed, the larger part anointed with human blood . . . (Anon. 1941; parentheses added).

He indicates three types of informants: elders (2), priests (3), and nobles (4). Each group would be able to present information concerning diverse institutions, practices, and religio-historical rationale. Some of this information would be contingent on the informant's pre-Columbian training or social position; hence the necessity for several types of informants.

Priests and nobles would appear to be the major informants for most of the data contained in the Codex Tudela and "Pinturas." Elders might, however, have been more appropriate for some of the practices described in the "daily ritual" section of the Codex Tudela, the "Speeches of the Elders," and perhaps "Hechicerías y Sortilegios."

Nobles or their offspring would have been easily available to Olmos at the College of Santa Cruz de Tlatelolco. Former priests and elders might have been easier to encounter in the various towns visited by Olmos in the Valley of Mexico and its environs. Torquemada (1943–44: 2:79) indicates, for instance, that Olmos had an informant named Lorenzo for data from the Texcoco area; the "Speeches" may have been collected from the elders of Cuernavaca. Mendieta (1945:1:158) states that Olmos also had an informant by the name of Don Andrés, an elder in Texcoco, whom he questioned concerning origin myths.

Olmos indicates that he personally interviewed the informants. He also states that he examined artwork and had his informants bring codices and artifacts for discussion. This is confirmed by Torquemada (1943–44:2:79). An Inquisition document, "Trial Pursued by Fray Andrés de Olmos against the Chief of Matlatlan," dating to 1540, indicates that he had in his possession confiscated pictorial documents.

Although further critical review is necessary, it would appear that at least a portion of Olmos's ethnographic works were written first in Nahuatl, the language of his informants. "Speeches of the Elders" was certainly recorded in the original language. "Hechicerías y Sortilegios," in Nahuatl except for a Spanish introduction, may represent one of the early stages of data summation. The Codex Tudela, which retains traces of indigenous couplets, is much nearer the final Spanish presentation to be found in the surviving unillustrated copy of "Pinturas."

The presentation of data follows the systematic nature of the interview procedure. Topics are discussed whenever possible with direct reference to specific paintings, drawings, artifacts, or places. Generally the salient aspects of a topic are presented in an ordered fashion. In the discussion of the eighteen-month calendar in the Codex Tuleda, for instance, the pertinent data such as feast name, duration, patron deity, ritual, and Julian correlation are given for each month before additional information of variable import is noted. In this particular case it appears that Olmos was using an outline, either from the interview or specifically for summation purposes.

Internal references to preceding or following sections, as well as the topical (divine to secular) ordering of the diverse sections of "Pinturas" and the Codex Tudela strongly suggest a systematic, holistic approach to the presentation of the ethnographic data. The scope is ambitious and, in terms of major indigenous institutions, rather complete. Although not encyclopedic, given the size of the work, the data included indicate an attempt to present the range of pre-Columbian culture and an understanding of some of its basic precepts.

Although the ethnographic works of Olmos are incomplete and may never be fully recovered, their data, methodology, and magnitude clearly place them among the earliest true ethnographies. Along these lines the Olmos works require comparison with the works of Sahagún, most of which were written at a later date, and in particular with the great Florentine Codex. It has not been my purpose to attempt here a detailed study of the relationships of the two sets of documents but rather to point out the nature of the corpus of Olmos's works and to suggest possible influences.

Perhaps the greatest influence that Sahagún could have derived from Olmos or his works is in the realm of methodology. Similarities are to be found in recording data in Nahuatl, interviewing informants, consulting indigenous documents, and in the systematic presentation of topics, the broad scope, and the formulation of various summations before the final presentation. Some of these categories are general and difficult to derive from a given source, while others are more specific and

74

perhaps more likely to have been copied. It is important to note, however, that the works of both men share all these points.

While it appears that a number of sections of Olmos's works were
circulating in the Mexico City area prior to, and conceivably after, the
middle of the sixteenth century, the likely point of intellectual contact
between the two men would have been the College of Santa Cruz de
Tlatelolco. Both were apparently at Tlatelolco late in the 1530s and
perhaps at some point in the 1540s. Both also drew informants from
the college and both may have begun their ethnographic investigations
as a result of the Fuenleal–Valencia order in the mid-1530s. It is highly
probable, if not certain, that they made contact, either directly, through
the use of the same informants, or through the availability of Olmos's
works. If this were the case we should expect to find some points of
topical overlap. Two such points may be data concerning the cult of
Ometochtli and the orations of the *Huehuetlatolli*.

The data concerning the pulque cult were derived from towns in
the Tepoztlan area and appear in the Codices Tudela and Magliabecchiano. Book 4 of the Florentine Codex presents data on Ometochtli. The paternal orations appear in the "Speeches of the Elders"
annexed to the *Arte Mexicano* and in Book 6 of the Florentine Codex. In
the case of the orations we know that the Olmos compilation was
circulating in midcentury, as it was partially utilized by Las Casas in his
Apologética historia sumaria. Although Las Casas met with Olmos in
1545, he states (1967:447) that Olmos sent him the data once he was
in Spain. He left for Spain in early 1547 and composed his *History*
between 1553 and 1559 (O'Gorman 1972:135ff.). The *Arte* was finished
in 1547, the same year as Sahagún's Book 6 and Fuenleal's trip to Spain
with a copy of "Pinturas." The presence of "Pinturas" in Spain prior to
this date is suggested by a brief treatise on laws that may have been
copied from it by Fray Andrés de Alcóbiz in Valladolid during 1543,
entitled "These Are the Laws That the Indians of New Spain, Anáhuac
or Mexico Had" (Alcóbiz, 1543).

These are only two of the possibilities that bear examination. A
detailed study of the two sets of works may produce further points of
topical contact. Other overlaps might be found in the use of pictorial
illustrations, as suggested earlier. Organizational similarities can be
examined also. Books 2 and 4, and the appendix of the latter, for in-

75

stance, in Sahagún's Florentine Codex and *General History* present the eighteen-month calendar, movable feast, year count, and tonalamatl in the same sequence as the Codex Tudela, giving similar weight to each.

While Olmos's works are earlier in date and may have influenced Sahagún in his approach, presentation, and choice of topics, they do not rival Sahagún's in extent of detail, nor do they detract from the contribution of Sahagún to anthropological and historical studies. All investigators receive stimulus from their surroundings, their peers, and their predecessors. In the early years of the colonial period in Mexico, the Franciscan world was not so large as to preclude contact, and it would seem unlikely that at any one time there would be many investigators pursuing pre-Columbian data in depth. It would have been advantageous, and necessary, to consult the works of others.

The great contributions of Olmos lie in the early date of his information and in his rigorous methodological approach, both of which are harbingers of anthropology in the Americas. Even in their surviving incompleteness his works are useful, especially when articulated to approximate their original form. His influence upon Sahagún, whether direct or indirect, appears to have been due to the same factors that make him notable today.

NOTES

1. The discussion in this paper of the Codex Tudela and its relationships is the result of investigations begun in 1968 in a seminar on Mexican manuscript painting under the direction of Dr. Donald Robertson. The seminar contributions are being prepared for publication under his editorship. Preliminary results of this continuing study by the writer were presented before the annual meeting of the American Anthropological Association at New Orleans, November 1969, and in "El Codice Tudela: Una Fuente Etnografica del siglo XVI" (Wilkerson 1971).

2. Pedro de Alvarado died in 1541 in Jalisco while the Marqués del Valle died in Spain in 1547. There is no evidence in the document that these two then-famous individuals had died yet. The impression is that of contemporaneity.

3. The first names of the two contemporary governors of Xochimilco are also given (Anon. 1941:239–40). Such information could help to tie the manuscript down to even less than the six-year period. León-Portilla, writing after the time of this investigation and using a similar contextual approach to "Pinturas," proposes 1531–37 as the time period (1969:41–42).

4. The "European" figures section follows a precise pattern moving from south to north. A letter from the *alcalde mayor* of Pánuco in 1553 (Paso y Troncoso 1939: 8:item 449), which mentions the evangelical labors of Olmos, refers to the Indians in the region as "Chichimec." Consequently the placement of the Chichimec figures

following the Huastec is in keeping with the nomenclature of the time. Since Olmos founded the monastery at Pánuco there is no question of his association with the Indians of the region. Meade (1950:380) places the founding possibly as late as 1532 while Ricard (1947:158) and Cuevas (1922:3:409) consider the date to be 1530. Kelly and Palerm (1952:30) believe that he was in the Totonac region before founding the Pánuco mission.

5. The Hueytlapan region stretched from the immediate area of the town itself toward the lowlands. Kubler (1948:461) indicates that religious construction began during the 1540s when Olmos was there. The same friar also renamed towns in the district (González 1581:153). Durán (1951:1:248) noted in his history that many Nahuatl speakers migrated to the *tierra caliente* because of successive droughts in the highlands. García Payón in his reconstruction of the mid-sixteenth-century demography of the area (1958, 1965) has shown that the entire area was composed of many towns that spoke either Nahuatl or Totonac or both. This would mean that there would be no lack of informants to supply information on the highland cultures, especially since the Totonac religion at the time was so permeated by highland attributes (as has been shown by García Payón [1971] and Melgarejo Vivanco [1966], in their treatment of Zempoala, the largest Totonac city).

6. At the end of Chapter 31, which deals, like the Codex Tudela, with the death of various social types, Cervantes de Salazar makes reference to the following:

> . . . having had recourse for the rest to a book that has been done on this, which
> I think will come out shortly . . . (Cervantes de Salazar 1914:56).

This corresponds to the data taken from Olmos's Summary and used by Mendieta, stating that there was a book of the calendar (1870:98). Certainly the unfinished nature of the Codex Tudela indicates that it was not ready for formal circulation, especially in an era when more manuscripts were available. On the whole it appears that Salazar had more information to work with than that contained solely in the Tudela Codex.

4

The Rhetorical Orations, or *Huehuetlatolli,* Collected by Sahagún*

T H E L M A D. S U L L I V A N

Escuela Nacional de Antropología de México

Of all the material gathered by Sahagún, none is as rich in language or as revealing of the pre-Hispanic Indian mind and thought as the rhetorical orations, generally called *huehuetlatolli.* There are some eighty-nine such orations, all told, scattered throughout the Madrid and Florentine codices, making these the richest repository of *huehuetlatolli* in all Nahuatl literature. Sixty make up Book 6 of the Florentine Codex, there is one in Book 12 of this same codex, and there are two in the "Primeros Memoriales." The twenty-six remaining orations can

---

* All translations of texts from Spanish and Nahuatl contained in this chapter are by the author. When they are from the Florentine Codex, the Nahuatl text of the Dibble and Anderson edition is cited by book and page number.

be found in corresponding texts of the Madrid and Florentine codices.[1]
(See Tables 9–14, pages 100–107 in this chapter.)

The authenticity of these orations—which was debated by a number
of Sahagún's contemporaries who saw, or wished to see, Indians as bar-
barians—is unquestionable to us today precisely for the reason that
Sahagún himself gave in his prologue to Book 6: ". . . it is not possible
for the human mind to invent what is written in this book, nor is there
a man living capable of inventing the language contained in it" (Sahagún 1956:2:54).

There are two other collections of *huehuetlatolli* of importance, one
gathered by Fray Andrés de Olmos in the sixteenth century (Bautista
1600) and one attributed to Carochi in the seventeenth century (Garibay 1943).[2] It is noteworthy that the three great Nahuatlatos among the
sixteenth- and seventeenth-century friars—Olmos, Sahagún, and Carochi
—collected these texts. The two best Nahuatl grammars extant are those
of Olmos (1875) and Carochi (1892), and had Sahagún's not been lost,
it is highly probable that his would have been added to the list. Indeed,
anyone concerned with the fine points of the Nahuatl language as well
as the ancient traditions of the Nahuas, as were these three, would be
interested in the stylistic, linguistic, and conceptual intricacies of the
huehuetlatolli.

What exactly are *huehuetlatolli?* Molina, in his dictionary (1970),
defines the term as "ancient history of sayings of the elders." Fray Juan
Bautista, who published the orations collected by Olmos in 1600 with
a rather free translation, entitled the book *Huehuetlatolli, O Pláticas de
los Viejos,* and this has generally been the accepted meaning of the
word. Both Garibay (1943:3; 1953–54:1:401ff; 1963:140) and León-
Portilla (1959:17–18), who refer to them as "didactic discourses," ad-
here to this interpretation and call them "Orations of the Elders" or
"of the Old Men." Garibay (1943:3) defines them as "orations and
doctrinal precepts by means of which the ancient Mexicans instructed
the children in good morals and in what could be called the practice
of social forms," and León-Portilla (1963:192) as "didactic discourses, or
exhortations addressed to the boys of the *Calmecac* or *Telpochcalli*, as
well as to adults, upon such occasions as marriage and funeral rites, for
the purpose of inculcating moral ideas and principles."

In his *Historia de la Literatura Náhuatl,* in the chapter entitled

The Rhetorical Orations, or Huehuetlatolli

"Discursos Didácticos," in which he discusses the *huehuetlatolli*, Garibay (1953–54:1:427) omits an analysis of the first nine chapters of Book 6 of the Florentine Codex, which are the prayers to the gods, giving as his reason that "it is not directly relevant to my subject." By the same token, in his introduction to the *huehuetlatolli* collected by Carochi, to which he himself gave the title "Huehuetlatolli, Documento A," he describes this group of texts as "not properly a *huehuetlatolli* but a miscellany of forms used in social intercourse" (Garibay 1943:3). In fact, it contains such texts as the salutations of a woman stopping by the house of her kinsman on her way to market; congratulations to a newly married couple and a series of orations by various people involved in this important event, including the matchmakers; orations to a ruler and his wife on the birth of their child; an oration addressed to a deceased ruler and one of condolence to his lords; a series of salutations by children to their elders and the elders' replies; and one by the elders to some singers, among others. Of the forty-eight separate texts, most of them fairly short, that comprise this series of orations, exactly two deal with the rearing of children. Nevertheless, Garibay (1953–54: 1:440) states that "their didactic character, their antiquity and the form in which they are preserved, prompted me to give them the title, *Huehuetlatolli*."

Similarly, the *Huehuetlatolli* of Olmos contains an oration on the occasion of one woman visiting another, a salutatory oration from a lord to a ruler, an oration of consolation from one lord to another dealing with a mishap that befell the latter, an address made by the lord of Texcoco to the people, another by the lords of Tlaxcala concerning the governing of the city, and others of a like nature, interspersed with what might be called "didactic discourses," such as those of a father to his son and a mother to her daughter, which deal with the social and moral aspects of their comportment.

In Book 6 of the Florentine Codex, too, the majority of the orations are nondidactic in character. In addition to the nine prayers to the gods at the beginning of the book, there is a series of orations delivered on the election of a new king which cover seven chapters of the book, and an extensive cycle of discourses, extending over eighteen chapters, dealing with marriage, pregnancy, childbirth, the naming of the child, and so forth, ending with the child's entrance into the calmecac, or telpochcalli.

81

Occasionally an instructive note is sounded in these orations, such as when the young groom is advised of his responsibilities as a husband, but as compared with the orations of the parents to their sons and daughters instructing them in a correct way of life and proper conduct in society—which, incidentally, span a scant six chapters in this book— they could scarcely be called didactic. The same is true of the *huehue-tlatolli* of the merchants found in Book 9, as well as others found in the Madrid and Florentine codices, which we will consider in more detail below.

Since the nine prayers in Book 6 are so patently nondidactic, why, if they are not relevant to the material contained in the book, as Garibay states, did Sahagún include them? Moreover, why did he place them at the beginning of the book and not put them at the end, or in an appendix, as he did with addenda in other books? Furthermore, we must ask, why is the "Huehuetlatolli, Documento A" almost entirely given over to discourses presented on social occasions, and why do we find texts of a similar socially ceremonial nature making up the bulk of the *Huehuetlatolli* of Olmos?

As remarked above, Molina gives the meaning of *huehuetlatolli* as "ancient history or sayings of the elders." The word is compounded of *huehue*, "old man" or "man of old," and *tlatolli*, which Molina defines as "word, oration, or language."

Thus *huehuetlatolli* can mean "the words of the elders" or "ancient," the "orations of the elders" or "ancients," or the "language of the elders" or "ancients." In my opinion it has all these meanings. The *huehuetlatolli* were the rhetorical orations in general—the prayers, discourses, salutations, and congratulatory speeches—in which the traditional religious, moral, and social concepts handed down from generation to generation were expressed in traditional language—that is, rhetorical language. Hence Sahagún's title to Book 6: "Of the Rhetoric and Moral Philosophy and Theology of the Mexican people, in which there are many niceties with respect to the elegance of their language and many fine things with respect to the moral virtues." (Sahagún 1956:2:51). And just before Chapter 1 is the statement, "Here begins the sixth book containing the prayers with which they prayed to the gods and the Rhetoric, and Moral Philosophy and Theology in one and the same context." (Sahagún 1956:2:55). "Moral Philosophy" in this case must be understood in the wider sixteenth-century sense of proper conduct, good manners, and correct behavior, as well as in its ethical sense.[3] The term "rhetoric" is similarly broad. Sahagún obviously is not referring to the ancient Greco-Roman art of oratory but to the humanistic rhetoric of his own time, which enjoyed a wider range of subject matter and style. As Garibay states with respect to Sahagún's use of these terms, as well as that of "theology," "It is pure analogy and one cannot apply to the procedures of the Mexican people those that were taken from the Greeks" (Sahagún 1956:2:48).

Nevertheless, there is a striking similarity between the humanistic rhetoric of the Renaissance, in which the imitation of great orators was fundamental to rhetorical training, and the method used by the Aztecs, and this similarity could not have escaped the friars. As Fray Juan de Tovar explained to Fray Joseph de Acosta (García Icazbalceta (1947: 4:92): ". . . in order to preserve word for word [the orations and poems] as declaimed by the orators and poets, the young lords who were to be their successors were drilled in them and, with constant repetition they committed them to memory without changing so much as a word, taking as their method the most famous orations composed in each era in order to instruct the young men who were to be orators. . . ." Basing his statement on earlier sources, Clavijero (1958:2:273ff.) also affirms that "those who were destined to be orators were instructed from childhood to speak well, and they made them learn by memory the most famous discourses of their forebears, which had been handed down from father to son. They particularly employed their eloquence in embassies, in deliberations in council and in congratulatory orations to new kings."

To speak well was fundamental to the education of the Aztecs. Pomar (n.d.:27) tells us: "To this house [calmecac] . . . came the sons of the king and of the other lords, and a few [sons] of commoners. They spent the day teaching them to speak well, to govern well, and to hear suits. . . ." And he goes on to say that the boys who went to the telpochcalli were taught the same things except for certain religious rites reserved exclusively for the priests. According to the Florentine Codex (Sahagún 1950–69:3:64), in the calmecac "they were thoroughly instructed in good speech [and] he who did not speak well, who did not greet people properly, they pricked [with maguey thorns]."

To the Aztecs, the importance of teaching a child to speak properly and to greet people properly extended beyond the social amenities normally associated with good breeding, refinement, and civility, although these characteristics were highly valued by this once rough and barbaric people. In the child who learned to speak with eloquence, to turn a mellifluous phrase, were the seeds of the future orator who would be made to learn the discourses of the great orators in the past, the *huehuetlatolli*, in which many of the religious and social traditions and much of the knowledge and lore of the ancients were preserved. The picture codices contained only the bold outlines of religious concepts, historical events, and socal practices, and this form of writing gives the lie to the old adage, "one picture is worth a thousand words." As Tovar so aptly expressed it (García Icazbalceta 1947:4:92), "Although they had diverse figures and characters with which they wrote, this was not as adequate as our writing to permit each one to say what was written, word for word, without variation; they [the words] could only agree [with the pictures] in concept." It was the words of the orators that brought alive and kept alive the traditions of the people. Thus Molina's definition, "ancient history or sayings of the elders," is figuratively, if not literally, correct. This is the essence of the *huehuetlatolli*, and nowhere is it better exemplified than in those collected by Sahagún.

Where did Sahagún collect them? Garibay (1953–54:1:426ff) has some contradictory things to say about Sahagún's sources which need to be reviewed in order to clarify this question. Fray Andrés de Olmos finished his *Arte de la lengua Mexicana,* to which the first part of his *huehuetlatolli* (the oration of the father to his son and the son's reply) was appended, on January 1, 1547, and Sahagún gathered the *huehue-tlatolli* contained in Book 6 in the same year.[4] Garibay thought, in view of these dates, that either Olmos and Sahagún had gathered the material in Texcoco in a collaborative effort or else that Sahagún had collected his *huehuetlatolli* under the supervision, and in emulation, of Olmos (Garibay 1953–54:1:426ff; Sahagún 1956:2:42). Probably because he could never satisfactorily explain away the notable discrepancies in style which, after a close study, would have to obviate the possibility of both series of *pláticas* coming from the same region, Garibay came to the conclusion, though he does not say how or why, that Sahagún gathered his material for Book 6 in Tlaltelolco (Sahagún 1956:2:43). In this opinion I concur. It is not certain where Olmos was

84

in the years 1546–47, nor for that matter where Sahagún was. We know, however, that in 1545, the year of the great plague, Sahagún was in Tlaltelolco tending the sick and burying the dead. When the plague was on the wane, in 1546, Sahagún was felled by it and nearly died. Though we have no record of Sahagún's whereabouts in 1547, the year that he gathered the *huehuetlatolli*, it is highly probable that, after so debilitating an illness, he remained in Tlaltelolco. Garibay considers the possibility that Sahagún might have acquired these texts in Tepepulco, the first site of his later researches for the projected *General History*, but the stylistic differences between the "Amonestaciones de los Magistrados" of the "Primeros Memoriales" and the *pláticas* of Book 6 of the Florentine Codex negate this theory completely. In linguistic style and usage, indeed, Book 6 bears a strong resemblance to the texts of the Madrid and Florentine codices that Sahagún gathered in Tlaltelolco or Tenochtitlan or both. The material is unmistakably from the same region. Undoubtedly Sahagún knew about Olmos' work; possibly he was even influenced by him. But it is equally possible that, as an earnest student of the Nahuatl language and customs, he collected the *huehuetlatolli* in Book 6 on his own initiative and for his own purposes. There is no question that, in depth and scope, the *pláticas* that Sahagún gathered far exceed those of Olmos.

Although, as Sahagún states, "the first turf was cut" for his *General History* in Tepepulco, where he went in the year 1558 (Sahagún 1956: 1:105), it would appear that, methodologically speaking, he had already made a beginning when he gathered the orations in 1547. The *pláticas* he took down were those of the nobles and wealthy merchants, rendered in rich and elegant language, probably the best example we have of Nahuatl rhetorical style. His informants, then as later, would have to have been principales, as he called them: priests, high-ranking dignitaries in civil and military affairs, former rulers, and the very wealthy merchants who themselves enjoyed the status of nobles. Only those who had heard the *pláticas* over and over, or had been trained in them, could have remembered them with such accuracy.

The *huehuetlatolli* of Sahagún, both those contained in Book 6 of the Florentine Codex and those found in other parts of the Florentine and Madrid codices, fall into the following general categories:

PRAYERS TO THE GODS

There are twelve prayers to the gods, eleven of them to Tezcatlipoca, ruler of heaven and earth and all mankind, who capriciously bestowed riches or poverty, sickness or health, honor or disgrace, and just as capriciously took them back. In these supplications he is invoked in time of plague to remove the pestilence, in time of want to send riches and abundance, in time of war to help vanquish the enemy, and in time of sickness to abate the suffering. He is also called upon to aid a newly elected ruler in his task of governing, to provide a new ruler when the old one dies, and to remove a bad king by doing away with him. In addition he is supplicated in two prayers by a confessor on behalf of a confessant, one text of which also contains the priest's admonitory oration to the confessant.

Seven of the prayers, and one to Tlaloc asking for rain in time of severe drought, were, as the texts state, rendered by priests. They are in Book 6, together with the prayer to Tezcatlipoca by a newly elected king. One of the confession prayers is in Book 1, and in Book 3 there are two prayers by a layman requesting relief from poverty and illness.

The nature and powers of Tezcatlipoca are nowhere more sharply etched than in these texts. There are, first of all, the names by which he is invoked: Tloque Nahuaque, literally "Lord of the Near, Lord of the Close," figuratively the supreme lord, the lord who is everywhere, in everything, upon whom all depend.[5] Other names are: Yohualli Ehecatl, "Night, Wind," that is, invisible and impalpable; Moyocoyatzin, "Capricious One"; Monenequi, "Tyrannical One"; Titlacahuan, "Our Master" (literally "we are his slaves"); Teimatini, "Knower of People"; Techichihuani, "Adorner of People"; Yaotl, "The Enemy"; Necoc Yaotl, "The Enemy on Both Sides"; Moquequeloa, "The Mocker"; Ipalnemoani, "Giver of Life" (literally "by virtue of whom one lives"); and Teyocoyani, "Creator of Man." They bespeak awesome and frightening powers, an arbitrariness against which man is powerless.

Nevertheless, as these prayers reveal, the pre-Hispanic Indian accommodated himself fairly well to these conditions. A certain pattern of interplay between man and deity emerges in these supplications, with the burden placed on the god. In the prayer to Tezcatlipoca in time

86

of plague, the catastrophe is viewed by the priest as a punishment visited upon the people, a manifestation of the deity's wrath. In a nicety of logic, the priest tells the god that "our tribute is death . . . all come to pay the tribute to death on earth" (Sahagún 1950–69:6:4); this being so, the priest asks why Tezcatlipoca does not permit each one to die in the manner fated for him, allowing those destined to suffer an ordinary death to go to Mictlan, the "Region of the Dead," below, and the warriors destined for death in battle, to Tonatiuh Ichan, the "House of the Sun."

Similarly, in the prayer in which Tezcatlipoca is asked to alleviate poverty, the priest beseeches "the lord of plenty, the lord of sweetness, of fragrance, of riches, of abundance" (Sahagún 1950–69:6:8) to give the poor and needy some respite from their misery, if only for a brief time. Since the deity can dispense and remove riches at will, what harm can it do for the poor to enjoy them for a while? Should their wealth make them heady, he can always strip them of it and give it to others who are more deserving.

Once again, in the prayer to Tlaloc, in time of drought, after describing the dire conditions of the people wracked by famine, the priest remarks that it would be better if the land were ravaged by plague or by war, for as those who die are given food offerings as provisions for their journey into the beyond, they would thus be provided with something to eat.

In the prayers that treat of the affairs of government, on the death of a king Tezcatlipoca is requested to choose a new ruler, who is regarded as the deity's representative on earth, to be mother and father to the "orphaned" city and, once elected, to guide him and prevent him from ruling badly. But if he cannot, or will not, then the god is asked at least to send him to the field of battle where he can die an honorable death and go "as a precious jade, a turquoise, an armlet" to the House of the Sun (Sahagún 1950–69:6:20). In the prayer in which Tezcatlipoca is asked to remove a bad king, besotted with privilege and power, this theme is amplified. The priest urges the deity to punish the offender at once, offering such alternatives as poverty, misery, or illness, although, says the priest, it would be better by far that the god mercifully put "his heart and body to rest" and let him go to join his ancestors in Mictlan, the Region of the Dead. The king himself, in a superb rogation characterized by an excess of humility, tells Tezcatlipoca that there are better people born under the same sign as he, destined from birth to rule, to become "the drums and flutes" of the lord. But since this is the way the deity has willed it, the king will govern the people in accordance with the guidance of the lord. Whichever road he indicates, the king will follow, the implication being that if the king rules badly it is because the deity, for reasons of his own, has so willed it.

In the series of orations having to do with confession, the priest, defending the penitent, reminds Tezcatlipoca that the confessant has placed himself in danger by exposing his transgressions, for they may arouse the deity to anger. The lord must keep in mind that what is done is done, and there is no undoing it, that a man's acts are predetermined from birth and are not entirely of his own doing.

The relationship between man and the aloof, arbitrary god who held his fate in his hands is less subtly, but more graphically, revealed in a short oration in Book 3 by a person afflicted with an illness. He makes a vow to Tezcatlipoca that if he is cured, he will spend all he has in his service. When he does not recover he becomes vexed with the god and calls him a bugger. To which the text comments, "Some he [Tezcatlipoca] cured, he was not angered by this, but others died" (Sahagún 1950–69:6:12).

COURT ORATIONS

There are nine court orations. Seven of them, which are in the Florentine Codex, Book 6, were delivered on the occasion of the election of a new king, and two, in the "Primeros Memoriales," were declaimed in the court of justice. The orations having to do with the election of a new ruler include those addressed to him on his accession; those made by him, or by a noble or high-ranking dignitary versed in the arts of oratory, in his behalf; an oration by the king to his lords and nobles; one by a dignitary to the lords and nobles extolling the king's address; and finally, one to the king on their behalf. The court orations constitute a whole ceremonial.

In the first oration to the new king, which is quite long, and which as Sahagún's title states, contains "*cenca ohovi in machiotlatolli: cenca quaqualli in tenonotzaliztlatolli*" ("very abtruse metaphors and excellent words of counsel") (Sahagún 1950–69:6:47), the king is told that Tezcatlipoca put a "sign" or a "mark" on him, that he marked him with "black ink, red ink," for this exalted position. It was ordained that, because he was "the thorn, the maguey shoot" his forebears left planted in the earth, he would take up "the load, the carrying frame," the burden of government, which they set down when they departed. Like Tezcatlipoca whom he represents, his power is absolute, and he can be arbitrary and capricious: he can speak and listen with compassionate "lips and ears of the lord," or he can strike with "his fangs and claws." Thus he is urged to

> Receive, speak to those who come in anguish,
> who come to receive what is fated for them . . .
> Take, reach for, arrive at the truth,
> for it is said, and it is true,
> that you are the substitute, the surrogate, of the
> Lord of All, the Supreme Lord,
> you are his drum, you are his flute;
> from within you he speaks   (Sahagún 1950–69:6:50).

Thus he is cautioned to rule with dignity, restraint, and justice; he is not to frighten people with a show of power, but to use his vast powers judiciously.

After hearing a less weighty and more conventional oration of felicitation, the king, or someone speaking in his behalf, thanks the speakers for their "words of motherliness and fatherliness" (Sahagún 1950–69: 6:61), the treasure of wisdom handed down to them which, like the swaddlings of a child, will fortify him and guide him in governing the people. It is not known what is fated for him. Perhaps his reign will be long and successful, the result of having ruled wisely, but perhaps he will rule badly and in a brief time the deity will remove him from office. As in all matters, it will be as the deity wills.

By far the longest and possibly the most informative oration of this series is that delivered by the king to the noble men and women, high functionaries, and great warriors, two-thirds of which is devoted to the evils of pulque. Its prolixity together with its severity of tone indicate that excessive drinking must have been a serious problem among the Aztecs. Pulque is likened to "a whirlwind, a cyclone that covers everything with evil, with wickedness" (Sahagún 1950–69:6:68). It is the root of all other transgressions, such as thievery and adultery. It makes people liars and braggarts, it reduces them and their families to poverty, and it crazes them. Hence inebriation, like thievery and adultery, is punishable by death. The king enjoins his subjects to devote themselves to the rigors and discipline of the battlefield and the military where

> ". . . the mother of the Sun, the father of the Sun, are born, come into being,
> the Tlacateccatl, the Tlacochcalcatl [the two high military commanders]
> who provide drink, who provide food,
> for the Sun and the Lord of the Earth" (Sahagún 1950–69:6:72).

If a man is a coward, however, he should devote himself to the cultivation of his lands to produce food for himself and the people. Eventually, one of them may be called to take the king's place or to govern in some other capacity in military or civilian affairs, and only a life of temperance and moderation in all things will make him fit for the task.

Two orations end this series, and, with it, the investiture ceremony. The first is addressed to those present—the nobles, lords, and warriors—and the second to the king on their behalf, lauding the newly elected king's words, "the precious jades, the precious turquoises" that he strewed before them, the teachings of the ancients which must serve as their guideline in life (Sahagún 1950–69:6:79).

In the first brief oration of the two in the "Primeros Memoriales" that belong in this series, a group of high functionaries and magistrates report to the king the cowardly conduct of a young warrior and suggest the sentence of death. The king agrees; they kill him and then report back to the king that the deed is done.

The second is an extremely lengthy oration involving four judges who speak successively to the people—lords, nobles, and commoners alike—about the neglect of their duties and their deplorable conduct. Parts of this text are dull and repetitious, and, excepting the oration of the fourth judge, none has the elegance and grace of the orations found in the Florentine Codex and other parts of the Madrid Codices. Nevertheless, it contains a great deal of ethnographic information, particularly with respect to the duties that the various high functionaries were expected to perform and the punishment for their neglect: either cutting off their locks (hairstyle was a symbol of rank), exile, or death.

ORATIONS OF PARENTS TO OFFSPRING

The series of orations rendered by a king, or noble, and his wife, to their children are six in number, and all are in Book 6 of the Florentine Codex. Four of these are addressed by the father to his sons. In the first, he instructs them in their duties as possible future rulers, exhorting them above all to be diligent in their devotions and in the propitiation of the gods, which will help them merit the kingship or else some high rank, for they were born to govern. Their task is to see to the ritual dancing and singing which give pleasure to the gods. They should also give attention to the crafts—featherwork, goldsmithery, and stonecutting—which in time of difficulty can buy food and drink for the people. He particularly exhorts them to see to the cultivation of the fields. "Where have I seen that one breakfasts, one dines on nobility?" he asks.

> The sustenances of life . . .
> are what walk, what move, what rejoice, what laugh . . .
> In all truth it is said, they are the lords, they are the rulers, they are
>   what conquer   (Sahagún 1950–69:6:91).

In the second oration, the young men are urged to live lives of true humility, as did their ancestors who achieved great wealth and honor. Their way of life was an example, "a light, a torch, a mirror," which they left to all (Sahagún 1950–69:6:107). To be meek, they are told, is to be noble and honored. True humility is rewarded with position, rank, and glory.

The third oration of the royal or noble father to his sons is on chastity and is probably the single most informative text on the Aztec concepts of purity and purification. The father enjoins his sons to lead chaste lives, or, should they marry, to be moderate in their sexual relations, because only the chaste or temperate are pleasing to the gods. According to this text those classed as pure, whose "hearts are as jades" (Sahagún 1950–69: 6:113), were the small children, the virgin youths, and the celibate priests and priestesses; those who died by drowning or were struck by lightning, who went to dwell in Tlalocan; and those who died in battle and went to the House of the Sun. The last two were regarded as having been marked for their fate by the gods of these places. It would appear from this text that death by drowning, being struck by lightning, and death in battle constituted acts of purification that made the individual desirable to the gods and eligible for those places of eternal delight and glory.

In contrast to the severe tone of these exhortatory addresses is the tender oration of the father to his daughter in which he tells her that the world is a place of great affliction mitigated only by a few pleasures; that she should give herself to a life of devotion and always comport herself in the manner becoming a noblewoman; that she should be diligent in learning and discharging her womanly tasks of weaving and preparing food; and finally that she should accept unhesitatingly and with good grace the husband chosen for her.

Finally, there are two parallel orations, one by the father to his son, the other by the mother to her daughter, instructing them in such mundane matters as the proper way to walk, talk, dress, eat, and how to conduct themselves in society generally, in which moderation in all things is stressed, the rule par excellence of Aztec life.

As Sahagún notes in his titles, these orations are rich both in language and in teachings and invaluable in what they reveal of the norms of conduct of the Aztecs. There is an emphasis on abstemiousness, austerity, proper conduct, and a regard for the opinions of others that bespeaks a rigidity controlled society.

ORATIONS OF THE MERCHANTS

With one exception only, the sixteen orations of the merchants which appear in Books 4, 5, and 9 of the Florentine Codex and in the corresponding texts of the Madrid Codices revolve around the three main events in a merchant's life: his departure for far-off regions, his return, and his sacrifice of slaves in propitiation of the gods. As in the case of the orations having to do with the newly elected king, these, too, are ceremonial in nature.

Three orations pertinent to the departure ceremony are found in Book 4 under the sign Ce Coatl, 1 Serpent, considered an auspicious day for departing, and there are five additional orations delivered on the same occasion in Book 9. The ceremony takes place before a large gathering at a feast given by the merchant who will lead the group. Those going out on the road for the first time, as well as the veterans, are addressed in a series of orations delivered by a merchant-elder, their mothers and fathers, and the old men and women of the community. They are exhorted to endure the hardships and perils of the road with courage and fortitude and if death is to be their fate, to meet it with valor, for death on the road for a merchant, like death in battle for a warrior, held the promise of a glorious afterlife in the House of the Sun. Devotion to the gods and humility toward others are stressed over and over again; the novices are instructed to serve their elders, to be humble toward them, to know their places always, and the experienced merchants are told to look after the youths and guide them. The leader of the group is particularly exhorted not to desert his companions, for whom he is responsible, along the way. A last exchange between the leader of the group and the elders and kin, in which he thanks them for their precious words and asks them to watch over his household, and the final farewell to the group, end this series of orations.

The next series was delivered when the merchant returned, at a ceremony symbolically called "the washing of the feet" (Sahagún 1950–69: 9:27ff.), which took place on two successive days and consisted of much eating, drinking, and speechmaking. On both occasions the returning merchant is addressed with extreme severity, despite his generosity and the obvious success of his trading expedition, not to mention his safe return. The elders question him closely about the honesty and diligence by which he acquired his goods. They speak to him so harshly, we are told, that they reduce him to tears. These are only ceremonial tears, however, for it quickly becomes clear that we are dealing with a set piece which, though ostensibly calculated to humble a merchant who has returned rich and prosperous from his journeys, is actually a reverse form of laudation. According to these texts, any merchant who made a display of his wealth ran the risk of being stripped of it by Moctezuma and put to death. Hence the merchants are cautioned again and again by the elders against any show of arrogance and ostentation, regardless of their riches (and the implication in these texts is that the merchants were extremely wealthy) and enjoined to lead sober and austere lives, dedicating themselves to the hardships of the road. Thus, we are told that the merchant-elders

"... admonished him [the merchant], they proffered him [words] full of sticks and stones, the words of the elders.

They heaped reprimands upon him that were like icy water, stinging
    nettles,
painful words that penetrate like a burning, a smoking stick.
They lashed out at him thus, so that his life would be longer"

(Sahagún 1950–69:9:42).

The last two series of orations in Book 9 concern the preparations for
the sacrificing of slaves in the fiesta of Panquetzaliztli, a celebration the
merchants shared with the warriors. They start with the announcement
of the returned merchant's vow to sacrifice slaves. This is followed by the
counsel of the merchant-elders on the order of rites, the details of the
feast that will accompany the event, their inspection of the preparations,
and their final words to the merchant containing the traditional exhorta-
tion to lead a life of humility, morality, and religious devotion.

Finally, there is an eloquent oration in Book 5, the Book of Omens,
rendered by the merchant-leader to his group when they have heard the
cry of a *huactli*, or laughing falcon—an omen that one of them would die,
fall ill, be devoured by wild beasts, or else that they would be robbed, or
that their goods would be carried off by the water. These, he tells them,
are the hazards of their calling, and they should prepare themselves to
die courageously and with dignity, and thus bring honor to those who
come after them.

ORATIONS RELATIVE TO
THE LIFE CYCLE

There are some forty orations relative to the life cycle of which thirty-
four are in Book 6 of the Florentine Codex, five in Book 3 and one in
Book 4; the last six have corresponding texts in the Madrid Codex of the
Royal Palace. With one exception, they are all orations of the nobles.
Since the majority are in Book 6 of the Florentine, it will be assumed,
unless otherwise indicated, that this is the source for the text under discussion.

Pregnancy

There are three series of orations on the occasion of the pregnancy of
a newly married woman, beginning with the announcement of the event

to the respective families, soon after conception, by two elders speaking on behalf of the prospective father. The second includes the felicitations to the pregnant woman by a member of the husband's family, when he gives her her first instructions on caring for herself and "the precious stone, the quetzal feather" (Sahagún 1950–69:6:135) she is carrying in her womb; an address to the parents of the couple by the same man; their reply;[6] and a short oration by the pregnant woman thanking them for their congratulatory and instructive words. The third series takes place during the last months of pregnancy when the families gather together for the purpose of engaging a midwife; it consists of an exchange of orations between the family and the midwife concerning the serious task that lies ahead, and the latter's instructions to the pregnant woman for a successful delivery, which include numerous superstitious beliefs concerning pregnancy and childbirth.

Childbirth

At the time of childbirth the pregnant woman is regarded as a warrior going into battle. There is a series of four orations by the midwife starting with one to the parturient woman during a delayed delivery urging her to fight her battle courageously. When she does, and the child is born, the midwife shouts the war cry which signifies, according to the text:

"... that the woman had fought her battle well,
that she had been a valiant warrior,
that she had taken a captive,
that she had captured a child" (Sahagún 1950–69:6:167).

Then the midwife addresses the child, welcoming him into the world, a harsh and unlovely place as she paints it, and performs the rite of cutting the umbilical cord and the consecration of the boy to the field of battle, or the girl to a life beside the hearth. This is followed by the bathing of the infant and an incantation invoking Chalchiuhtlicue, goddess of water, to exorcise the evil and filth with which the child was born.

Here again, we are dealing with a ceremonial, and now follow numerous congratulatory orations: from the midwife to the new mother; from the two families to the midwife on her successful delivery of the child and her reply cautioning the families against becoming presumptuous because of the birth of the baby; orations by a noble elder of the city as well as those by ambassadors of neighboring states addressed to the two families and to the infant with the reverence due a future ruler. Including three orations of the commoners, there are twelve on the congratulatory theme. They follow a general formula, if not a particular order, and more or less the same ground is covered in all of them: a precious stone, a quetzal feather, has been born into a world full of pain and affliction. The child is the hair, nails, thorn, spine—that is, the offshoot—of his ancestors, and in him their glory is brought to life once more. What is fated for him? Will he live or will he die before reaching maturity? Will he bring glory to his ancestors or shame?

Following these is another series of orations at the time of the name-giving. In a brief account of this ceremony in Book 4, under the sign Ce Cuauhtli, a favorable sign for this event, there is a short oration to the child by the old men and women, welcoming him into the world, and one to the mother instructing her in caring for herself and the baby during the first weeks after parturition. In Book 6 are the incantations and orations of the midwife four days after birth, when she again bathes the child to purify him or her and also performs the name-giving ceremony and the placing of the child in the cradle for the first time.

Infancy and Childhood

The orations dealing with this portion of the child's life are seven in number. The first is delivered by the parents soon after the child's birth when the boy or girl is promised either to the calmecac and consecrated to Quetzalcoatl and the priesthood, or to the telpochcalli and consecrated to Tezcatlipoca and the military. At the time the boy or girl is actually entered in the school, the parents invite the instructors of the telpochcalli or the priests from the calmecac to a feast in their home where, in a series of brief orations found in the appendix to Book 3 of the Florentine Codex, the parents turn the child over to the priests or warriors to be educated. They accept the charge without guaranteeing the outcome, for, as they tell the parents, the boy or girl will develop in accordance with the fate determined by the sign under which he or she was born. Ending this group of orations are those to the boy by his father and to the girl by an old woman, in Book 6, in which they are told that they must now leave the comforts of their home and dedicate themselves to a life of devotion to the gods, austerity, obedience, and learning.

Marriage

In a series of oratorical exchanges between father and son and the father and the masters of the telpochcalli, which are too brief properly to be classed as orations, the decision is reached that the boy should marry and permission is granted that he leave his school. A prospective bride is chosen for him at a gathering of the family and kin, matchmakers are dispatched to ask for her hand, and after four visits to the girl's family and what Sahagún designates as "much speechifying," little of which is included in these texts, the bride's family gives its consent. Properly speaking, three orations are attendant upon the occasion of marriage. In the first, addressed to the bride by a member of the groom's family before she is carried to the groom's house for the wedding ceremony, she is told that she is now separating herself forever from her childhood and her family. She must now comport herself as a proper married woman and discharge her marital duties with diligence. The remaining two are delivered after the wedding ceremony, and they contain more specific words of counsel to the bride and groom by their respective in-laws.

Death

There are two orations to the dead. One, in Book 6 of the Florentine Codex, is addressed by the midwife to the woman who has died in childbirth with the child a captive in her womb and who became deified at the moment of her demise. In it the midwife eloquently bids her farewell and sends her off on her well-earned journey to the glorious House of the Sun where she will join her sister *mocihuaquetzque*, women warriors, who carry the sun on its course from midday to sundown. The second oration is contained in the appendix to Book 3 of the Florentine Codex and in the corresponding text of the Madrid Codex of the Royal Palace. It contains the words spoken to one who has died an ordinary death and is destined to go to Mictlan, the final abode of all, "a place without a chimney, place without a vent" (Sahagún 1950–69:3:39), and also contains some words of condolence to the bereaved family.

MISCELLANEOUS

Lastly, there are two orations which do not fit into any of the other categories. Both are short. One, which occurs in Book 5, "The Book of Omens," contains the words of comfort spoken by a *tonalpouhqui*, a soothsayer, to someone who has heard a wild beast howl in the night, which was regarded as an omen of death or disaster. He advises the person in question not to place the blame upon the animal but to accept his fate as the will of the lord. The other, in Book 12, is Moctezuma's speech to Cortés on his arrival in Mexico-Tenochtitlan, an oration of great elegance and dignity in which the Indian monarch bows to his fate and welcomes Cortés as the next ruler of the land and successor to the throne that he, Moctezuma, has only been holding for him.

As Sahagún himself notes in the titles, both in Nahuatl and in Spanish, that he gave these prayers and orations, they are replete with exquisite figures of speech and elegant phrases. Indeed, no study of *huehuetlatolli* would be complete without some comments on style, but this is a subject that requires and deserves a separate consideration and wider treatment than can be given at this time.

Briefly, the rhetorical orations are characterized by the extensive use of metaphor, complementary phrasing, synonyms, and redundancy, as the reader may have noted in some of the texts and phrases quoted. In the majority of cases the words or phrases are paired and thus give a definite rhythmic pattern to the oration. Nahuatl rhetoric is richly poetic and imaginative.

Observe, for example, the paired words and phrases and the use of metaphor in the following text from the prayer to Tlaloc, in time of drought and famine:

"The sustenances of life are no more, they have vanished;
the gods, the providers, have carried them off,
they have hidden them away in Tlalocan.
They have sealed in a coffer, they have locked in a box

their verdure, their freshness,
the cuphea, the fleabane, the purselane, the fig-marigold . . ."
(Sahagún 1950–69:6:36).

Particularly to be noted are the metaphors formed of two words (occasionally more) which together have a single meaning, a type of figure characteristic of the Nahuatl language.

Metaphor	Literal Meaning	Metaphorical Meaning
Atl, tepetl	Water, mountain	City
Teuhtli, tlazolli	Dirt, filth	Evil, vice
Mixtitlan, ayauhtitlan	Out of the clouds, out of the mists	A wonder
Cuitlapilli, atlapalli	Tail, wing	The common people
Iztlactli, tencualactli	Saliva, spittle	Falsehood
Petlatl, icpalli	Mat, seat	Authority, the throne

Over and over one meets the same figures and the same phrases but always with some slight variation. That they are the product of the indigenous mind and culture, as Sahagún stated, is undeniable; they never could have been invented by a Spaniard. The rounded periods, the attention to detail, the emphasis on austerity, the preoccupation with death recall the monumentality, the realism, and the severity of Aztec sculpture. While the orations appear to be set in an established framework, within that framework they move and flow with a high degree of freedom and imagination. To us they seem repetitious, but to those who depended upon them for the transmission of their traditions, the set phrases could never fail to call up the desired images. This, primarily, was their purpose.

The classification and syntheses presented here of the rhetorical orations, or *huehuetlatolli*, collected by Sahagún demonstrate that these were not didactic discourses, as Garibay and Leon-Portilla define them, nor, in Soustelle's words (1956:223), "precepts of the elders" ("*preceptos de los ancianos*"), but were the orations handed down from generation to generation and delivered on key occasions, both religious and secular, for the purpose of perpetuating and preserving the religious, social, moral, and even historical traditions of a people whose form of picture writing was inadequate for this task. The series of orations on the investiture of the king, those on the departure and return of the mer-

TABLE 9
PRAYERS TO THE GODS

Addressed to	Subject	Orator	Florentine Codex	Madrid Codex of the Royal Palace	Madrid Codex of the Royal Academy
Tezcatlipoca	Want	Layman	3:11	137v	
Tezcatlipoca	Illness	Layman	3:12	138r–39v	
Tezcatlipoca	Plague	Priest	6:1–5		
Tezcatlipoca	Want	Priest	6:7–10		
Tezcatlipoca	War	Priest	6:11–15		
Tezcatlipoca	Election of king	Priest	6:17–20		
Tezcatlipoca	Replacement of dead king	Priest	6:21–25		
Tezcatlipoca	Removal of bad king	Priest	6:25–28		
Tezcatlipoca	Confession	Priest	1:8–11	49r–51v	
Tezcatlipoca	Confession	Priest	6:30–31		
Tezcatlipoca	Aid in ruling	Newly elected king	6:41–45		
Tlaloc	Drought	Priest	6:35–40		

TABLE 10
COURT ORATIONS

Addressed to	Subject	Orator	Florentine Codex	Madrid Codex of the Royal Palace	Madrid Codex of the Royal Academy
King	His election	Lord or noble	6:47–55		
King	His election	Lord or noble	6:57–59		
Lords and nobles	Gratitude for good wishes	King	6:61–62		
Lords and nobles	Gratitude for good wishes	Lord or noble on behalf of king	6:63–65		
Lords and nobles	Exhortation to moral life	King	6:67–77		
Lords and nobles	Lauding the oration of king	Lord or noble	6:79–82		
King	Gratitude for king's counsel	Elderly lord	6:83–85		
King	Cowardly warrior	Group of lords and nobles			65r
Lords, nobles, and commoners	Neglect of duties and immorality	4 judges			61v–64v

TABLE 11
ORATIONS OF PARENTS TO OFFSPRING

Addressed to	Subject	Orator	Florentine Codex	Madrid Codex of the Royal Palace	Madrid Codex of the Royal Academy
Sons	Duties as future rulers	Royal father	6:87–92		
Son	Humility	Royal father	6:105–11		
Son	Chastity	Royal father	6:113–19		
Son	Conduct in society	Royal father	6:121–26		
Daughter	Way of life	Royal father	6:93–98		
Daughter	Conduct in society	Royal mother	6:99–103		

TABLE 12
ORATIONS OF THE MERCHANTS

Addressed to	Subject	Orator	Florentine Codex	Madrid Codex of the Royal Palace	Madrid Codex of the Royal Academy
Novice merchant	Departure	Old merchants	4:61–64	216v–18v	
Veteran merchant	Departure	Old merchants	4:65–67	218v–20r	
Merchants and families	Departure	Merchant-leader	9:12		29r–29v
Merchant	Departure	Merchant-elder	9:13		29v
Merchant	Requesting he take son	Parents of novice	9:14		29v–30r
Novice merchant	Departure	Parents	9:14		30r
Merchant-elders	Departure	Merchant-leader	9:15		30r
Merchants	Departure	Merchant-elders	9:15		30r–30v
Merchant-elder	Return: 1st day, "washing of feet"	Returning merchant	9:27, 28		33r, 33v
Merchant	Return: 1st day	Merchant-elder	9:27, 29		33v–34r
Merchant	Return: 2d day	Merchant-elder	9:42–43		38r–38v
Merchant-guests	Vow to sacrifice slaves	Merchant	9:52–53		40v–41r
Merchant	Preparations for sacrifice of slaves	Merchant-elders	9:55–57		41r–41v
Group of merchants	Hearing a laughing falcon—evil omen	Merchant-leader	5:153–54	244v–45r	

TABLE 13
ORATIONS RELATIVE TO THE LIFE CYCLE

Addressed to	Subject	Orator	Florentine Codex	Madrid Codex of the Royal Palace	Madrid Codex of the Royal Academy
Families of married couple	Announcement of pregnancy	2 old men on behalf of husband	6:135–36		
Husband	Announcement of pregnancy	Elder on behalf of families	6:136–39		
Pregnant woman	Prenatal care	In-law	6:141–43		
Families of married couple	Prenatal care	In-law	6:143–44		
In-laws	Gratitude for their words	Parents of pregnant woman	6:144–46		
Old men	Gratitude for their words	Pregnant woman	6:146–47		
Families of married couple	Engaging midwife	Old man	6:149–50		
Midwife	Request for services	Old woman	6:151–52		
Families of married couple	Acceptance of case	Midwife	6:152–55		
Women kin	Care of pregnant woman	Midwife	6:158		
Parturient woman	Delivery	Midwife	6:160		
Infant	On his birth	Midwife	6:167–69		
Infant	Cutting of umbilical cord	Midwife	6:171–73		
Chalchiuhtlicue	Bathing the newborn baby	Midwife	6:175–77		
Mother of baby	Successful delivery	Midwife	6:179		

Addressed to	Subject	Orator	Florentine Codex	Madrid Codex of the Royal Palace	Madrid Codex of the Royal Academy
Midwife	Successful delivery	Old woman	6:179–80		
Families of married couple	Humility on birth of child	Midwife	6:180–82		
Infant	On his birth	Ruler, lord, or merchant	6:183–85		
Old men and women caring for baby	Care of child	Ruler, lord, or merchant	6:185–87		
Father of child	Felicitations	Ruler, lord, or merchant	6:187–88		
Infant and parents	On his birth	Ambassador	6:189–90		
Ambassador	Gratitude for oration	Old man	6:190–92		
Infant of commoners	On his birth	?	6:192–94		
Mother (commoner)	Successful delivery	?	6:194–95		
Father (commoner)	Felicitations	?	6:195–96		
Infant	On his birth	Old men	4:114	235r–35v	
Mother	Care of child	Old men	4:114–15	235v	
Chalchiuhtlicue	Name giving (boy)	Midwife	6:201–4		
Chalchiuhtlicue	Name giving (girl)	Midwife	6:205–7		
Quetzalcoatl	Promise of child to calmecac or telpochcalli	Parents	6:208–11		
Boy	Entering the calmecac or telpochcalli	Old man	6:213–16		
Girl	or telpochcalli	Old woman	6:216–18		

TABLE 13, cont'd

Addressed to	Subject	Orator	Florentine Codex	Madrid Codex of the Royal Palace	Madrid Codex of the Royal Academy
Telpochtlatoque	Entering child in telpochcalli	Parents	3:49–50	152r–52v	
Parents	Receiving child in telpochcalli	Telpochtlatoque	3:50–51	152v–53v	
Priests of calmecac	Entering child in calmecac	Parents	3:59–60	156r–57r	
Parents	Receiving child in calmecac	Priest	3:60–61	157r–57v	
Son	Marriage	Father	6:127		
Father	Marriage	Son	6:127		
Telpochtlatoque	Permission to leave telpochcalli	Father	6:128		
Father	Permission granted	Telpochtlatoque	6:128		
Bride	Conduct as married woman	Old man	6:130		
Bride	Conduct as married woman	Old woman (in-law)	6:132		
Groom	Conduct as husband	Mother-in-law	6:133		
Parturient woman	Death	Midwife	6:164–65		
Deceased	Death	?	3:39–40	129r–30v	
Kin of deceased	Death	?	3:40		

TABLE 14
MISCELLANEOUS ORATIONS

Addressed to	Subject	Orator	Florentine Codex	Madrid Codex of the Royal Palace	Madrid Codex of the Royal Academy
Man	Howl of beast—bad omen	Priest	5:151–52	243v–44r	
Fernando Cortés	Welcome to Tenochtitlan	Moctezuma	12:42		

chants, as well as those on the occasions of marriage, pregnancy, and childbirth make it abundantly clear that the *huehuetlatolli* was an enculturistic and rhetorical device which played an integral part in these ceremonials. The numerous orations in which an orator speaks on behalf of a king, or noble, or the family, testify to the formal nature of these discourses, and the following statement made by the informant found in the orations of the merchants further substantiates this:

> "And they (the elders) delivered their words, their utterances . . .
> only accompanied by food and drink;
> it was then that the words of wisdom came forth"
>
> (Sahagún 1950–69:9:30).

Even the orations of the parents to their children, parts of which have the specific purpose of inculcating the children with the traditional mores and norms of conduct, have a formal quality. Although the texts do not specify this, they sound as though they might have been delivered before a group of people, possibly at a coming of age ceremony for which, as in the case of the announcement of pregnancy, all the kin gathered, and so were not intimate talks between the parents and their children.

To date, I have encountered the word *huehuetlatolli* only once in the Sahagún manuscripts (Sahagún 1950–69:9:42; corresponding to the Madrid Codex of the Royal Academy 38r), in one of the orations of the merchants, a text that has already been cited in these pages (see p. 93):

> . . . *quinonotza, quimaca in teyo, in quauhyo, in ueuetlatolli:* They admonished him, they proffered him [words] full of sticks and stones, *the words of the elders* (or words of the ancients) . . .

Here the term *huehuetlatolli* is associated with counsel and correction, but the words of correction are traditional; the person addressed had done nothing wrong.

Thus, the *huehuetlatolli* were the rhetorical orations rendered on a diversity of ceremonial occasions. As an old man tells an envoy who brings greetings to a newborn child and his parents, they are,

> ". . . [the words] which the men, the women of old left you,
> handed down to you,
> which are carefully folded away, stored away, in your entrails,
> in your throat" (Sahagún 1950–69:6:190).

That is, they are both the "words of the elders" and the "words of the ancients," the traditions that were handed down from father to son. By the same token, as in the case of the prayers, they are both the language of the elders and of the ancients, the rhetorical, ritual, and ceremonial language of what these and other texts reveal to have been an inordinately ritualistic and ceremonial people.

NOTES

1. The books in the Madrid Codices that might have corresponded to 6 and 12 of the Florentine are missing from those manuscripts. Of the material contained in the "Primeros Memoriales," which was apparently the data Sahagún gathered in Tepepulco between 1558 and 1561, only a minimal part was later incorporated in the Florentine Codex, and this did not include the two *huehuetlatolli* cited here. H. B. Nicholson discusses the correspondence of texts in "Primeros Memoriales" and the Florentine Codex at length in his forthcoming article, "Sahagún's Primeros Memoriales, Tepepulco, 1558–1561," to be published in the *Handbook of Middle American Indians* (Nicholson: in press).

2. At the end of this group of texts is the following statement: "These fragments of excellent Mexican were written by Don Miguel, Maestro de P. Oracio." Garibay (1953:1:440) thinks that P. Oracio is none other than P. Horacio Carochi, with which I am inclined to agree.

3. The term "moral" is derived from the Latin *moralis*, "custom, manner," and was sometimes used strictly in this sense, as for example, Acosta's *Historia Natural y Moral de las Indias* (Acosta 1962).

4. At the end of that book is the statement: "It was translated into the Spanish language by the said father Fray Bernardino de Sahagún thirty years after it was written in the Mexican language, in this year of 1577."

5. Carochi (1892: 419) defines the names as "apud quem sunt omnia, or qui est iuxta omnia," which Paredes (1910: 35) amplifies into "with whom and in whom we live; and who is near, present, and immediate to everything."

6. Sahagún says that the reply is made on behalf of the woman's parents, but this is not specified in the Nahuatl text (Sahagún 1956:2:166; 1950–69:6:144).

5

The Research Method of Fray Bernardino de Sahagún: The Questionnaires*

ALFREDO LÓPEZ AUSTIN

Universidad Nacional Autónoma de México

INTRODUCTION

It has been justly asserted by Jiménez Moreno (Sahagún 1938:xvi) that Sahagún followed for his time the most rigorous and demanding methods in his study of the culture of the Nahua people.

In describing the steps which permitted him to obtain the rich material that was to reach its full expression in the *General History of the Things of New Spain* and in the parallel manuscript in Nahuatl that is included in the Florentine Codex, Sahagún mentions as his starting point a draft in Spanish, a "memoir of all the subjects that had to be treated" (Sahagún 1956:1:105), which, had it been preserved for us, would permit us to appraise accurately each of his books. From it we could deter-

---

* A Spanish version of this paper is scheduled for publication by the Instituto de Investigaciones Sociales of the Universidad Nacional Autónoma de México.

mine the degree of the contribution of the native informants to the work, not just to attribute to one or another the glory of the results of the enterprise, but also to provide the historian who consults this masterwork with standards of judgment that would permit accurate evaluation of the information it contains.

In spite of the lack of the draft plan, abundant valuable and contradictory opinions exist on the role of Sahagún on the one hand and of the informants on the other (Garibay in Sahagún 1956:1:11; García Icazbalceta 1954:375; Robertson 1966:625–26, n.26; Jiménez Moreno in Sahagún 1938:liii; Anderson 1960:35). But it is essential to try to reconstruct the method followed by Sahagún in order to determine surer limits in the investigation of the problem.

The present study attempts to ascertain as far as possible the origin of the content of the questionnaires Sahagún used and the way the contributors answered him. This intention can be justly contested by adducing the necessity of first having the complete translation of the Nahuatl documents, but one can reply that the growing use of the texts that are being translated day by day makes an effort of this sort necessary, despite its wholly provisional character. Eventually the draft plan will be reconstructed in more detail, but in the meantime this approximation will have some utility.

SAHAGÚN'S PURPOSES

According to the author himself, the research was conducted with the fundamental goal of creating an appropriate instrument for preaching the Christian doctrine in New Spain, and for its proper conservation among the natives:

> ... It was ordered me as holy obedience to my superior prelate to write in the Mexican tongue what I thought would be useful for the doctrine, culture, and subsistence of the Christianity of these natives of this New Spain, and for the aid of the workers and ministers who indoctrinate them (Sahagún 1956:1:105).

Quite apart from the fact that he began the investigation some time before receiving the order from the provincial, Sahagún's motives seem totally directed towards the goal he himself notes. He chose as specific purposes of his work the knowledge of the former religion, in order to prevent the return to idolatry (as did Acosta 1962: 14, 45, 215, 278, et al.), the recording of an extensive Nahuatl vocabulary which would help in preaching, and the disclosure of the old customs in order to correct the false opinion that the natives possessed a low cultural level before the arrival of the Spaniards (Acosta 1962:318).

Sahagún expresses the first specific purpose in the prologue of his *General History*:

> A doctor cannot correctly apply medicines to the ill without first knowing from what disposition and cause the sickness proceeds; therefore a good physician should be knowledgeable in medicines and in sicknesses so as to apply correctly to each disease the corrective medicine; and the preachers and confessors, being doctors of the soul, should be experienced in the medicines and illnesses of the spirit in order to cure the spiritual ills: the preacher [should know] of the vices of the republic in order to direct his teachings against them, and the confessor in order to know what to ask, and to understand what is said relevant to his charge; it is highly useful that they know what is relevant to the exercise of their offices, nor should the ministers be careless in this conversion, believing that among this people there are no sins other than drunkenness, theft, and lust, because there are many graver sins among them which are in dire need of remedy: the sins of idolatry, idolatrous rites and beliefs, omens, superstitions, and idolatrous ceremonies have not yet totally disappeared.
>
> In order to preach against these things and even to know whether they exist, it is indispensable to know how they were used in the time of their idolatry. For in the absence of this knowledge they do many idolatrous things in our presence without our understanding; and some say in excusing themselves that these are stupidities or childishness, not knowing the root of their creation—which is mere idolatry, and the confessors do not even ask or believe such things to exist, not knowing even the language for asking them, nor would they understand it even if they were told. So that the ministers of the Gospel who will succeed those who came first in the cultivation of this new vineyard of the Lord will have no occasion to complain about the first [of us] for having left in the dark the things of these natives of New Spain, I, Fray Bernardino de Sahagún . . . wrote twelve books of the things—divine, or better idolatrous, and human and natural—of this New Spain (Sahagún 1956:1:27–28).

A little further on he mentions the purpose of obtaining from the books he had collected the necessary vocabulary to make a dictionary and of creating a corpus of works which did not exist in a land without phonetic writing:

> When this work was begun, those who knew of it began to say a dictionary was being made, and even now many ask me: How is the dictionary coming along? It would certainly be highly advantageous to prepare such a useful work for those who want to learn this Mexican language, as Ambrosio Calepino did for those wanting to learn Latin and the meanings of its words, but there has certainly been no opportunity because Calepino took the words and their meanings, their errors, and their metaphors from the reading of the poets and orators and Latin authors, substantiating everything he said with the authors' sayings, a foundation that I have not had due to the lack of letters and writing among this people; but whoever would want to do it could do so with facility, because by my labor twelve books have been written in the proper and natural language of this Mexican tongue, which besides being an entertaining and profitable composition presents all the ways of speaking and all the words this language uses, just as well substantiated and true as those written by Virgil, Cicero, and the other Latin authors (Sahagún 1956:1:31–32).

But Sahagún does not mention the goals that the Franciscans had for the firm establishment of Christianity in New Spain, which undoubtedly influenced his objectives. This is no place to go into detail about the politico-religious utopia of the Franciscans (Maravall 1949; 199–228, *passim*; Nicolau D'Olwer 1952:155–70); nevertheless we can refer briefly to Sahagún's personal ideas. Although he dares not say, with Acosta, that the triumph of the church in the New World "will be a kingdom, not for the Spanish nor for the Europeans but for Christ Our Lord" (Acosta 1962:45), Sahagún does nonetheless justify the establishment in New Spain of a government quite different from the Spanish one. He tells us that the weather and constellations of this land make the men—natives or foreigners—incline toward lust and sensuality; the natives in their gentile days counteracted this influence by exercises performed with iron discipline, which were lost with the implantation of soft European customs. It was essential to collect and record the testimonials of the old life, to separate the young Indians as much from their fathers (and hence idolatry) as from the Spaniards (and hence corruption), to initiate them into a truly Christian life, and then, after suppressing everything idolatrous in the pre-Hispanic norms and practices, to reimplant these prac-tices for the benefit of Christ (Sahagún 1956:3:158–61). The land that the infidel and the heretic had alienated from the church (Sahagún 1956:1:31) was being recovered in New Spain, whose men had sufficient capacity—as Sahagún was demonstrating in his work—to initiate there the Republic of Christ. For this reason, he could compare the Nahuas to the Greeks and Romans (Sahagún 1956:2:53).

Sahagún's work, as many have already pointed out (León-Portilla 1958b:12), could not have been the result of a merely academic restlessness. The epoch did not permit it, and the active life dedicated to evangelization gave Sahagún no time for it. But what about his dictionary? It was not the result of disinterested study either (Nicolau D'Olwer 1952:171). It is true that in that period the Nahuatl that had been recorded was known only to Fray Alonso de Molina, Sahagún himself, and the old men born before the arrival of the whites (García Icazbalceta 1941:61; Mendieta 1945:114), even though Olmos and Motolinía were not far behind, but the language had to be recorded because it was the vehicle with which to penetrate the native mind (León-Portilla, 1966b: 21) and because it was to be retaught to the young Nahuas as a cultured language once the Republic of Christ was established.

The Franciscan dreams were not realized. Without them, the work of Sahagún lost much of its original meaning. That work continues today to serve other different but no less noble goals, maintaining its usefulness on the solidity of an extraordinary method.

SAHAGÚN'S METHOD

Sahagún himself provides us with the pertinent information about the steps followed in the collection of the material for his work (see also García Icazbalceta 1954; Jiménez Moreno in Sahagún 1938; Garibay in Sahagún 1956; Toro 1924; León-Portilla 1958b, 1966b; Ricard 1947: 124–25; Nicolau D'Olwer 1952; Anderson 1960). Once the draft outline was prepared, which in this case should be understood to mean only the initial plan and not the developed questionnaire, he asked in the Acolhua village of Tepepulco for the services of people knowledgeable about native antiquity:

> In the said village I had all the leaders assembled, together with the lord of the village, Don Diego de Mendoza, an old man of great distinction and ability, very experienced in all civil, military and

political, and even idolatrous matters. Having met with them, I proposed what I intended to do and I asked that they give me qualified
and experienced persons with whom I could talk and who would be
able to answer what I asked. They answered that they would discuss
the proposition and give me an answer another day, and thus they
took leave of me. Another day the lord and the leaders came and,
having made a solemn speech, as they used to do then, they pointed
out to me ten or twelve leading elders and told me I could speak
with them and that they would truly answer everything that might
be asked of them. There were also four Latinists, to whom I had
taught grammar a few years earlier in the College of the Holy Cross
in Tlaltelolco.

With these leaders and grammarians who were also leaders I con-
versed many days, nearly two years, following the order of the draft
outline I had made (Sahagún 1956: 1:105–6).

We have then: an investigator who adds to a profound knowledge of
the language the proper character to enter into contact with the informants—"gentle, humble, poor, and in his conversation prudent and af-
fable to all" (Mendieta 1945:4:114–15); a people of cultural importance
ruled by the son-in-law of the famous Ixtlilxochitl II, lord of Texcoco
(García Icazbalceta 1954:345); ten or twelve cultured elders willing to
serve as informants; and four youths who have been influenced by both
cultures, willing to serve as intermediaries in the gathering of information
(Anderson 1960:35; Ricard in Garibay, 1953–54:2:345). One more element must be mentioned: the pictorial codices that served as a basis for
the inquiry.

> All the things we discussed they gave to me by means of paintings,
> for that was the writing they had used, the grammarians saying them
> in their language and writing the statement beneath the painting
> (Sahagún 1956:1:105–6).

And further on:

> These people had no letters nor any characters, nor did they know
> how to read or write; they communicated by means of images and
> paintings, and all their antiquities and the books they had about
> them were painted with figures and images in such a way that they
> knew and had memory of the things their ancestors had done and
> had left in their annals, more than a thousand years back before the
> arrival of the Spanish in this land.

116

Most of these books and writings were burned at the time of the destruction of the other idolatries, but many hidden ones which we have now seen did survive and are still kept, from which we have understood their antiquities (Sahagún 1956:2:165).

This is to say that Sahagún obtained information directly derived from the pictorial codices and that he used this system to record the information obtained and, as will be seen later on, to interrogate the Nahua elders.

The work of Tepepulco, schematic if compared to what followed, was the foundation that permitted Sahagún to obtain greater information from the Mexicans among whom he went to live in 1560.

At the time of the Chapter at which Father Francisco Toral, who gave me this charge, celebrated his seventh year, I was transferred from Tepepulco; taking all my writings I went to live at Santiago del Tlaltelolco, where, assembling all the leaders, I proposed to them the business of my writings and asked them to designate for me several able leaders with whom I could examine and discuss the writings I had brought from Tepepulco. The governor and the mayors pointed out to me eight or ten leaders chosen from among all of them, very skillful in their language and in the things of their antiquities, with whom (in addition to four or five collegiates, all of whom were trilingual), while closed off in the college for a period of more than a year, everything I had brought from Tepepulco was corrected and expanded, all of which had to be rewritten from a terrible copy because it had been written hurriedly.

Having done what has been related in Tlaltelolco, I came to stay at St. Francis of Mexico with all my writings, where for a period of three years I read and reread these writings of mine by myself, went back and corrected them, and divided them into books, into twelve books, and each book into chapters and some books into chapters and paragraphs . . . and the Mexicans added and corrected many things in the twelve books while they were being put into smooth copy, so that the first strainers through which my works were sifted were those of Tepepulco, the second those of Tlaltelolco, the third those of Mexico; and in all of these scrutinies there were college-trained grammarians (Sahagún 1956:1:106–7).

At the present time four stages of the work in question are known through documentation: (1) a brief schematic plan which may well be identified with the information received in Tepepulco and which Paso y Troncoso baptized with the name "Primeros Memoriales"; (2) an extensive manuscript later divided into two parts which have come to be called the Madrid Codex of the Royal Academy of History and the Madrid Codex of the Royal Palace, which, as Ramírez (1903b:6) correctly states, could originally have been a smooth copy (although written in various hands) but was later converted into a rough draft; (3) a beautiful and extensive bilingual manuscript now known as the Florentine Codex, subsequent to the Madrid Codices, the Nahuatl column of which Sahagún must have considered definitive (Garibay 1961:8), the Spanish column constituting a version (not a literal translation) of the *General History of the Things of New Spain*; and finally (4) there exist among the pages of the Madrid Codex passages known as "Memoriales con Escolios" in which Sahagún translated the Nahuatl text word for word and with ample explanations. This translation constitutes an unfinished foundation for the dictionary, which was also never finished. It can be said that the first three stages, which are the important ones for our purposes, mark the work done in Tepepulco, Mexico-Tlaltelolco, and Mexico-Tenochtitlan, respectively. The difference between the latter two is not as great as has been claimed. In Mexico-Tenochtitlan, Sahagún gave his work final divisions into books, chapters, and paragraphs; the grammarians added the specific headings in Nahuatl, polished the language (but not excessively), omitted things by error or mistranscribed them, and added beautiful illustrations, albeit with marked European influence. For purposes of investigation the Tlaltelolcan and Tenochtitlan documents constitute a unit, so much so that the book corresponding to the conquest preserves, even after its passage into the document elaborated in Mexico-Tenochtitlan, its totally Tlaltelolcan character.

Therefore two stages can be considered fundamental to the Franciscan's investigation: the initial one of Tepepulco, which has as a result the information contained in the "Primeros Memoriales," and the investigation of Tlaltelolco, from which derive the Madrid and Florentine codices, even though the latter was done in Mexico-Tenochtitlan. Further on we shall see the most notable differences between Sahagún's first and second contacts with the native informants.

The result is a priceless work. One notes in it a continual departure from the original plan, since it appears that it was not intended to be a book in Spanish (Garibay 1953–54:2:65); rather the work took on a very different shape which depended on the particular circumstances of the subject matter, the formation of the questionnaires, and the will of the native elders, on contradictions in the text derived from the differences among the informants, and on the *General History*—even on frequent errors by the Franciscan who, despite his knowledge of the language, misinterpreted several passages (Garibay in Sahagún 1956:1:12; Anderson 1960:41). All of this is helpful in judging the authenticity of the work's contents. It is an encyclopedia of the Nahua people, planned and directed by Fray Bernardino de Sahagún, and formed from the material supplied by the native elders who lived fully within the world preceding the conquest.

Once the author himself has explained the process he followed and has presented the two principal stages of its development, the question of the originality of his method arises. In spite of Chavero's assurance that no historian had used this method before (Chavero n.d.:34), it is known that Olmos had already initiated the collection of the *huehuetlatolli*, or ancient speeches, and that he and Ramírez de Fuenleal had used the pictorial codices as a basis for the acquisition of information, steps that were followed by Tovar, Durán, Alva Ixtlilxochitl, and Alvarado Tezozómoc, among others (Garibay 1953–54:2:71–73, 1961:14). Moreover, Olmos may have used the question method to obtain the information which was the foundation of his work, and it would not be farfetched to think that Durán may have done the same thing. I think the problem of originality is secondary. Sahagún's importance rests on the results of his efforts. The method emerged from the contact between the cultures. Nahuatl man, upon being questioned either about the history of his people, or about his ancient customs, or even, during confession, about his sins, brought forth, with a peculiar sense of authenticating his words, the pictographic document which was both a mnemonic device and a proof. This was the basis of the Nahua's knowledge, which could be written down immediately by the translators or provisionally recorded verbatim when the Latin system of writing was adapted to the native language. It was also of interest from the beginning to record the chants of the ancient religion in order to try to shape the new ones on this foundation, and to record the *huehuetlatolli* with all their valuable information on the ancient morals. This made the system of verbatim transcription unquestionably preferable to that of simultaneous translation—at least for the friars who knew the language —and it was only a short step from verbatim transcription to the formulation of the questionnaires.

THE GENERAL PLAN OF THE WORK

Indicated as antecedents and possible inspirations to Sahagún's work are the *Archaeology* of Flavius Josephus, the *History of Animals* and *Parts of Animals* of Aristotle, the works of Albert of Cologne, and especially the *Natural History* of Pliny (Garibay 1953–54:2:57–71) and *On the Properties of Things* by the Franciscan Bartholomew de Glanville (Robertson 1966:*passim*). Sahagún could have known them all, both in New Spain and in Salamanca, where he was a student, and they are all examples of a continuous and evolving line of human thought that originates with the systematic Greek studies of animals, passes through the Latin natural histories, and arrives in the New World in the form of medieval encyclopedias which included all beings in rigorous hierarchical order, beginning with the Trinity and ending with mineral forms.

In spite of the continuous variations in the Franciscan's plans, they all follow a scholastic and medieval hierarchy, adapted of course to the religion and customs of the ancient inhabitants of New Spain. In the index of the successive arrangements of the *General History* provided to us by Jiménez Moreno (Sahagún 1938:illustration between xl & xli), we can see that in the "Primeros Memoriales" Sahagún began with the gods, continued with heaven and hell, went on to the lordships, and concluded with earthly things. Already in the Madrid Codices the books on the natural things are placed fourth. In the design of Mexico-Tenochtitlan the book on rhetoric and moral philosophy and the one on the conquest are included. Up to the Madrid Codices the hierarchy is strict; in the definitive presentation of the work, Sahagún had already introduced modifications that can make one who does not know the previous plans doubt the hierarchical order that ruled the distribution of subjects.

The book corresponding to the gods was divided into a treatise on the gods, an account of the religious celebrations, and a description of the places the Nahuas believed men went after death. It is, in sum, a study of divinity, of the divine-human relationship as worship, and of the divine-human relationship as punishment and reward—the latter, at least, from the Christian viewpoint. The last of these three books was subsequently modified for the reasons listed below; but still, in the prologue of the *General History*, Sahagún says that the third will treat of the "immortality of the soul and the places where they said souls go upon leaving the body, and of the vows and offerings they made for the dead" (Sahagún 1956:1:28).

Afterward come the books of heaven, which should logically treat of heaven as an entity related to the secrets of man's soul—judicial astrology—and of heaven as a physical body—natural astrology. Between these two themes, which constitute a book apiece, another was initially placed treating omens and predictions, which were tied in some way to the theme of judicial astrology, according to Sahagún. Later yet came the book of rhetoric, moral philosophy, and theology, which is assumed to have been completed much earlier but which was not included in the original plan as part of the body of the work. After some hesitation, Sahagún felt it pertinent to place this treatise in sixth place among his books. His reason is unclear; perhaps he considered that it was necessary to situate the Nahuas' knowledge of philosophy and theology, expressed in rhetoric, before the treatment of their knowledge of heaven as a physical entity.

Heavenly things are followed by the human: first of all the social divisions in hierarchical order, starting with the lords, going on to the merchants and officials, and concluding with the vices and virtues of all men; secondly man as a physical being, with the parts of the human body and diseases and their remedies; thirdly man as a member of national groups.

Animals, plants, and minerals—the eleventh book—occupy the next place. Actually the encyclopedia ends here. But just as there existed an independent treatise on rhetoric which had to be interpolated as a book (Book 6), so Sahagún possessed a valuable history of the conquest as told by the conquered. He simply chose to include it at the end; it remains a mere addition to the general conception which, but for its value, could be considered a leftover.

SAHAGÚN'S QUESTIONNAIRES

Sahagún's three specific purposes—to know the ancient religion, to create or inspire texts from which a rich vocabulary could be obtained, and to record the Nahua's great cultural possessions—largely determined the method he followed in his books, a method which varies considerably. Sometimes it seems as though he had only the linguistic aim in mind, and even in this case he sometimes collected vocabulary by means of a constant set of questions and sometimes permitted the informants to give him whatever sentences and speeches they chose. He was conscious that the materials obtained by the first system were sometimes only valuable for the formation of his planned dictionary, so he provided no Spanish translations of these in his *General History* (see Chapter 27, Book 10). In other cases he included translations but warned the reader of the Nahuatl text of the trouble they could cause:

> Another thing about the language which will also annoy those who may understand it, is that for one thing there are many synonymous names, and one way of speaking and one sentence is said in many ways. It became a challenge to know and write down all the words for each thing and all the ways of saying one sentence, and not only in this book (7) but in the whole work (Sahagún 1956:2:256).

In the chapters where the informants answered under pressure of a questionnaire, the questions are shown in a more or less clear form. The comparison of the contents of the paragraphs gives an approximate idea of the list of questions. Of course the approximation will be closer when each book has been analyzed on the basis of a complete translation.

FIRST BOOK
In Which Are Treated the Gods Worshiped by the Natives of this Land of New Spain

Paragraphs 5 and 10 of the "Primeros Memoriales," which treat respectively the ornaments and the powers of the gods, can be considered antecedents to the first books of the Madrid and Florentine codices. The positions of the figures and of the text of paragraph 5 lead to the supposition that they were copied or drawn from memory in the pages of "Primeros Memoriales" and that on the basis of the pictures the Franciscan followed along asking for their meaning. The grammarians wrote to the left of the gods' figures a brief description of the ornaments, which were all the elder informants had described. The rigidity of the language suggests that the informants were repeating phrases learned in the calmecac; these schools were attended almost exclusively by the *pipiltin*, or nobles. At the end of the list, however, the uniformity of the answers breaks down; the reason is easy to guess, since the many small figures that appear there are not really gods but rather the images of the mountains, the *tepictoton*, and Sahagún must have asked for their meaning, what they are made of, and why they had those adornments. The answer to the latter question, to the effect that the figures are dressed like Tlaloc because they bring rain, perhaps motivated Sahagún to initiate a new interrogation, this time to find out each god's powers. This question is answered in paragraph 10, only for the main gods and always in a very rigid and laconic fashion.

In spite of the brevity of the information received in Tepepulco, Sahagún arrived at an analysis of the situation which permitted him once he reached Mexico-Tlaltelolco to shape an interview. First of all, he could already rely on a list of the gods as a foundation, even though the Tlaltelolcans' revision caused the suppression of those considered repetitious (Xochipilli is eliminated because he is already mentioned under his name Macuilxochitl) and of those that were unimportant to the Mexicans. Each god's name constituted a heading, which formed the guideline on which the questions were formulated:

1. What were the titles, the attributes, or the characteristics of the god?
2. What were his powers?
3. What ceremonies were performed in his honor?
4. What was his attire?

The order of the questions must be supposed to have been strict, since it varies in only one case. Not all the questions are answered under each heading. The answer to the first question is more or less rigid, abounding in participles, which may reflect the memory of instruction in school. As the topics proceed, the answers become more spontaneous and free, including various names of the divinities, villages that particularly worshiped them, things the gods had invented, histories of the deities, and the like. The answer to the second question seems freer, although it is brief. Here Sahagún permits the informants spontaneous exposition, and he even seems to formulate cues or circumstantial questions, motivated by the preceding answers, when he thinks he sees something interesting. The answer to the third question is very brief in the early sections, but as the chapters advance it appears that the informants gain confidence and talk freely, making valuable contributions. They talk about the month during which the god was feasted, about the places of worship, about the guilds that dedicated particular service to him, and in the case of Tlazolteotl they include important words of the confession made to the goddess by those burdened with guilt from transgressions, especially sexual ones. The answer to the fourth question is rigid. It is only missing in cases like that of Tezcatlipoca, in which the Mexicans were talking about the supreme deity and not about the specific god with this name and hence could not describe his dress because they conceived of him as invisible and intangible. This answer is strict and brief, as in the case of Tepepulco, where it is based on what was learned in school and perhaps was also aided by figures. But the content is different from that of the first responses.

The answers show that the informants are cultured and educated men of pre-Hispanic Mexico. However, they may not have been priests before the conquest: the importance they give to Yacatecuhtli, to travel, and to the feasts given to the organized merchants makes one suppose that at least some of them belonged to that merchants' guild, a fact not to be wondered at if notable Tlaltelolcans were chosen. As experienced men they had sufficient preparation to answer Sahagún's questions on the meanings of obscure terms. Thus in Chapter 1 they say in reference to Huitzilopochtli, ". . . *Tepan quitlaza in xiuhcoatl, in mamalhuaztli, q. n. yaoyutl, teuatl, tlachinolli*" (". . . he casts over the people the turquoise serpent, the lighter of the flame"). This signifies war, the divine water, the hearth fire—the informants give themselves the luxury of answering with another *disfrasismo* (divine water, hearth fire)—which is a synonym for war in elegant speech.

Although this is not the place to discuss Sahagún's translation in the *General History*, one can respond to the indictment of the informants for having referred to their ancient gods by comparisons with the Greco-

Roman deities. Some have considered this a sign of a high degree of acculturation, which has been linked in ill-founded criticism to the forgetting of the old beliefs. It was not the informants, however, who compared the Nahuatl gods to those of Mediterranean antiquity: in the Madrid Codex the comparison is found in the margin in Sahagún's handwriting. Such comparisons continue into the *General History*, but they are not written in Nahuatl, not even in the Florentine Codex.

SECOND BOOK
Which Discusses the Calendar, Feasts and Ceremonies,
Sacrifices, and Solemnities Which These Natives of New Spain
Performed in Honor of Their Gods

The second book can be divided according to method into the main body and first appendix, which treat the religious ceremonies, and then into each of the remaining appendices, on the buildings of the great temple, the offerings and rites, the ministers of the gods, the striking of the hours and oaths, the ritual hymns, and the priestesses. I shall examine most closely the means used by Sahagún to obtain information about the ceremonies and the hymns, mentioning only in passing matters which concern the other appendices. It should be noted that Chapters 1–19 of the *General History* do not proceed directly from any Nahuatl manuscript.

The antecedent to the main body of the second book is in the "Primeros Memoriales." A small codex including drawings of the main events of the feasts is the foundation used by Sahagún to formulate the questions, but one should consider that in this case the drawings are included more to aid the informants than to help Sahagún, because he asks about the feasts one by one with a predetermined questionnaire. The questions are:

1. What is the name of this feast (in reference to the rectangle containing the drawing)?
2. Why is it called that (when the name arouses his curiosity)?
3. What human sacrifices or offerings were made for this feast?
4. How was the ceremony performed?
5. On what date of the Julian calendar did this month fall?

The order varies only in the material on the first two monthly feasts.

The answers are brief, although those that correspond to the fourth question are more detailed. The last chapter, on the feast of Atamalcualiztli, does not follow any questionnaire and is substantially more extensive.

Once in Mexico-Tenochtitlan, Sahagún had no need of the outline. The order of the headings was that of the Nahua months (or that of the nonmonthly feasts) and the Franciscan quite rightly believed that he would receive more valuable information if he let the informants narrate freely the course of the ceremonies. It was just a directed interview, not structured by a questionnaire, although the informants themselves had as guidelines the important moments of the ceremonies that received special names in Nahuatl. For example, *netzompaco*, "the hair is washed," during Tozoztontli; *calonohuac*, "the retreat was made in the houses," in Huei Tozoztli; and *toxcachocholoa*, "the leaps of Toxcatl are made," during the month of that name. Sahagún intervened only with circumstantial questions and perhaps with prompting.

The freedom of exposition allowed the informants can be proved by their constant use of connecting terms, which show that the Franciscan rarely intervened. Among them can be noted *niman ye ic, mec, niman, auh in icuac i*, and the preterit perfect used as a connective between paragraphs. There is also the indication that the informants finished their statements with phrases like *ye ixquich, nican tlami*, or *nican tzonquiza* ("that is enough," "here it concludes," "here it ends"). Furthermore, the answers do not correspond to information learned in school but to a memory of the splendor of the past. This is indicated by the predominant use of the preterit imperfect and by descriptions more of living social customs than of an abstract succession of religious rites. Some of Sahagún's circumstantial questions can be guessed. As an example I cite a request for information on a variety of corn unknown to him—*cuappachcintli*. The informant answers, "*Yuhquin cuappachtli itlachieliz*" ("it resembles shrub hay").

The hymns and the material composing the sixth book are the first fruits of Sahagún's work, for it is calculated that they were collected between 1547 and 1558 (Garibay 1958:10). The Franciscan intervened little in collecting this material; he asked the elders for the hymns and ordered the collection of the poems. Perhaps he inquired later about the meaning of these extremely obscure texts, but if so he did not interrogate the right people, or perhaps he did not insist in the face of the informants' reticence (Garibay 1958:23). His failure to discover the meaning of these texts may be due in part to his inexperience as a text collector, but undoubtedly he was also strongly motivated by his aversion to materials he judged diabolical.

The question about the great temple of Mexico-Tenochtitlan is answered with an overly schematic drawing of the plan in the native fashion, and fifteen names of buildings existing within the enclosure. In Mexico-Tlaltelolco, as we would expect, the list grows, and brief descriptions are given with it. The rites are also accorded brief descriptions corresponding to requests for explanations of the previously sketched figures. The informants first drew the religious pose; then to the left they put down the name of the rite. Sahagún asked for an amplification, and this was given and written in the blank spaces. The variable amount of amplification filled the spaces for the figures or crossed into the next answers, thus making it necessary to draw lines of demarcation to prevent the attribution of a text to the wrong heading. The information is not exactly that learned in school, as is proved by the use of the preterit imperfect and by the existence of words like *diablome* and *juramento*. The priests' section is also very brief. Sahagún first asked their names, as can be seen in a list of only five names which appears in the "Primeros Memoriales" (Sahagún 1905–8:6:(2):41), and in a fuller one which later served as a basis for questions about their activities. In the second list the names of the ministers were placed at equal distances on the pages; having made the list, the Franciscan initiated the questioning, asking only for an explanation. The answers, some long and some short, occasionally made the estimated space insufficient. The past imperfect was again used here. (On the appendices, see also León-Portilla 1958a.)

THIRD BOOK
The Beginning of the Gods

As previously noted, this book was originally concerned with the place the Nahuas believed the dead went. Sahagún must have considered the antecedent of Book 3, from Tepepulco, a failure. In that village he had asked to be told only of the world beyond, and the result was four texts:

about the different things that are lost in the world of the dead, about the place to which those who died young went, about the offerings for Mictlantecuhtli and Mictecacihuatl, and about a woman who was resurrected and who told what she had seen in the other life. There may have been more collected from another manuscript in addition to this story; the texts seem to have been mixed up during their transfer to the "Primeros Memoriales," and the story was not even concluded (unless perhaps the following page was lost). The exposition in all these texts is completely free, and their information, which may have been useful, was disregarded by Sahagún. When he asks in Mexico-Tlaltelolco about the places the dead went, he does not even notice the omission of the Chichihuacuauhco, the paradise of dead children, of which he should have had knowledge from the Tepepulco data. Possibly he remembers the resurrected woman, but the text he uses is different and is in another section of his work. In Tlaltelolco he poses the initial question about the places the dead went and uses the names as headings. He may have added circumstantial questions upon hearing the statements. In the other two places he asks who went where after he realizes that the manner of dying determined the destination. The answers seem completely free; most are given by the informants on the basis of funeral prayers.

In discussing the first book, I mentioned that the informants had answered the first questions briefly and that as the interrogation advanced the answers became richer and more spontaneous. The result was a markedly uneven book in which the four gods of greatest importance did not receive sufficient attention. Sahagún, conscious of this weakness, reinterrogated the informants, but, uneven as the first book was, he refused to take it apart and amend it with this new information. The new material had such value that it could constitute an independent book; it became the third book in the final work, in which the original main theme was relegated to an appendix. The problem was to give it an appropriate title, and Sahagún did not hesitate to choose one that was fully related only to the first chapter and only slightly to the rest: "The Beginning of the Gods." Nevertheless the final order is given in Tenochtitlan, for even in the Madrid Codex of the Royal Palace the texts concerning the other life precede those narrating the origin of Huitzilopochtli.

Sahagún asked for additional information only on the four major gods.

As Garibay affirms (Sahagún 1956:1:256), the Nahuas answered with a beautiful fragment of an epic when referring to Huitzilopochtli. They gave brief explanations, perhaps in answer to Sahagún's circumstantial questions, upon finishing their statements, and they closed by saying *"ye ixquich,"* "that is enough." The Franciscan evidently did not agree, as he continued to question them about the religious ceremonies, particularly the communion, related to the Mexican god. In this latter part, the answer is very similar to that of the main body of the second book.

Tezcatlipoca was next, and the informants were unable to answer in a similar fashion about the supreme divinity, invisible and untouchable, creator of history but without a history. They answered with small prayers directed to him, and with the many names given him, with a few explanations of these names, and with information about the places where he was worshiped.

Tlaloc was described next, but the texts referring to him were used to enrich the seventh book. Another epic was offered about Quetzalcoatl, making this book, so haphazardly formed, one of the most beautiful of the work.

In the appendix were included two more texts which would have been more appropriate in other books: one concerning education and one dealing with the priesthood. The first may have as an Acolhuan antecedent a free and extensive statement, which appears in the "Primeros Memoriales," about the activities of boys and girls in their respective schools and the functions of the teachers (Sahagún 1905–8:6(2):130). Nevertheless Sahagún paid little attention to such matters among the Mexicans, for he does not discuss the theme of the girls' school. He used the names of the two boys' schools as headings and asked:

1. How did men offer their sons to these schools?
2. How did the young men live in them?
3. How were transgressors of the rules punished?

As in previous instances the informants based their information on well-known speeches, which were used to answer the first question both for the telpochcalli and the calmecac. The second answer is based on school teachings, also known by memory, and since the informants mention punishment, the third question is not answered. From the text referring to the priesthood the following questions may be inferred:

1. What hierarchy existed in the priesthood?

2. What was the social origin of the two highest priests?

3. What were the ranks of those who served in the temple?

The wording of this last question is suggested to me by a note in the margin in Sahagún's own hand.

FOURTH BOOK
On Judicial Astrology or The Art of Divining Used by These Mexicans to Know Which Days Were Fortunate and Which Were Unfortunate and What Conditions Would Be Met by Those Born on the Days Attributed to the Signs or Symbols Which Are Placed Here, This Seeming More Like Black Magic than Astrology

Even in the title one notes Sahagún's aversion to this subject; what he called "judicial astrology" was not adjusted to the course of the stars —reason enough to consider it false and belonging to magic. But from the "Primeros Memoriales" on, he was determined to understand a system as foreign to him as the calendar of 260 days. He had recorded with drawings the signs of the days, divided into twenty groups of 13. Before each group was written the information on the destinies, from which the following questionnaire arises:

1. Was the sign that started the 13-day group good or bad?
2. What fate did the noblemen born under it have?
3. What fate did commoners born under it have?
4. What fate did noblewomen born under it have?
5. What fate did common women born under it have?

Undoubtedly the informants had previously told Sahagún that it was customary to answer separately as to the fortunes of males and females, nobles and commoners. The order of the questions is not strict, and they are seldom all answered. The answers are brief. The information given by the Acolhuas will in some cases differ from that of the Mexicans.

The Tepepulco data certainly served as a basis for the questionnaire Sahagún later formulated for the Mexicans, but the fact that in their extensive information the Mexicans referred not only to the initial days of the groups of thirteen but also to intermediate signs of great significance makes one believe that either they had on hand a table of days similar to the one the Franciscan had made in Tepepulco or they knew with precision and by memory the order of the signs. Sahagún used the initial signs of the thirteen-day groups as headings; the Mexicans established the intermediate signs of importance as well, and the following questionnaire was used:

1. What sign begins the thirteen-day group?
2. What signs follow?
3. In general terms are they good or bad?
4. What is the fate of the noble born that day?
5. And of the commoner?
6. Of the woman?
7. What is the fate of one born on this day who does not act correctly?
8. And of one who does?
9. On what day is it convenient to offer to the water one born under this sign?

As can be supposed, the analysis of the situation which permitted Sahagún to formulate questions 1–8 is based on the answers from Tepepulco, while the knowledge of the possibility of changing destiny by offering the infant to the water on various dates could have been acquired in previous conversations. Sahagún soon realized that in several of the groups of thirteen days there was an easily understood relation between the sign and the fate, and the question of why it was favorable or unfavorable became very important.

The increasing confidence acquired by the informants as they gave their answers made them hasten their responses to the Franciscan's questions or vary the imposed order in their accounts. Sahagún realized the value of the spontaneous information he was receiving, so he let them expound freely, answering questions in the order they wished and narrating digressions that occupy whole chapters. In return, he also began formulating circumstantial questions related neither to the initial questionnaire nor to the theme of the book.

The answers are extensive and spontaneous, not based upon a rigorously memorized knowledge such as the *tonalpouhque* or readers of fates may have possessed. The style, elegant but occasionally arcane, is the same when they refer to the destinies as when they digress. When they decline to go into further detail, one may suppose they don't have any more information. Moreover, the great importance placed on the speeches and customs of the organized merchants leads again to the assumption that at least some of the elders belonged to that guild. It is not surprising, on the other hand, that an educated person should know the science of destinies, even if not with the specialist's depth, if it was taught in the calmecac.

Besides the fact that this tonalamatl, or book of destinies, is of prime importance, its living picture of the ancient Nahua enhances its merits. In it is found information about drunkards, about merchants' speeches, about the ceremony of offering infants to the water, about the witch doctors known as *temacpalitotique*, and other subjects.

FIFTH BOOK
Which Treats the Omens and Forecasts Which These Natives Took from Certain Birds, Animals, and Were-Animals in Divining Things of the Future

In Tepepulco Sahagún simply asks for a list of the ancient omens and obtains a summary statement listing them as cause and effect. This is accompanied by another similar list on the meaning of dreams, which unfortunately was not developed in Tlaltelolco. The first is doubtless the basis for the ample information received later from the Mexicans, for with almost insignificant modifications it constitutes a simple questionnaire:

1. What is the omen concerning . . . ?
2. How were the effects of the omen counteracted?

Other questions, relating to the sounds produced by the animals or their appearance, are occasionally added with the clear and simple purpose of obtaining a vocabulary rather than some other kind of information. The questions are answered freely at some length, but with little intention of giving more information than is requested.

Then in Tlaltelolco there follows a second part of the work relating to superstitions, which was to become an appendix. It does not seem to have either a structure or guidelines in the form of headings. The informants speak one after another with no more order than that determined by mere associations of ideas. They begin by describing a superstition about a flower and continue with two other such descriptions; they speak of the action of stepping over a child, which impedes his growth, and this gives them the opportunity to warn of another action producing the same damage; they refer to the consequences of eating from the pot, continue with what is said of tamales stuck to the pot, then mention the dangers of the battlefield. They go on to state the obligation of leaving the umbilical cords of children on such a field; this suggests the theme of the pregnant woman and then of the woman in labor; the superstition about the three stones of the hearth is followed by the one about the tortilla on the griddle, and then the one about the grindstone. After speaking of the newborn child they go back to the pregnant woman. It seems that they are responding only to the Franciscan's urging that they mention yet another superstition.

SIXTH BOOK
Of the Rhetoric, Moral Philosophy, and Theology of the Mexican People, Where There Are Very Curious Things Concerning the Skills of Their Language, and Very Delicate Things Concerning the Moral Virtues

If, as has been said, this book is incorporated into Sahagún's work by forcing the general plan to a certain extent, that does not mean that its inclusion is inappropriate. For the Franciscan's purpose of having in hand sufficient material for a return to strict morality, no other part of his work is more essential. For those trying to gain an acquaintance with the people of ancient Mexico, whether in the sphere of ethnohistory or that of literature or of the broadest humanism, no other book among the twelve has the value of the sixth book.

The date of the collection of the material should be fixed, as has been noted, between 1547 and 1558. The fact that by the first of these dates Fray Andrés de Olmos had already included part of his *huehuetlatolli* in his *Arte de la lengua mexicana* has led to the belief that the two Franciscans worked together or that Sahagún was inspired by his fellow friar (Garibay in Sahagún 1956:2:41–42). The texts referring to modes of courtesy and censure between nobles and commoners which appear in the "Primeros Memoriales" should not be considered as antecedent but as a pale parallel to Book 6. The discourses of the sixth book follow a much more ambitious plan both in contents and in selection. They can be classified as prayers to the gods, speeches of the king, paternal

133

exhortations, speeches for ceremonies and solemn occasions—marriage, pregnancy, childbirth, addressing the newborn, cutting the umbilical cord, washing the infant, salutations of ambassadors to the parents of a noble child, offering to the water, offering to the temple—and proverbs, riddles, and metaphors. Antecedents to the structure of this last part have been sought in the *Book of Proverbs* (Sullivan 1963:94), Erasmus's *Proverbs*, and the *Diálogo de la Lengua* by Juan de Valdés (Garibay in Sahagún 1956:2:46). The idea of hierarchy that appears first in Book 6 will recur below.

The opinion that specialists were consulted for this book (Garibay in Sahagún 1956:2:43) seems correct, particularly in reference to the speeches pronounced by the midwife. The Franciscan had only to ask that prayers, speeches, proverbs, riddles, and metaphors be mentioned, perhaps with an outline of the themes noted, but without knowing beforehand, for example, that he would obtain a prayer which asks a god for the death of the governing tyrant. However, not everything is strictly an account of such literary material. There is valuable free exposition which connects some speeches with others and explicates the themes treated. One may cite a brief item about the villages that worshiped Tlazolteotl, where the speeches of confession are given; the account of the marriage ceremonies; and the medical and magical care of the pregnant woman by the midwife. It seems unquestionable that much of this information was solicited by Sahagún. But did he solicit it during the collection of the material, or afterward in Tlaltelolco or Tenochtitlan when he arranged his texts in order? The necessary linkage between certain parts seems to indicate that the formulation of the questions took place during the gathering of the data.

SEVENTH BOOK
Which Treats the Natural Astrology Attained by
These Natives of This New Spain

If Sahagún could have avoided treating this subject without damaging the general plan of the work, he would probably have eliminated it and thus deprived us of some truly valuable information. As he addresses himself to the reader at the beginning of this book, he says:

The reader will have reason to be annoyed at the reading of this seventh book, and all the more so if he understands the Indian language as well as the Spanish, because in Spanish the language gets very base, and the material touched on in this seventh book is very vulgarly treated. This is because the natives themselves related the things treated in this book in a vulgar fashion, the way they understand them, and in a vulgar language, and it was thus translated in Spanish in a vulgar style and with low level of understanding, pretending only to know and to write what they understood on this subject of astrology and natural philosophy, which is very little and very lowly (Sahagún 1956:2:256).

He could not be more unjust. This book is a personal failure; it is worth a great deal in certain chapters, but they are precisely those where his questionnaire did not interfere. Sahagún asked about the nature of the sky with totally Occidental expectations, perhaps anticipating replies which might deal with celestial spheres, the density of strata, universal rotation, the origin of temperature variation in attractions and repulsions of cold and heat, explanation of climates in different latitudes and altitudes, chronometry—all this and more constituting the celestial science of his time. His intentions, however, were confronted with an unexpected cultural barrier. If he attacks the Indians for their low level of understanding, they must have felt the same way about his intelligence when confronted with questions they considered ingenuous in their lack of knowledge. If Sahagún had understood something about the clash of ideas, perhaps his book would be one of the best sources on the cosmic vision of the Nahuas, discussing the upper to lower floors, the course of the stars through them, the supporting trees—information that is seldom available from other sources.

His failure in this book is foreshadowed in the "Primeros Memoriales." As on previous occasions, he asked that drawings be made on the right side of the sheets; thus he obtained pictures of the sun, the moon, the eclipses of these two bodies, three constellations, Venus, a comet, the star arrow, two more constellations, and also the meteors, which represent the wind, lightning, rain, the rainbow, ice, clouds, and hail. The following information was given to him: that the sun was worshiped so many times a day; that the moon was venerated by those of Xaltocan; that people were terrified by the eclipse of the sun, believing the star would end and the monsters called *tzitzimime* would descend; that blood sacrifices were made at eclipses of the sun; that pregnant women were frightened of eclipses of the moon because they believed that they might cause their children to turn into rats; that children were shaved every month so they would not get sick; and that the constellation of Mamalhuaztli served to indicate the time when fire should be offered or flutes should be played. There is silence about the other constellations, of which they could say nothing, but Sahagún is told that Venus shines brightly, that the comet announces a war or the death of a nobleman, that the star arrow worms dogs and rabbits, that the constellation of Xonecuilli shines brightly, that the constellation Colotl shines brightly, that the wind produces effects depending on the place from which it proceeds, that lightning bolts are made by the Tlaloque, that rain is made by the Tlaloque, and so forth.

All of this he should have put aside, but upon arriving in Tlaltelolco he insisted on his routine. He asks, "What names does the star receive?" and he is answered more or less satisfactorily. He then asks about its nature, and he is answered as to its appearance and phases when possible, with an ingenuousness suggesting that the informants tried to answer the questions at the level on which they were asked. Faced with this attitude, Sahagún has to return to the matter of worship, which is what the elders will discuss most freely, and with that is coupled the matter of the ills caused by the celestial bodies and the ways of avoiding them.

The gap of understanding between questionnaire and informants is so great that the Franciscan can follow only two roads: he searches for vocabulary on the subject, and he lets the Nahuas express their ideas freely. Thus arises, in an explanation of why a rabbit is seen on the moon, what Garibay considers the prose version of a sacred epic poem (Sahagún 1956:2:251), a text of immense ethnological and literary value.

When Sahagún returns to the meteors he finds that everything leads to the Tlaloque. He therefore includes the information on Tlaloc, in order, I believe, to correct some of the imbalance of the first book.

After speaking of meteors, and perhaps acting on the suggestion of the section in the "Primeros Memoriales" that the winds influence people according to the direction they come from, he asks about the course of the years, knowing that according to the Nahuas they run in a spiral in space, ending a cycle in thirteen horizontal revolutions at the completion of a "century" of fifty-two years. Building on this information and on a note from Tepepulco about the feast at the end of the period, he urges a free description of the ceremony. Related to this theme is that of the calamities expected every year 2 Rabbit, the account of which is also quite free.

Sahagún was either unconscious or unappreciative of the value of the information he had received, perhaps because he was annoyed at his relative failure.

EIGHTH BOOK
Of the Kings and Lords and of the Way They Held
Their Elections and the Government of Their Kingdoms

I shall consider this book succinctly. The diversity of the subjects and forms of the questionnaires do not permit a more detailed description here.

When asked about matters of lordship, the informants thought Sahagún wanted information on the history of the lords, and so they gave him a copy of the pictorial codices that contained very brief accounts of the lives of the rulers. Their explanation in Nahuatl was noted in the margin. The Acolhuas referred to the rulers of Tenochtitlan, Texcoco, and Huexotla. The Tlaltelolcans added their own. These are poor texts, entirely in Nahuatl style, with very brief narrations of little value. They are not at all comparable to other codices which, under the same pre-Hispanic norms, had furnished the Nahuas for centuries with the knowledge of their past. Despite the fact that his question was misunderstood and that this information brought nothing new, Sahagún not only collected it, but also included it in the Florentine Codex and translated it into the *General History*. Moreover, he did the same with similar fragmentary information about Tula, about the forewarnings of the arrival of the Spaniards, and about the notable things about Mexico up to 1530.

He continues with the attire of the lords and with the finery they used in their dances. Both in Tepepulco and in Tlaltelolco these are simple vocabulary lists, which do not coincide. In the second part some of the ornaments are sketchily described.

For the lords' pastimes there is a simple mention of eight recreational activities in the "Primeros Memoriales;" these serve as headings for the fuller treatment by the Mexicans.

In treating the furniture used by the rulers, Sahagún was also satisfied with a mere vocabulary. The lists are different in the first and second collections. The experience of Tepepulco only aided him in clarifying terms, since household furniture was initially translated as *tlatquitl* ("goods"), and the first answers included flowers, tobacco, fine food, cacao, and the like.

In relation to military dress, Sahagún follows a double procedure in Tepepulco. In one case he asks for names and then, in the margin, requests amplification. In the other he asks for drawings, first of attire and then of insignia, and he asks for amplification of the former and only the name of the latter. In the Mexican information there are only names, a real shame considering the rich information that could have been obtained on the basis of the beautiful Acolhuan drawings.

In the "Primeros Memoriales" there are questions for both nobles and commoners about food:

1. What were the foods of the nobles?
2. What were their drinks?
3. What meats did they consume?
4. What did the commoners eat?

Not only do the informants answer the direct question, but they also tell what the complementary dishes were. In Tlaltelolco the questions were:

1. What did the lords eat?
2. How was the food served?

The responses are very meagerly developed.

In Tepepulco he asked only for the names of the royal houses, and later he tried to use the nine mentioned as a base in Tepepulco, allowing the Mexicans to amplify their answers freely. More and more buildings appeared on the list, and Sahagún abandoned the questionnaire made with the Acolhuan information.

In relation to women's attire, the Franciscan asks the Tepepulcan women what clothes they wear and how they adorn themselves. In Tlaltelolco he successively asks about blouses, skirts, earplugs, facial shaving, coiffure, care of the body, and the manners of courtesy. In both cases the anwers are simple statements. To learn the activities of the noblewomen he asks only for vocabulary, although the answers in Tepepulco include the occupations of common women.

When he is asking about the rule of the republic, Sahagún pays closer attention. In Tepepulco he obtained a long list of the activities of the ruler, some topics of which were briefly developed to the right of the list. He chose those that seemed most important to him and in Tlaltelolco he asked for amplification on the following:

1. War
2. Selection of judges
3. Preparation of dances
4. Organization of guards and protection of the city
5. Amusement of the people
6. Concession of grants to the village

The answers were free and quite extensive. Afterward, and separately, a seventh question was answered on the running of the market. His questions about the selection of the lord suggest that he had first asked about the system and then about the ceremony.

All this has another Acolhuan antecedent—a text that begins with the history of the Chichimecas and ends with a long list of what they obtained by their conquests and power.

The final report of this book presents a problem. In the Madrid Codex, apart from what concerns the lordship, there are answers to the following questions concerning education:

1. How was a common child educated from birth on?
2. What were the levels of ascent in the telpochcalli to reach the rank of *tecuhtli?*
3. How were the sons of lords and leaders educated?

The answers were transfered to the Florentine Codex incorrectly, for only the third and second ones were taken and they were so placed as to imply that it was the sons of nobles who rose in the telpochcalli to become *tetecuhtin.*

NINTH BOOK
On the Merchants and Artisans of Gold, Precious Stones, and Rich Feathers

The most important part of this book, that concerned with the merchants, has been carefully studied by Angel María Garibay K. in his *Vida Económica de Tenochtitlan* (Garibay 1961), where his Spanish translation appears. Here, consequently, I shall simply relate how Sahagún obtained this material, repeating the idea that he got all of it in Tlaltelolco, the merchant capital, undoubtedly from the Pochtecas themselves. Because of the method followed, these texts should be divided into three parts: (a) the history of the Pochtecas or organized merchants, chapters 1 and 2; (b) data on their customs and activities, end of chapter 2 and all of chapter 5; and (c) customs and ceremonies of the Pochtecas, described in passing in the rest of these texts. In the first part, Sahagún asks in general about the history of the Pochtecas, and the answer comes almost certainly from a historical pictorial codex peculiar to that group, of definite pre-Hispanic style and high quality. In the second part one notes the constant questioning of the Franciscan. The answers are open and precise but not elegant, partly because the questionnaire does not appear to have been structured. It is probable that in the third part Sahagún asked about broad areas; the answers are free and very elegant, giving the correct structure of the temporal order of the ceremonies. The firm, sure narration is very similar to that of the religious ceremonies in the second book, but it is reinforced by long speeches.

As for the artisans, the different occupations constituted the headings. With that outline Sahagún poses the following questions:

1. What are they called and why? (If the name derives from the origin, the informants allude to it; if the occupations are subdivided the different names are explained.)

2. What particular gods did they venerate?

3. How are their gods attired?

4. How were they worshiped? (The answers include the dates, sacrifices, dances, economic collaboration for the buying of slaves and so on—all at length.)

5. What do they produce?

6. How did each occupation work? (When there are several methods, the answer is given separately for each. It is extensively explained in the logical order of the process, even depicting the tools.)

In the case of the *amantecas*, or makers of feather mosaics, circumstantial questions seem to have been asked, mainly in order to ascertain the importance of the occupation during pre-Hispanic times and the causes of contemporary decadence.

TENTH BOOK
Of the Vices and Virtues of this Indian People,
of the Interior and Exterior Parts of the Body, of the
Sicknesses and Countervailing Medicines, and of the Nations
Which Have Come to This Land

This book can be divided by reason of method into the following parts: (a) kinship, age, occupation, and offices; (b) parts of the human body; (c) illnesses and medicines; and (d) nations.

The title "dictionary in action" which Jourdanet and Siméon gave to the tenth and eleventh books of this work (Sahagún 1880: 593–94, 597) is readily applicable to the first part. Already in the "Primeros Memoriales" one sees the clear intention of simply making a vocabulary on these subjects, except for a relatively full treatment of the procedures of magicians and curers. The headings of the Mexican data were previously provided by the Tlaltelolcans themselves, a fact which can be noted mainly in the degrees of kinship established by the Nahuatl and not the European system, and in the lists of noble persons, which include many metaphorical names of the sons of the *pipiltin* and hence leave no reason for independent expansion. The questions are simple:

1. What is the . . . ?
2. What is a good one like?
3. What is a bad one like?

(This antithesis is believed to have derived from Theophrastus [Garibay in Sahagún 1956:2:88–89] or from Bartholomew de Glanville [Robertson 1966:624–25].) The second question disappears for obvious reasons when the subject is the owl man, the libertine, the homosexual, the madman, or the prostitute. The two last questions are often swamped by the interest in information, as in the case of the vendors of colors, rabbit fur, jars, paper, and saltpeter. For in spite of Sahagún's almost completely linguistic intention in this part, the answers, at first brief, become more extensive, employing adverbs and adjectives and presenting more valuable material, perhaps at the instigation of Sahagún himself. The texts thus come to constitute a reflection both of pre-Hispanic life and of life in Sahagún's time, in which vendors of European paper, Old

World animals, candles, or shoes appear. The interest in forming a vocabulary is not in recording a language that is about to disappear, but in recording one destined to be revived and augmented with new material.

The second section, concerning the parts of the human body, is meant only to provide vocabulary. In the "Primeros Memoriales" the list of parts (in the first person plural possessive, the usual form in Nahuatl in referring to the human body) carries on its right from one to four verbs related to the name. In Tlaltelolco the list of organs is notably extended; it includes synonyms and orders the parts of the body by regions or by nature, and the list of adjectives and verbs that can be applied to the parts in question grows inordinately. This explains why Sahagún would not have judged it prudent to make a Spanish translation of that veritable arsenal of words. A good opportunity was lost for learning the Nahuas' conception of the different parts of the human body (see Dibble 1959; Rogers & Anderson 1965).

The chapter dedicated to medicines and illnesses is completely different. A great interest in native medicine was shared among Sahagún, the College of Santa Cruz de Tlaltelolco, to which he dedicated so many years, and the Spaniards in general. Sahagún began collecting information on the subject in Tepepulco, and two different lists exist in the "Primeros Memoriales" (one in good handwriting and the other in bad) in which the names of illnesses are recorded to the left and then in a few words to the right either the medicine or a notation that the illness is incurable.

In Tlaltelolco the names of the informants are occasionally noted. They are all native doctors, and they are distributed among the headings by specialty, including diseases of the head, eyes, nose, and teeth; of the neck and throat; of the chest and back; of the stomach and bladder; and diseases of the skin, diarrhea, foot diseases, obstruction of the urinary ducts, fever, and finally wounds and fractures.

The process of elaboration can be followed through comparison of the Madrid Codex of the Royal Academy of History and the Florentine Codex. (A) One or several Nahua doctors edited the first five paragraphs of the chapter. This version is in the Madrid Codex with corrections and additions made when the text was written. (B) Later the doctors mentioned as informants revised and corrected the first five paragraphs and added another at the end, declaring their names. (C) Sahagún ordered that this revision, corrected and amended, should pass on into the Florentine Codex, considering it definitive with one more addition, placed at the end of the fifth paragraph. (D) Later one or several doctors—presumably different from those previously mentioned—corrected and eliminated important parts and added the text of the Madrid Codex—all possibly without Sahagún's authorization, since one of the additions can be considered suspiciously idolatrous.

The part concerning the nations that inhabited this land is not easy to analyze. The text is inconsistent within each paragraph; in no case are all the questions formulated; their order is not fixed; there does not exist as in other parts a regular ascent or descent to the questionnaire; the narration touches several points which could well constitute another answer later on; the informants take the liberty of adding what they think is important; the questions are many and cannot all be answered under each heading. Nevertheless, from the analysis of each individual chapter, one discovers that a questionnaire exists (see León-Portilla 1965:17–18). From it the following questions can be cited:

1. What is the origin of these people?
2. What places do they inhabit, and what are their characteristics and products?
3. What are the names given to this group, and what is their etymological origin?
4. What is their degree of culture?
5. What are their most important occupations?
6. In what arts do they excel?
7. What were their cultural contributions?
8. What were their gods, and how were they worshiped?
9. What are their moral virtues?
10. What are their defects?
11. What is their physical appearance?
12. What are their foods, and how do they prepare them?
13. How do they dress?
14. How do they wear their hair?
15. What type of government do they have?
16. What language do they speak?
17. Into how many groups are they divided or to what group do they belong?

18. How is the family organized?

19. What education do their children receive?

In addition to the frequency with which these themes are treated, the existence of the questions is revealed by the informants when they refer to an interruption by the Franciscan. The following phrases are examples: *"izcatqui in imitlacauhca, in imacualtiliz in otomi,"* "behold the vices, the defects of the Otomis"; *"izca in quichihua,"* "behold what they did"; *"oc izca centlamantli iniyeliz, in innemiliz otomi,"* "behold the form of conduct, another fact of the life of the Otomis." On other occasions the informants themselves take the initiative: *"oc izca achiton, in no monequiz mitoz in intechcopa toltecah,"* "behold here even a little more that it is necessary to say about the Toltecs."

The answers are free, derived from common knowledge, but they are of great importance, fluid, and do not pretend to be spoken in elegant language.

ELEVENTH BOOK
On the Properties of the Animals, Birds, Fish, Trees, Grass, Flowers, Metals and Stones, and on Colors

Even the initial description of the eleventh book in the Florentine Codex calls it a "forest, garden, orchard of the Mexican language." In fact, Book 11 does contain a great deal that is of purely linguistic interest, but its importance as natural history is also great. The informants who contributed descriptions of plants and animals known only in distant regions must have been expeditionary merchants or workers in the palace gardens that sheltered exotic plants (or had drawings of them on its walls), and in the animal house (Garibay in Sahagún 1956:3:216–17) that so intimidated the Spanish.

The plants and animals are classified according both to biological kinship and to means of utilization. Even though the big chapter headings are hierarchically established by Sahagún, the classification into paragraphs and the lists of species appear to have been made by the Nahuas. This can be seen in the double classification, which may refer the description of aquatic animals to previous passages on birds or mammals, or may cause the serpent that lives in anthills, *tzicanantli*, to be mentioned not among those of its order but next to the ants. As rudimentary as Euro-

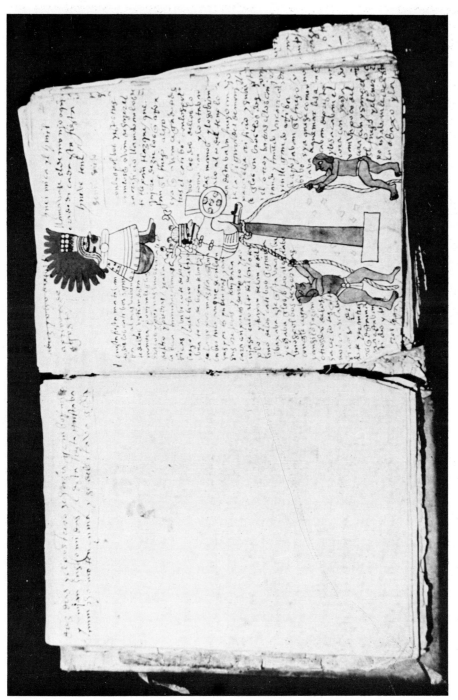

PLATE 1. Section on Xochipilli, Codex Tudela, folio 29r. From copy in Latin
American Library, Tulane University.

PLATE 2. Beginning of Chapter 8, "On the Manner in Which the Elders Relate History, Particularly Mythical Orations," Fray Andrés de Olmos, "Arte de la Lengua Mexicana" (1547), folios 209v-11r. From copy in Latin American Library, Tulane University.

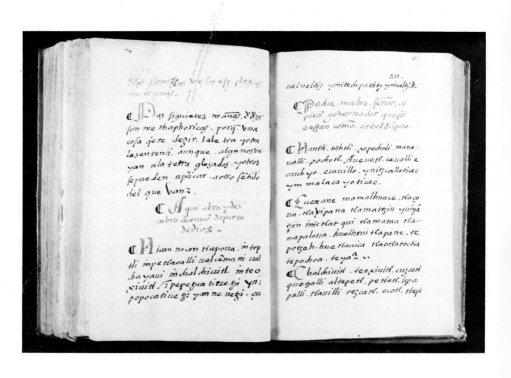

PLATE 3. St. Jerome, from *Vitae Patrum* (Toledo, Juan de Ayala, 1553). Reproduced from James Patrick Ronaldson, *Early Book Illustration in Spain*, Introduction by Konrad Haebler (London, 1926).

PLATE 4. Scenes from Gold Working. Florentine Codex, Book 9. Laurentian Library, Florence.

PLATE 5. Scene from Gold Working showing tile floor, plateresque column and base, and landscape. Florentine Codex, Book 9. Laurentian Library, Florence.

PLATE 6. Temples and Ball Court. Codex Nuttall, p. 2. British Museum, London.

PLATE 7. Buildings in elevation generated from the plan. Florentine Codex, Book 2. Laurentian Library, Florence. (From Paso y Troncoso, Lam. XV, fig. 51.)

PLATE 8. Temple in elevation, pyramid in perspective, staircase lacking. Florentine Codex, Book 9. Laurentian Library, Florence.

PLATE 9. Scene of singing, on a tile floor. Florentine Codex, Book 9. Laurentian Library, Florence.

pean biological classification was in those days, these liberties would have been unpardonable in a European work.

The variety of questionnaires utilized and the scope of the subject make it necessary that I present here only the most outstanding examples. Furthermore, many of the problems mentioned in connection with the questionnaire on the nations also apply to this book.

The following is the approximate order of the questions posed with reference to quadrupeds, which I obtained by numerical majority of sequences:

1. What is the name (or names) of the animal?
2. What animals does it resemble?
3. Where does it live?
4. Why does it receive this name?
5. What does it look like?
6. What habits does it have?
7. What does it feed on?
8. How does it hunt?
9. What sounds does it make?

On rare occasions a question aimed simply at vocabulary is added even though it has no relation to the subject. The question alluding to appearance is the most frequent and best elaborated; the one on habits also becomes extensive and of considerable importance. Several phrases which imply answering can be discovered: *"inic tlama,"* "it hunts like this"; *"inic itlacual,"* "this is their food"; *"inic maci,"* "this is how it is hunted"; *"auh in ieliz,"* "and its way of life."

The texts referring to birds are collected with the same questionnaire in a more variable order, and answers about habitat and appearance predominate. Special questions begin to emerge: whether they migrate and when, how many eggs they lay, what the eggs are like, whether they are edible birds and what their meat is like (of lake birds), how they hunt (of predators), how they sing (of songbirds). The question on the origin of the name is asked more frequently (unless it is spontaneously volunteered because the name is onomatopoetic). Instead of saying what animal the bird in question is similar to, the informants cite its classification. Thus the answers are, "It is a duck," or, "It is an eagle." The digressions gain importance because of the liberty Sahagún allows the informants in the interest of more information. The answers are of average length when they refer to the appearance, and brief for the rest, with important exceptions. At the end we find an extensive vocabulary on the anatomy of birds, included perhaps because so many different kinds of feathers are mentioned in the chapter on predators.

In sections on snakes and insects, the questionnaire is enlarged with the obvious questions on whether or not they are poisonous and how they attack.

In the paragraph on fruit trees the questioning is on the appearance of the tree and characteristics of its fruit; the need for words for the vocabulary is stressed, and the reply is often a verb in the first person singular. For example, "*nictzetzeloa, nictequi, nixococihui*," "I shake [the tree] so the fruit will fall," "I cut [the fruit]," "my teeth ache [when I eat the fruit]." Despite this emphasis on vocabulary, it is obvious that Sahagún insisted that the first two questions be answered also with syntactically uninvolved words—words that could be used in the dictionary. One sees the corresponding tendency of the informants to free themselves from this kind of expression, which they manage to do by clarifications about the environment, medicines, and the like. In referring to flowering trees, the second question (What does it resemble?) is replaced by one on the trees' characteristics.

In the paragraph on edible plants the questions are (without the rigorous order of a questionnaire) : Where do they grow? What is the origin of their name? What is their appearance? What do they taste like? How are they eaten? A demand for vocabulary follows. The one on grasses asks what they look like, what they are used for, and where they are produced, and vocabulary is demanded. In the one on mushrooms, questions are added on whether they are medicinal, whether they are edible, and how they are prepared. In the one on hallucinogens, the effects they produce on the organism and the mind are requested.

Those referring to trees in general, to the parts of the tree, to the wood, the forest, the garden, and flowers in general are exclusively linguistic. The answers are single words; verbs in the first person singular; similarly applicable adjectives; terms of location and quantity; names for the processes of germination, maturation, and withering; and phrases and sayings.

In the section relating to precious stones and minerals, the questions are in no strict order: Where does the name come from? What is their appearance? Who can use them? (Of precious stones.) How are they polished or used? What value do they have? A demand for vocabulary is answered with verbs in the first person singular. The first question must have been asked overinsistently, for *"acampa quiza in itoca,"* "the name comes from nowhere," or something similar, is a frequent response.

When colors are treated, if the subject is a raw material, the Franciscan asks for the origin of the name; whether it is animal, vegetable, or mineral; where it it is produced; how the product is made; the color derived from it; and finally vocabulary. When talking of already manufactured dyestuffs he asks for the origin of the name, the chromatic tones, and the mode of production, and demands vocabulary.

I have saved for last the section about medicines in the seventh chapter of the book. I do so because the evidence of the authors (Sahagún 1956: 3:326), as in the case of illness and medicine, indicates that it was entrusted to specialists; the answers are quite free and extensive in comparison with the rest of the book, there is no demand for vocabulary, and there is no relation between the medicinal plants, animals, and minerals described here and the mention of the same ones in the rest of the treatise on natural history. Everything indicates that it is not only an independent work but also a very different one, inserted into the eleventh book (see chapter 9 of the present volume).

The questionnaire, with little variation in order and a high degree of completeness in the answers, is as follows:

1. What is it? (In the case of plants: What part of the plant is it?)
2. What does it look like?
3. What does it cure?
4. How is the medicine prepared?
5. How is it administered?
6. Where is it found?

TWELFTH BOOK
Which Treats the Conquest of Mexico

The problems posed by this history of the conquest are many, and the solutions scholars have proposed on the matter very contradictory (Ramírez 1903a; Chavero n.d.; Boban 1891; García Icazbalceta 1954; Garibay in Sahagún 1956; Jiménez Moreno in Sahagún 1938; León-Portilla 1961; Nicolau D'Olwer 1952). Nevertheless, the method used was simple: Sahagún collected from the native informants of Tlaltelolco their narration of the fall of Mexico. The Nahuatl style is unmistakable: the characteristic connectives of uninterrupted narrative abound, particularly those formed with the word *auh* and a verb in the preterit perfect which refers to the last thing mentioned in the previous paragraph. The description contains long lists of functionaries and the typically native kinds of speeches that often give body to history. There is no doubt that the history originated in Tlaltelolco, since the role played by the Mexicans of the northern city is judged to be greater than that of its sister city of Tenochtitlan, and there are phrases exalting Tlaltelolco's value: ". . . *ayatle huel quichiuhque; yuhquin tetitech onehuaco; yehica ca in tlatilulque cenca mochicauhque*," "[Alvarado's men] could do nothing; it was as if they had come up against a rock, for the Tlaltelolcans made themselves very strong." We may be sure that this was not dictated by Tenochcas.

Sahagún only divided the book into chapters, and not even always in the right places, for between chapters 21 and 22 and between 33 and 34 he chopped off the informants' sentences.

CONCLUSION

New questions arise upon ending this first approximation of Sahagún's method. Three important ones may be mentioned: What is the degree of veracity in the informants' answers? To what degree can the answers be considered reflections of the ancient culture rather than merely the personal or class attitudes of the elderly informants, since they all belonged to the upper stratum of Nahuatl society? How reliably did Sahagún employ the data he was given? Some questions can already be answered with the material presented here, but the necessary comparisons of these data with those from other sources and of all the Nahuatl manuscripts with one another and with the *General History* have not yet been made. We have taken only the first step.

The Research Method of Sahagún

The analysis of the method of this work shows that the method cannot be regarded as the transplantation of a Christian Occidental mode of inquiry—it is not one man's reanimation of the medieval encyclopedia through humanism. Nor is it the last fruit of the millennial tradition of the corn growers nor the perfection of the old colored glyph. It arose as a new reality which is neither sum nor average of an old one, and it is still charged with understanding and misunderstanding. It bore the mark of an unrealized dream, and it persists as a reality that was never dreamed of, a source of knowledge about Nahuatl man, and, in the last analysis, about all men.

6

The Treatment of Architecture in the Florentine Codex of Sahagún

DONALD ROBERTSON

Newcomb College, Tulane University

The works of Sahagún constitute one of the greatest single sources of information on sixteenth-century Mexico that has come down to us. During that fascinating century, pre-Hispanic or native culture and native styles of art were in decline but still retained a remarkable degree of vitality. The massive introduction to Mexico of Spanish culture and Spanish art with their own intrinsic diversity created additional diversity. In the course of the century new cultural patterns and new colonial styles of art emerged.

The colonial Florentine Codex means something new and different to each scholar or student who discovers it for the first time. For those who have longer associations with it, the manuscript can still open new vistas, perhaps not to supersede earlier interests, but to enrich them and to provide new materials and new ways of approaching the ethnohistory of colonial Mexico. In this chapter I shall approach the illustrations or vignettes as addenda to the text, ancillary to deciphering the meaning of the work. In manuscripts from earlier in the sixteenth century the illustrations may carry the full burden of meaning or a clearly greater burden than they do in the Sahagún work, but the important point is that the illustrations in this manuscript still play an important role as direct bearers of information. At the same time, proper interpretation of their relation to the text throws light upon the equally important relation of the painter of the pictures to the compiler of the written text, and thus to the intellectual ambience that drew forth the work.

In this chapter I use only the first eleven books of the Florentine Codex, since the codex makes a more logical whole if Book 12 is excluded. At some time in the future one would hope to have the twelfth book and the earlier versions of the text included in a larger study of the Sahaguntine corpus of illustrations. The reproductions that illustrate this chapter are from Sahagún 1905–8. They are also reprinted in Sahagún 1950–69. Plate numbers refer to the former, figure numbers to both.

The present discussion will illustrate the high degree of Spanish influence on the illustrations showing architecture in the Florentine Codex, both in terms of the Spanish architectural forms appearing in the manuscript and in the treatment of pre-Hispanic or native forms. A brief exploration of the nature of Spanish architectural traits in the codex will be followed by a parallel discussion of depictions of native architecture. By Spanish architecture and architectural traits we mean those shapes and forms common to Spanish architecture and absent from pre-Hispanic architecture. By native architecture we mean those shapes and forms common to pre-Hispanic architecture in Mexico and absent from Spanish architecture.

Architecture in the Florentine Codex appears in drawings and paintings showing both the colonial traditions newly established and currently evolving and the older traditions of the pre-Hispanic native world. In the first, the forms and shapes of Spanish Renaissance architecture appear in surprisingly detailed vignettes scattered through the text (Sahagún 1905–8, 1950–69). In the second, a wide diversity of shapes and forms appears throughout the text and is also gathered in larger concentrations in Book 11, Chapter 12, paragraph 9.

The Treatment of Architecture in the Florentine Codex

EUROPEAN ARCHITECTURE

Sources for the Sahaguntine versions of European architecture include, of course, buildings actually built in New Spain either by untrained monk-architects or by professional architects from Spain, imported Spanish and other prints, and, less frequently, paintings (Kubler 1948).

What was the Spanish architecture imported into Mexico like, and how was it imported? The sixteenth century in Spain itself was a time of amalgamation of styles (Bevan 1938, 1950; Chueca Goitia 1953; Kubler & Soria 1959). Attributed to the emperor Charles V is the Moorish or, perhaps better, Mudejar pavillion in the Alcázar of Seville. Gothic forms from the late traditions of that style persisted, while the new Renaissance style called plateresque appears in the Casa de Ayuntamiento of Seville. Another stream in Spanish architecture and decoration of this dynamic century was the Renaissance purism associated with the name of the great Spanish architect Herrera, exemplified in the Escorial of Philip II and earlier in the palace begun but not finished for Charles V in the grounds of the Alhambra in Granada.

All of these ingredients of Spanish architecture and decoration appear in Mexico: the Mudejar work of the ceilings at San Francisco, Tlaxcala; the Gothic convento churches of the early sixteenth century; the plateresque decoration of their portals; and the purism of the churches of Cuilapan and later the great cathedrals (Kubler 1948).

In the drawings in Sahagún's work there are almost no visible traces of the Mudejar or of the Herreran and earlier purism (Robertson 1959:167–78). What we do see over and over again is the portrayal of plateresque details in columns, capitals, pedestals, decoration of archivolts, and the use of arches to span openings. Tile floors drawn with perspective indicate varying levels of understanding of this complex language of visual representation. Called *plateresque* because of its imagined similarity to the work of the silversmith, it is more a new style of decoration than a new style of construction. Vaults, for instance, continue the same structural pattern as in the late Gothic, but their undersurfaces are given a Renaissance look by the use of decorative detailing. The same is true of door and window openings.

Plateresque, then, is basically a style of two-dimensional surface decoration that is easily represented in drawing and painting. Elements of the plateresque which appear both in the Ayuntamiento of Seville, built by Diego de Riaño in the third decade of the sixteenth century, and in the illuminations from Book 10 of the Florentine Codex are elaborate bases with decorative sculptural reliefs, bold and complex moldings, and pilasters with sunken panels supporting round-arched openings for doors and windows. Transmittal of the aesthetic of the plateresque to the New World was facilitated by travelers to America going through the port of Seville, where, during times of waiting for passage, the Ayuntamiento building would have been constantly before their eyes. Members of the regular clergy, for instance, would have seen this building when it was still new in the mid-sixteenth century; it was thus able to exert a strong influence on buildings to be erected under their amateur supervision later in the New World.

The High Renaissance facade of the Palace of Charles V in the Alhambra at Granada, also in the Andalusian south of Spain, demonstrates an element of this later phase of Spanish architecture. Its highly rusticated basement, with its deep separation resulting in emphasis upon the individual blocks of masonry that form the flat arches of the windows of the lowest floor, is echoed time and again in Book 9 of the Florentine Codex.

Strict relationships linking buildings in Seville and Granada to Sahagún are not provable, nor are they proposed here. What we want to demonstrate is the fact that New Spain and Old Spain share common systems of shapes and forms and common ways of putting them together. The link between the *posa* at Huejotzingo (Kubler 1948: fig. 385) and the illuminations of Book 9, Chapter 16 of the Florentine Codex (Plate lviii, fig. 59), for instance, is a more direct one, since they are both parts of the Franciscan environment in Mexico itself. Here we see the relatively simple capital, neither Corinthian nor Ionic, but if anything a variation on the theme of the Tuscan order, appearing as a series of half-round moldings surrounding a cylindrical (or sometimes a truncated conical) capital. In both the drawing and the actual building the forms represent that erosion of the fine details of the classic capital that Kubler would associate with forms produced at a significant remove from the metropolitan center, in this case Spain, their point of immediate origin (Kubler 1961, 1964, 1966).

154

The column from the *portería* at Huejotzingo, its short proportions giving it a relatively squat look, with a girdle, as it were, of leaf forms and even a bit of woven basketry design surcharged upon the shaft, makes a close parallel with the column from Book 11, Chapter 12 of Sahagún's work (Plate cxxviii, fig. 827), borne out even by the rudimentary Corinthian capital crowning each.

The beautiful plateresque columns of the facade at Acolman are examples of plateresque work in Mexico of the highest order of delicacy and authenticity. The parallel with the Sahaguntine drawing from Book 11, Chapter 12, paragraph 3 (Plate cxxviii, fig. 822) is indicated by the similarity of proportion—each is tall in relation to diameter—and by the interruption of the simplicity of the shaft of the column by horizonal rings of decorative form. The drawing, being so small in scale, has had, of course, to sacrifice some of the delicate detail of the plateresque addenda to the classic orders.

Architectural representations in the Sahagún manuscript show that by far the greatest European influences stem from prints rather than from any other single source. Conventions of perspective for representing exterior and interior, use of tile floors to indicate perspective space, even such devices as small landscape scenes viewed through doorways or windows, all seem to have their precedent in prints (Lyell 1926; García Icazbalceta 1954). Prints used to illustrate books seem to have been more important than prints that circulated as single leaves with devotional images of, for example, the Holy Family, the Saints, or the Fathers of the Church, although this is difficult to prove. Few of the single prints have survived as prints, but some have come down to us in mural painting copies.

The influence of Spanish easel painting is probably minimal, since not many paintings were brought into New Spain. Those that were brought in would have been concentrated in the main churches of the capital and would have been placed in retablos; therefore they could not have been studied in such detail or as close at hand as the books in a monastic library.

The influence of prints imported from Europe upon sculpture adorning actual architecture has become well known through the relationship of the print from the *Flos Sanctorum*, Zaragosa, 1521, to the third *posa* chapel at Calpan in the state of Puebla (Kubler 1948:figs. 390, 391).

Changes in the carved relief from the print can be accounted for by the changed shape of the field, the changed medium, and, probably more importantly, the fact that the Calpan sculpture was made in Mexico several decades after the Spanish print.

Similarly, mural paintings in Mexico also show the influence of, if not direct derivation from, book illustrations from the mother country. The *St. Jerome in His Study* (Plate 3 in the present volume) from Juan de Ayala's *Vitae Patrum*, Toledo, 1553, reflects the common vocabulary of forms in the writing desk, for example, and the common vocabulary of spatial organization in the placing of the figures in a relatively limited space and the extension of that space into the space of nature by landscape seen through windowlike openings (Lyell 1926:fig. 186).

It is in the parallel of the works of Sahagún's artists to those of other painters at work in the colony that we see, as we would expect, the closest similarities. In a mural from Actopan, so representative of other murals—some lost to us, some preserved to us—we can see the common factors linking the muralist working on a large scale with the miniaturist working on such a small scale, both deriving ultimately from imported prints such as the *St. Jerome* mentioned earlier. At Actopan we would call attention to the seated figure of a saint in the middle register (Toussaint 1948:fig. 42; 1967:fig. 127). Between two fine examples of plateresque columns, before a background suggesting the extension of space by a landscape seen over a low parapetlike wall, the figure of the saint is placed on a most striking floor. Deriving from the patterns of tile floors laid in checkerboard fashion, the design suggests forms we shall see repeated over and over again in Sahagún's illustrations. As in the paintings from Book 9, Chapter 20 (Plate lxi), the individual tiles may be square or rectangular. In many examples, patterns that seem to suggest shading along a diagonal line lose the softness of edge suggesting shading, which turns the tiles into a series of triangles, or, in some cases, more complex patterns suggesting hourglasses. These patterns of tiling are most significant elements in European prints and in the Sahaguntine illuminations, for they not only establish a ground for standing figures or for the furniture of seated figures; they also establish, through their patterns of convergent lines (sometimes parallel, sometimes seeming to converge to a common vanishing point), patterns of perspective seeking to define with a certain precision, if not quasi-mathematical regularity, exact, almost measurable space and the location of figures placed in that space. The drawings from Sahagún demonstrate some of the variations on the theme of the tile floor common in the manuscript. In one type, which appears relatively rarely, the diagonals of the tiles converge to the back of the space depicted.

Two scenes in Book 9 (Plate lvii, Figs. 52, 56; Plate 4 in the present volume) show in one instance the use of the tiled floor to determine exterior space, in the other the ability of the artist to convey the appearance of space without the crutch, as it were, of the regular floor. Each scene achieves the same satisfactory effect of a significant space for the figures, reinforced by the use of light and shade contrasts.

The famous scene of the goldworker (Plate 5 in the present volume) from Book 9, Chapter 16 (Plate lviii, Fig. 59) demonstrates the use of the tile floor as part of the depiction of interior space. Here too we see the Tuscan capital, column, and base, the latter bearing the letter A, presumably the initial of the artist. Again, the proficiency of the artist in using patterns of light and shade to define space is apparent.

The Florentine Codex demonstrates the high degree of fidelity of the Sahaguntine artists to the Renaissance architecture of the colonial period which surrounded them and to the canons established by painters and printmakers from Mexico and Spain.

NATIVE ARCHITECTURE

Native-style architecture, or architecture assumed to be in the pre-Hispanic form and tradition, appears in illuminations throughout the Sahaguntine opus, with an especially direct concentration in Book 11, Chapter 12, paragraph 9, dedicated to the various kinds of houses. Sources for comparison with the pre-Hispanic architecture are not as clearcut; the relations are not as close as they are in the case of colonial forms. We have chosen to compare the drawings with a pre-Hispanic work, the *Codex Nuttall* (Nuttall 1902:2) admitting its Mixtec origin, which places it at some remove from the area in which Sahagún and his artists were working. This manuscript, however, is of the Mixteca-Puebla tradition as Vaillant (1960) has defined it, and subsequent work has confirmed this large cultural unity.

A more direct link between the Sahagún drawings and the architecture of the pre-Hispanic past might lie in actual architectural remains which still stand and thus were available for study by the artists working with Sahagún. For instance, the main bulk of Tenayuca Pyramid was still standing. Even if it was in a somewhat ruinous state, surely enough was visible to act as a guide to the artists even in Sahagún's time. Other remains now lost might also have been present as models.

But, as we shall see, the artists seem not to have been influenced by actual buildings as much as by graphic traditions which had already drifted further and further from the buildings themselves and seem to have hardened into patterns, in some cases meaningful in only their most general outlines. This is especially true of the pyramids.

The majority of the architectural representations in the Florentine Codex do not use the plan which in the pre-Hispanic tradition seems to have been the standard way of recording the ball court. In the *Codex Nuttall*, for instance, the ball court (see Plate 6 of the present volume) is shown in plan with more in the way of symbolic detail, such as *greca* panels for toponymic identification, than the ball court of Book 8, Chapter 17 (Plate li, fig. 91) of the Florentine Codex. Here the European nature of the players with their unified design contrasts with the unitary composition of the *Codex Nuttall* figures (Robertson 1959). We might note that the walls of the court are shown with a linear pattern suggesting regular-coursed ashlar masonry. No such patterns appear in the older manuscript, and we may conclude that they are much more likely to be of European than of native origin.

The representation of a group of buildings has already been noted for the Nuttall manuscript, where the buildings are arranged in registers, "higher" representing "further back in space"—in other words, there is no use of perspective (Robertson 1959). The lack of perspective also appears in the fact that the registers are in a lateral elevation with the exception of the ball court drawn in plan. The colonial manuscript, on the other hand, shows in Book 8, Chapter 17 (Plate li, fig. 90) a group of buildings surrounding a courtyard drawn as though the elevations were generated from a plan (see Plate 7 in the present volume). Although perhaps a more ambitious attempt to represent space, it is more confusing than the group drawn in the native convention, since it tries to show two aspects in the same drawing—plan and elevation—and avoids the solution provided by traditional European perspective, a solution which could have shown relations from a single point of view rather than several.

The representations of a standardized form representing "house" or "*calli*" in the two manuscripts show some interesting variations. In both there is a strong pattern of posts and lintels to define the structure and the form of the doorway. In both the building is placed upon a low platform. In both there is a decorative panel over the lintel in a sort of attic story. Differences emerge, however, in the use of a series of over-lapping forms to define the wall in the Nuttall houses, lacking in the *calli* form in the Florentine Codex. It is a recognition of the native way of thinking of walls in more dynamic terms than we are accustomed to in the European tradition.

For us the wall is a flat plane, a potential field for decoration of various kinds—plateresque or Baroque, where each style will treat the wall ac-cording to its own patterns. In the native tradition the wall is a series of dynamic planes—three in the Nuttall drawings, two at Teotihuacán, where the *tablero-talud* form of the facades of pyramid stages repeats in the inner surfaces of the porches of the palaces. In other words, a tradition as old as Teotihuacán continuing through the Mixtec drawings and the temple on the Pyramid of Teopanzolco, for instance, is lost to Sahagún's artist, or if it survives, it is only in the form of two pairs of short horizontal parallel lines, one on each side of the facade.

The remains of architecture from south central Mexico are perhaps better evidence for the native traditions the Saguntine artists were attempting to recapture. An important trait in late pre-Hispanic pyramid design can be seen in the Pyramid of Tenayuca (Anon. 1935:Plate 24), where two staircases mount the front of the pyramid, each flanked by a low framing element (*alfarda*). It is the form of this framing element and not the quality of the staircases which is of diagnostic importance, for here we see most clearly that toward the top of the staircase it is broken by a small molding and that it changes its angle above the molding. The result is a sort of small platform jutting out from the area of the platform proper. The Anderson and Dibble translation (Book 11, Chapter 12, paragraph 9) suggests reference to this change of angle: "This *Teocalli* has levels, a landing, a stairway, a junction . . ." (Saha-gún 1950–69:12:269). Does this "junction" refer to the meeting point or "knee" of the change of angle in the framing elements of the staircase?

The illustration from Book 2, Chapter 21 (Plate x, fig. 8) shows this molding marking the change of angle, but in comparison with the actual remains of pyramids the molding is too large and too low; the indication of a change of angle is not made successfully.

The temple from Book 2, Chapter 24 (Plate xi, fig. 17) showing human sacrifice indicates that the artist is in trouble. He has projected the molding marking the change of angle so that part of it seems to go around the whole building, while in the drawing from Book 9, Chapter 30 (Plate lv, fig. 30) there is no boundary to the staircase. There is no molding marking the change of angle, and the "levels" of the translation seem to be actually a continuation of the staircase around the building shown on at least three sides through the use of perspective in contrast, we might note, with the temple, which is shown in elevation only (see Plate 8 in the present volume).

A bit more satisfactory is the scene of human sacrifice from Book 1, Chapter 2 (Plate vi, fig. 28), where the "levels" are clearly distinguished from the stairs and the *alfardas* are shown with the diagnostic molding marking the change in angle. The molding, however, seems far too low to be accurate. The whole, drawn in direct elevation with no attempt at perspective, avoids problems tackled in the burning temple of Book 8, Chapter 6 (Plate xlvii, fig. 56). Here the perspective of the lower level is in pretty good shape. The perspective in the topmost level not only shows the building from a higher viewpoint than that of the lower level, but it is also noncongruent, since it is a "reverse" perspective in that the lateral boundaries of the platform diverge rather than converge as they move back into space.

The scene representing the conquest of a city from Book 8, Chapter 17 (Plate l, fig. 80) has the perspective of the top platform in a converging pattern but is not in accord with the pyramid, which is surely in direct elevation. The temple is not really committed, since it is above the eye level and would properly be seen in what looks like an elevation drawing even if the platform itself were shown in a three-dimensional rendering. It is in the drawing of the ceremonies on the elevation of a new ruler in Book 8, Chapter 18 (Plate lii, Fig. 93) that we see the completeness of the misunderstanding of this important diagnostic feature. Here the *alfardas* with their hourglass shape—nipped in at the waist, as it were, rather than at the neck—are used as decorations for the temple walls flanking the posts of the lintel construction. Surely this artist had never seen a temple, and surely he did not realize the importance in pyramid design of this key element. Having seen it somewhere, probably flanking a staircase, he treats it as a mere decorative adjunct to be placed at will.

Difficulty with drawing the facade of a pyramid continues even into the section of the manuscript specifically devoted to architecture, where the most proficient and knowledgeable artists would surely have been called upon. The building of a pyramid from Book 11, Chapter 12, paragraph 9 (Plate cxxxi, fig. 885) and the drawing of a pyramid with twin temples (Plate cxxxi, fig. 884) both show the changing angle of the *alfarda* but with its diagnostic molding placed too low. Furthermore, no distinction is made between stairs and levels of the pyramid. Notice here the appearance of tile floors in front of the pyramids to develop the illusion of space in front of and flanking the low projecting platform. This is clearly the tile flooring introduced via prints from Europe used with a higher degree of clarity than the other spatial relationships in these two drawings of pyramids.

Tile floors used in the context of native architecture abound. One of the most successful but in some ways odd examples (Plate 9 in this volume) is the scene of singing from Book 9, Chapter 8, paragraph 1 (Plate lv, fig. 31). Here, as a matter of fact, the Nahuatl text indicates that the singing took place in a courtyard with "a covering of straw." There is no indication that the tile floor represents anything but a European convention used to enhance the three-dimensional quality of the scene. The illustration in Book 9, Chapter 2 (Plate liii, fig. 9) showing a Tlacaxipeualiztli scene before Ahuitzotl is a nice example of several divergent traits; it uses the tile floor to indicate space through two series of parallel lines converging. It also shows Ahuitzotl seated in front of a building drawn in perspective showing both walls, and it exhibits the use of a pattern suggesting the regular courses of ashlar masonry. Behind is a round-arched doorway complete with the voussoirs of Spanish Renaissance architecture. Both the round-arched doorway and the ashlar masonry are surely out of place in a pre-Hispanic context.

The merchant's court of Book 9, Chapter 5 (Plate liv, fig. 20) is most confusing and confused, for it shows in the foreground our familiar tile floor drawn in the pattern of ashlar masonry laid in regular courses with broken joints. It also shows the main building using the diagonal patterning of tile flooring as a surface wall pattern. The terrace in front of the building, in other words, uses patterns appropriate to walls. The walls are shown in patterns appropriate to a terrace, and both ignore the fact that pre-Hispanic wall surfaces, as well as floors, exterior and interior, were typically covered with a layer of plaster and painted; regular-coursed masonry, had it been used, would not have shown. Remaining buildings all indicate that irregular, noncoursed masonry was the technique used in the late pre-Conquest period. In the details of the masonry of the Pyramid of Tenayuca, for instance, the stones are irregular in size, the joints not systematically broken, and the only regular patterning is the "long-and-short work" used to stiffen the corners of the pyramid or the edges of the *alfarda* so that they will maintain crispness of outline. This long-and-short work, indicative of Aztec construction, does not, incidentally, appear in the drawings of pyramids or *alfardas* by Sahagún's artists.

This confusion—or at least lack of knowledge of pre-Hispanic masonry techniques—is also apparent in the two vignettes from Book 2, Chapter 38 (Plate xv, fig. 49). In one, *Ixcoçauhqui*, the wall of a building is shown in the checkerboard pattern of a tile floor where all the squares are the same color. In the other (Plate xv, fig. 48), the checkerboard pattern with diagonals is used for the wall of a building, but we have seen earlier that this is a variation on the patternings of tiled floors! In both these buildings, we might add, a compound or double beam is used as a lintel and appears to be a variation on the established pattern coming directly from native pre-Hispanic traditions.

Different types of buildings are seen in a series of illuminations from Book 11, Chapter 12, paragraph 9 (Plates cxxxi–cxxxiv). The terseness of the text in this section is disappointing when compared with the diversity of illustration. To understand and work closely with them in detail it is probably best to work in close association with a Nahuatlato. Here we can best make some general comments by pointing out, for instance, indications that the influence of European forms and ways of thought are extremely strong, even when native or pre-Hispanic buildings are supposedly being represented. We have already pointed out the difficulty the artist had with the teocalli. The types shown in Plate cxxxii are interesting, since all but three show the tile floor patterning, and one of these, the *tecpilcalli* (Plate cxxxii, fig. 890), might possibly have had one, but the drawing is probably incomplete. Buildings with flat arches, Corinthian capitals, two stories, and regular-coursed masonry are surely more colonial than pre-Hispanic.

The two facades identified as the *tecpancalli*, with their short brackets to support the door lintel, both have other suspiciously European traits —the upper with its carefully detailed ashlar masonry laid in regular beds and broken joints, and the lower with banded masonry. The bracket suggests the form used to help support the ceiling beams of New Mexico mission buildings or half of a so-called *zapata* capital, common in Spanish wooden architecture.

In closing we return to Book 8, Chapter 5 (Plate xlvii, fig. 55) representing Tollan, where we see the ultimate in pre-Hispanic architecture: the ruins of the great Toltec capital, Tula, represented by an arcade of wooden beams supported by Tuscan capitals of the type common in conventos of the time and by a broken arch, which really belongs in our earlier section dealing with colonial forms. Behind the colonnade, tucked away in the background, is a true native-style post-and-lintel building.

This demonstration shows that the artists of Sahagún depicted colonial architecture quite accurately. The rendering of the colonial forms and shapes representing the Spanish traditions in New Spain shows us that the artist knew them intimately. They were a part of his daily life, and thus there are few lapses when they are painted. Not only the forms but the technical skills of the Spanish artist are used with assurance. Perspective, light and shade, the ability to show space, mass, and volume, and the ability to place the human figure convincingly in an interior or an exterior space all show how "Spanish" the background of Sahagún's artists was.

The native component in the illustrations of the manuscript, on the other hand, shows knowledge of pre-Hispanic forms in widely varying degrees of proficiency. At times the artist seems to be working from drawn or painted models; at other times he seems to have abandoned the model and struck out on his own, and the results demonstrate how minimal the understanding of native forms can be. We have chosen to concentrate on the less self-conscious examples of native architecture scattered throughout the text, since here the artist is working with his guard down. He shows a temple as a setting for a native action where the action is the point of the drawing, not the temple as such. In the section dealing with architecture per se, where the artist is quite consciously trying to show architecture from his past, we feel that a careful and critical analysis using the skills of the Nahuatlato is called for. Even here, however, lapses do occur, indicating a lack of familiarity with this aspect of native pre-Hispanic culture.

The question I have raised here is: If the illustrations of architecture and the devices used to present architecture are so acculturated, so close to the Spanish present and so far from the native past, is it not incumbent upon us to examine the texts for similar signs of Spanish rather than native points of view?

7

The Last Years of Fray Bernardino De Sahagún (1585–90): The Rescue of the Confiscated Work and the Seraphic Conflicts. New Unpublished Documents.

GEORGES BAUDOT

Université de Toulouse

SAHAGÚN AND COMMISSARY FRAY ALONSO PONCE. NEW DOCUMENTS FOR THE PERIOD *1586–87*.

Among the innumerable obscurities shadowing many years of Sahagún's biography, those that refer to the final stage of his life attract attention because of the uncertain context in which they occur. New facts concerning this late period in the biography of Fray Bernardino would hold no interest were it not for the ever-present and productive desire to highlight a life so intimately tied to a great work. All details are important for the proper consideration of this work. Sahagún's last years are fundamental if we remember the importance of certain dates. In 1584–85, stripped of the most complete texts of his *General History* by the 1577 royal rulings of confiscation, Sahagún rewrote part of his work, helped by some materials left to him and by his memory, and guided by a specific end. We shall consider all this further on. Let us point out at once, however, that we owe to this period such important works as "Calendario Mexicano, Latino y Castellano" (Sahagún 1585b), "Arte Adivinatoria" (Sahagún 1585a), "Libro de la Conquista" (Sahagún 1585c) in a new edition, and perhaps also the famous "Vocabulario Trilingüe" (Sahagún 1585d). It is useful to examine the archives for information about such a productive period in the life of a man well over eighty years old and in broken health.

We already know that these years were not a period of peace in Sahagún's life. In 1886, García Icazbalceta (1954:332–33) described Sahagún's role in the conflicts of the Seraphic order which shook his Province between 1584 and 1587. These conflicts were brought about by the differences between the recently named commissary general, Fray Alonso Ponce, and the Provincial, Father Pedro de San Sebastián. Basing his account on Father Ponce's *Viaje* (1873:1:78, 238, 250, 251, 280; 2:166, 216, 282, 287, 499), García Icazbalceta traced the dispute in broad strokes, insisting on the insignificance and even the weakness of Sahagún —in spite of the fact that the supreme responsibilities of the Franciscan order in New Spain fell several times on Fray Bernardino. It is useful to underline here that García Icazbalceta's sources are exclusively Father Ponce's opinions. Thus, according to Father Ponce and hence García Icazbalceta, the facts are these.

Father Ponce arrives in Mexico in 1584 as commissary general of New Spain. The Provincial, Father Pedro de San Sebastián, not only denies him a visit to the Province of the Holy Gospel, but also has him arrested and banished to Guatemala, with the decisive aid of the viceroy, the Marqués de Villamanrique, and of his wife, Doña Blanca de Velasco. Naturally the consequences are serious. On June 29, 1585, the Franciscan chapter names Sahagún first definitor, and so on March 9, 1586, Father Ponce, on his way to Guatemala as a prisoner and in accordance with the Franciscan constitutions, orders that Sahagún govern the Province as substitute commissary general. Sahagún accepts the post, but not for long, renouncing it as soon as the viceroy asks for his credentials. Not happy over resigning so easily, on April 8, 1586 Fray Bernardino declares in writing that he supports the Provincial, Father Pedro de San Sebastián, as legitimate prelate, and that he rejects the present and future censures and excommunications of the exiled commissary general. In the same vein, still as definitor, Sahagún signs a letter on May 16, 1587 in which he refuses to recognize Father Ponce as commissary, and on July 6, 1587, he introduces a suit before the Audiencia against Father Ponce's legitimacy as commissary general. Father Ponce eventually excommunicated all the definitors, including Sahagún, on December 19, 1587. This excommunication must have been somewhat academic, as Fray Bernardino did not leave his office as definitor until the new Chapter was celebrated on January 29, 1589. Thus far, these are the occurrences related by García Icazbalceta.

Of course it is necessary to clarify Sahagún's seemingly contradictory attitude, since he was a man little given to noisy rebellion. Sahagún's biographers have tried to do so. Thus, recapitulating García Icazbalceta's account and adding to the preceding documentation only a letter by Fray Gerónimo de Mendieta dated March 16, 1586 (García Icazbalceta 1892:2:doc. lxvi; 53) intended to appease spirits and to avoid the taking of "evidence from those who accept Father Sahagún as prelate and those who do not," Luis Nicolau D'Olwer (1952:126–31) managed to understand the reason for what had happened. For Nicolau D'Olwer the conflict of 1584–87 is just another episode in the fight for control of the order that divided the seraphic friars in New Spain into "Creoles" and "Peninsulars." Father Alonso Ponce, a Peninsular, appeared then to be an adversary of the Creoles. Nicolau D'Olwer's explanation, however, contains a patent contradiction. He bases his theory on Mendieta, who declared that the Creole tendency was

> . . . against the feelings of all the old and expert priests who have been in this land, who felt unanimously that when the religion of Saint Francis *no longer was harvested* in the Indies *by friars from Spain it would be a lost thing* . . . (Cuevas 1914:54:298; emphasis mine).

Nicolau D'Olwer accepts the idea that Sahagún's position on this matter coincided with Fray Gerónimo's. But if Sahagún, with Mendieta, was so firm a backer of Peninsular recruitment, why did he renounce the office of commissary and unite himself eagerly to those who disavowed Father Ponce, the most important exponent of the supposed Peninsularist theses? Mendieta could have spoken on behalf of Father Ponce, since he was a Peninsular, but he intervened in the conflict only in order to make peace between the opposing factions, and he kept his distance from everyone. Sahagún clearly took a position against the commissary general from Spain; the following documents, presented here for the first time, confirm this fact. So treating the problem as a quarrel between the Creoles and the Peninsulars does not seem to be getting us anywhere.

A fact mentioned by Nicolau D'Olwer, who did not understand its true importance, can be a first clue. Upon his arrival in Mexico, Father Ponce was solemnly received in the Convent of Tlatelolco, Sahagún's see, on October 15, 1584. The students of the College of Tlatelolco, native Mexicans who were thoroughly Latinized, offered the new commissary general a welcome impregnated with a strong Mexicanist or indigenist spirit, perhaps inspired by Sahagún but in any case very much in accord with the orientation of the college and its teachers, the Franciscan ethnographers. It does not seem likely that Father Ponce could have fully appreciated the atmosphere revealed by such a welcome (Ponce 1873 2:223). But Father Ponce's "peninsularism" was simply a declared "anti-indigenism," which was to be expected in a high official coming from the metropolis in 1584, only six years after the censures that confiscated Sahagún's work. The Peninsular seraphic recruitment advocated by Sahagún could apply only to men like himself or his elders—Motolinía and Olmos—convinced Mexicanists concerned with a particular political and religious orientation for Mexico, almost always protected by the viceroys and inspired by an evangelizing zeal of unquestionable millenarian intentions.

Already it seems that things were more complex than can be explained by an antagonism between Creolists and Peninsularists. Rather the events seem to be rooted in one of the constant directions of seraphic history in sixteenth-century Mexico. To make sure of this, let us examine the unpublished documentation offered by the General Archive of the Nation in Mexico and the General Archive of the Indies in Seville. These materials will enable us to follow Sahagún's career more closely during these crucial years.

The first relevant document is an account of a curious Inquisition trial held against the Provincial, Father Pedro de San Sebastián, in which Fray Bernardino de Sahagún and his friends, among them an outstanding figure, Fray Alonso de Molina, were involved. Its date—April 1586—is early and, of course, within the limits of the conflict. The document refers to events that occurred when Father Ponce placed the government of the Franciscan Province in Sahagún's hands in March 1586. The seraphic controversies must not have gone well in the Province of the Holy Gospel, for the materials of the trial are made up of denunciations by Franciscans arrested by order of the viceroy, on the eve of their forced repatriation to Spain via the prison of San Juan de Ulúa. The accusations are serious, and they recall many other similar accusations leveled against Motolinía and his coreligionists almost sixty years earlier, in 1529 (Baudot 1964). In sum, the Franciscans were accused of wanting to consider Mexico as an autonomous entity in both political and religious matters, and to make the viceroy its head.

The document is located in the General Archive of the Nation in Mexico (Inquisition section, Vol. 120, doc. 12; 25 folios with internal numeration). On the cover it carries the title "Mexico. April 1586. Trial against Fray Pedro de San Sebastián, Provincial of the Order of St. Francis; Fray Pedro Oroz, Guardian of Santiago Tlatelolco; Fray Fulano de Chaves, Guardian of the Convent of Guamantla. Information. Words against the excommunications." (In the margin is noted, "It was not pursued.")

On Folio 1 there is a first denunciation by Father Antonio de Torres, dated San Juan de Ulúa, April 11, 1586, telling how some seraphic friars arrested by order of the viceroy in the process of being transferred to Spain accused their superiors in Mexico of heretical words:

> . . . I present to Your Majesty how I have heard these present friars of St. Francis who came to this island as prisoners by order of the Viceroy to be sent to Spain, quote from certain of their friars, especially the Guardians of Mexico and Guamantla, scandalous words and very bad-sounding propositions to the effect of paying little attention to ecclesiastic censures and making the Viceroy head of these Kingdoms both temporal and spiritual, which is a Lutheran heresy now so current in England. . . .

The accusers—in Folio 3 Fray Juan Cansino and in Folio 5 Fray Andrés Velez—explain the charges they were formulating against their fellow priests. Thus in Folio 3 Fray Juan Cansino declares:

> . . . professed friar and priest of the Order of St. Francis, who was imprisoned by order of the Viceroy, Marqués de Villamanrique, and who still is, in the port of San Juan de Ulúa . . . said that . . . it was about the *eighth or tenth of last March* when, being in the

169

Convent of St. Francis in Mexico in joint congregation at the sound of the bell . . . it must have been approximately eleven o'clock more or less . . . the aforesaid Fray Andrés Velez, companion of the witness, had just finished notifying the aforesaid Fray Pedro de Oroz and all the congregation of a letter patent from Fray Alonso Ponce, Commissary General of the aforesaid Order, which commanded under pain of major excommunication, sentence having been brought, that from then on they accept *Fray Bernardino de Sahagún as Provincial Commissary,* because he had suspended Fray Pedro de San Sebastián from the office of Provincial; and he particularly ordered Fray Pedro de Oroz in the aforesaid patent to give favor and assistance to the dissemination of the order under pain of major excommunication . . . to which the aforesaid Fray Pedro de Oroz answered that he would obey it if the Lord Viceroy should order him to . . . and the aforesaid Fray Pedro de Oroz answered that wherever the Viceroy intervened there was no excommunication nor obedience to a prelate . . . he said twice: *here we have a head to obey, who is the Viceroy.* (Emphasis mine.)

Further on, in Folio 4, Fray Pedro de San Sebastián seems to have said:

. . . *that there was no other Pope in the Indies but the Viceroy.* . . . (Emphasis mine.)

In Folio 5 Fray Andrés Velez's declaration is almost identical:

. . . that, being in the Convent of the Lord St. Francis of the city of Mexico *on the eleventh day of the month of March* . . . in order to announce to the Father Fray Pedro de Oroz, Guardian of the aforesaid Convent, a letter patent of Father Fray Alonso Ponce, Commissary General of the aforesaid Order . . . in which he commanded under pain of major excommunication, sentence having been brought, that they not obey Father Fray Pedro de San Sebastián, Provincial of the aforesaid Order, for as long as the visit he was making he held him suspended, and that he had *named in his place Father Fray Bernardino de Sahagún,* whom he ordered them to obey . . . *the aforesaid Father Fray Bernardino de Sahagún being taken as Commissary Provincial of this Province and obeyed as such.* . . . (Emphasis mine.)

According to the document, the reactions of Fray Pedro de Oroz and Fray Pedro de San Sebastián (which I have not transcribed so as not to lengthen this account unnecessarily) are of the same nature as the above-mentioned.

The charges were to be made on April 30, 1586, under the care of Dr. Lobo Guerrero, attorney of the Holy See:

> . . . against Fray Pedro de San Sebastián, Provincial of the aforesaid Order, and Fray Pedro de Oroz, Guardian of Santiago Tlatelolco, and Fray Fulano de Chaves, Guardian of Guamantla, about scandalous propositions and words . . .

In fact it appears that Fray Pedro de Oroz had changed guardianship in the meantime, as indicated during the trial by Licenciado Bonilla from Veracruz, April 30, 1586 (Folio 8r):

> . . . Fray Pedro Oroz, at present Guardian of the Convent of Santiago . . .

The ratification of the declarations against the seraphic authorities of Mexico took place on May 11, 1586 (Folio 10ff.). Finally (in Folio 11v) we see a name that gives a more indigenist tone to the trial, that of Fray Alonso de Molina, here accused for his famous preface to the *Vocabulario*, in a context that leaves little room for doubt:

> . . . said that in a vocabulary of the Mexican language composed by Fray Alonso de Molina of the aforesaid Order . . . he says these words in dedicating the aforesaid book to the Viceroy, "*Your Excellency being head of this new Church.* . . ." (Emphasis mine.)

We have seen already that from April 8, 1586 on, Sahagún supported the followers of Fray Pedro de San Sebastián. But his activity was not limited to this. Before the letter of May 16, 1587, in which, according to García Icazbalceta, he renewed his support of the Provincial, the General Archive of the Indies in Seville offers us four other letters signed by him in a very shaky hand, which leave no doubt of his allegiance. These letters give no indication that he was afflicted with the weaknesses and problems of age. Having renounced the office of commissary, he had only to keep away from the quarrel. But he did not falter in stamping his signature and using all his authority on behalf of a cause which he must have judged to be his own.

In the General Archives of the Indies in Seville (Section Audiencia de México, No. 287) there is a series of letters directed to the king or to the Council of the Indies, including four letters, with various copies, each with Sahagún's signature, almost illegible and suggestive of his age and illness. They are:

1) *May 30, 1586.*

Your Most Catholic Royal Majesty.—Since our ministry is to treat and publish the truth, especially for one who values it as much as Your Majesty, we the Provincials and Definitors of the Order of St. Francis in the Province of Mexico have determined to say what we think, what we feel to be such in the matters of your Auditors Pedro Farfán, Palacios, and Robles, whom the visiting Archbishop has suspended from their offices. It is not our intention to treat secret and private matters, because only God is a judge of them. But in all that is and has been public concerning the good government and dispatch of the ministry, favor and protection of this new Church and of the poor native Indians, the quieting and pacification of these Kingdoms together with pious and Christian demonstrations, they have come with truly singular care and diligence, and all the Republic cries and will cry for them, because it believes them priests and righteous servants of Your Royal Crown; feeling that the aforesaid Visitor has done them an injustice, motivated by the ancient passion he has had towards them for not caring for his private matters and interests from the time of Don Martín Enríquez, your Viceroy, on, and aligning himself in this passion with Dr. Farfán since it was he who attended your Viceroy, Don Martín Enríquez, in all things in the meetings he held with the aforesaid Archbishop. For the love of Jesus Christ, let them be heard and favored by Your Majesty, sending them to exercise their offices, for thus will be continued the service of Your Majesty, whom this same God keep in the health this Religion desires.

Mexico, May 30, 1586. Your Most Catholic Royal Majesty, your Chaplains Minor kiss the hand of Your Majesty.

Fray Pedro de San Sebastián, Provincial.
Fray Pedro Oroz
FRAY BERNARDINO DE SAHAGÚN
Fray Rodrigo de San Luis
Fray Pedro de Requena
Fray Francisco Vásquez
(Holographic signatures; also a duplicate with holographic signatures.)

This first plea in favor of the Audiencia, by which the New Spain Franciscans were protected in their quarrel with Father Ponce, is followed a little more than five months later by a much more explicit document.

2) *November 8, 1586.*

Your Most Catholic Royal Majesty.—It is with great pain and

feeling that we write this to Your Majesty, we the Provincial and Definitors of the Province of the Holy Gospel of Mexico of the Order of St. Francis, on behalf of the five hundred friars who belong to it and who are living in the strictest perfection of our estate possible and discharging your Royal conscience in what we unworthily have in our charge. We have always tried to live in maximum peace, love, and charity among ourselves, edifying the towns as should be done; our clothing and nakedness and *ways being quite different from those that our Religion uses over there, possessing no property at all,* so that according to all, this was one of the most perfect Provinces in the Order. Our grave sins or the envy of Satan have been the cause for making this happy state lose its character—perfection, peace, charity and regular observance being darkened *by the Commissary named Fray Alonso Ponce, who came here two years ago* and who is of such a character that neither our clamors nor the pleas and mandates of your pacific Viceroy and Royal Audiencia have been or are powerful enough to bring him to the path. From which it is inferred that if the Royal authority cannot be established over him and he does not obey it, what will the poor subjects do! We have written about it several times to our superiors and to the Commissary of the Indies who attends that Court, but since they are each other's creatures, they have not wished to remedy matters up to this point, not wanting to hear nor pay attention to two serious friars and servants of God whom, in the name of this Province, we have sent, called Fray Rodrigo Durán, Custodian, and Fray Cristóbal Hernández.

We come humbly to Your Majesty as sole protector, patron and most powerful King and Lord, and with due respect we beg that he have pity on us and send us a peaceful prelate without passion, who will be such if he comes from Your Royal hands and Council, ordering the Commissary who is now here to leave his office forthwith, that we may not be completely destroyed. As proof of all this, we defer to what your Viceroy and Royal Audiencia may report, for they know it well and sympathize with our works as one who sees and has seen them, [and they] have protected and do protect us. We await the remedy from heaven and Your Majesty, hoping for it with all possible speed, and praying that Our Lord keep and prosper the life and health of Your Majesty as is necessary for the maintenance of His Catholic Church.

Mexico, November 8, 1586. Your Most Catholic Royal Majesty, we Your least Chaplains kiss Your Majesty's Royal hands.

Fray Pedro de San Sebastián, Provincial.

Fray Pedro Oroz

FRAY BERNARDINO DE SAHAGÚN
Fray Rodrigo de San Luis
Fray Pedro de Requena
Fray Francisco Vásquez
(Autographic signatures. Three copies of identical text, all with autographic signatures. The third copy is dated Mexico, November 8 of 86 and January 30 of 87, *sic*; emphasis mine.)

Three points particularly stand out in this text. First, the open hostility toward Father Ponce, who is accused of wanting to destroy the Franciscan work in New Spain; second, the constant support that the signers of the plea receive from the viceroy and the Audiencia; and last, and in our opinion most important, the insistence of the signers upon the exemplarity of the religious life of the order in New Spain, founded on evangelic poverty and considered to be essentially different from the life carried on by the order in Spain. Thus, a phrase like "ways being quite different from those that our Religion uses over there, possessing no property at all" echoes the reform of Father Juan de Guadalupe, which prevailed in the Province of San Gabriel de Extremadura in Spain and of which the "first twelve" apostles to New Spain were initiates, with Fray Martín de Valencia and Motolinía at their head. Thus it is equally obvious that in 1586 the spirit which encouraged primitive evangelization with obvious apocalyptic overtones was kept alive, and that this conception of the seraphic work in Mexico counted both on the support of the viceroy and on the hostility of the high officials from the peninsula. Finally, it is clear that Sahagún adhered to such ideas and ways of imagining his work, since during this conflict he clearly placed himself on the side of those who espoused them and confirmed the fact in writing. Undoubtedly the seraphic conflict set in motion by Father Ponce, a friend of the archbishop and therefore of the secular clergy, now takes on new dimensions. Sahagún's attitude also begins to seem logical throughout the occurrences that illuminate this dispute. Was it not perhaps a matter of defending the deep significance of all his work in Mexico? The following documents (ibid.) confirm the revealing elements and details of this explanation.

3) *April 16, 1587.*
Sire.—Via the mail fleet we gave Your Majesty an account of how beaten and persecuted we are, with no peace nor solace nor even honor *because of the revolutions, altercations and revolts of Fray*

Alonso Ponce, our Commissary, as your Viceroy and Royal Audiencia must have reported; and likewise *how the Archbishop of this city and Don Luis de Velasco had conspired to support the cause of the aforesaid Commissary, since they were of his party and opinion,* using as a trick that others be asked and presenting them as witnesses so that Your Majesty would credit them more, *the Archbishop doing it for self interest, since by reason of friendship with the Commissary he was going to receive half of the convents and doctrines of this Province,* contrary to the Royal Charter of Your Majesty, whom we humbly ask and petition for the same thing as in the last letters: that he not credit what is said about our affairs by the aforesaid Archbishop nor by Don Luis de Velasco, for their cunning and trickery are proven. The Royal Audiencia and all the world that sympathizes with us will be of another heart, openness, and Christianity; and hence we await the remedy by Your Majesty as we have asked and pleaded. And confident, we end with the hope that Our Lord keep Your Majesty's Catholic person.
Mexico, April 16, 1587.
Fray Pedro de San Sebastián, Provincial.
Fray Pedro Oroz
FRAY BERNARDINO DE SAHAGÚN
Fray Rodrigo de San Luis
Fray Pedro de Requena
Fray Francisco Vázquez (Emphasis mine.)

It is fitting to point out here the role of the archbishop of Mexico, who renews and continues the attitude already manifested by his predecessor, Fray Alonso de Montúfar in 1558 (Baudot 1965). Montúfar was opposed to the Franciscan ambitions and intentions concerning the native world and the establishment of the church there. Like Montúfar before him, Archbishop Moya de Contreras epitomizes the effort to impose a secular clergy in order to replace the friars and ensure a church in conformity with the colonial attitudes of the metropolis. In the sixteenth century this effort would never meet with the favor of the successive viceroys. They had to support the Franciscans, from Motolinía on, who had argued for an increase in viceregal authority and who even strove for viceregal autonomy. The last document of this group (ibid.) addresses this matter.

4) *April 16, 1587.*
   Sire.—With the obligation of Chaplains Minor and faithful vassals of Your Majesty we have reported on our own behalf and on

behalf of this Province of the Holy Gospel of the Order of St. Francis, *whose leaders we unworthily are,* what we feel about the government of the Marqués de Villamanrique, Viceroy of this New Spain. For what is good and what is bad, especially in governmental matters, should be reported by the ministers of God to their absent King so that he will be sure in his heart of knowing what is involved. The case is, most Christian and powerful King, that your Viceroy is abhorred and hated by many, and the cause, known as if seen and touched every hour, is that he is the most careful and solicitous in what concerns your Royal service of all those we have known during fifty years. And because he tried to recover your Royal Hacienda from private persons who had been usurping it for many years and curbed besides the liberties of republics and offices which have not known before what it was to have either a man or a head as they do now. Truly we, the dispassionate who are before you, believe that it was God's choice that Your Majesty made in this man, for the reformation of great excesses that were generally current in this Kingdom and also as an example of life for Christian people, accompanying him in everything with singular wisdom and prudence his wife Doña Blanca; for which they deserve the reward and esteem of Your Royal person, to whom may the sovereign Majesty of God give many years of life with an eternal crown of glory.
Mexico, April 16, 1587.
Fray Pedro de San Sebastián
Fray Pedro Oroz
FRAY BERNARDINO DE SAHAGÚN
Fray Rodrigo de San Luis
Fray Francisco Vázquez
Fray Pedro de Requena (Emphasis mine.)

That Sahagún's position remained firm throughout the conflict, and that his signature manifested a deliberate intention to intervene, becomes quite clear through his last involvement, about a month before the excommunication proclaimed by Father Ponce. Seeing that no one yielded in the controversy, the viceroy assembled the seraphic authorities on November 2, 1587, to prepare an official deposition of the Order on the case. The unpublished documentation concerning it is also preserved in the General Archive of the Indies in Seville (Section Audiencia de México, No. 21, Section 3, Documents 21, 23, 23a). It consists of the following pieces:

176

Doc. 21: The viceroy's opinion favorable to the Franciscans of Mexico and hostile to Father Ponce.

Doc. 23: Letter from the viceroy dated November 3, 1587, reporting on the meeting of the previous day concerning the role that should be played by Father Ponce in Mexico and stressing the general hostility of the Franciscan dignitaries toward the commissary general.

Doc. 23a: Testimony of the opinions and vows given by the friars of the Order of St. Francis about the reception of Fray Alonso Ponce, commissary, to the exercise of his office, at the meeting which the viceroy, Marqués de Villamanrique, called for this purpose.

We shall examine this last document more carefully, because it is the most revealing. It is joined to the viceroy's letter of November 3, 1587. We abstract from its contents the parts that most directly concern Sahagún's activity at the meeting.

(Folio 2r) In the city of Mexico on the second day of November of the year 1587, the Most Excellent Don Álvaro Manrique de Cúñiga, Marqués de Villamanrique, Viceroy . . . called to his presence the priests of the Province of the Holy Gospel of this New Spain, to wit: Fray Pedro Oroz, Guardian of the Convent of Santiago Tlaltelolco and Provincial of this Province . . . *and Fray Bernardino de Sahagún, Discreto and former Definitor of this Province.* . . . (Emphasis mine.)

(Folio 4r) . . . and then Father Sahagún said that for brevity's sake he does not want to repeat the words already spoken [by Father Pedro Oroz], but rather taking the substance from them says that for the remedy of these past problems which have resulted from Fray Alonso Ponce's regime, and so that those who are presently eminent desist, it is very necessary that it be processed through the state and the said Fray Alonso be ordered not to reside in this Province nor have any jurisdiction in it himself or through another; and this is his opinion and the substance of all that he declared. . . .

The opinions of the other speakers testify to the enormous authority Sahagún had in his order at that date, for in general the others defer to his opinions:

(Folio 6v) . . . Fray Luis de Villamayor said that in everything and for everything he defers and conforms to the opinions of Fray Bernardino de Sahagún . . . and then Fray Alonso de Paterna said that he defers to the opinion of Fray Pedro Oroz and Fray Bernardino de Sahagún . . . etc. . . . etc. . . .

As we can see, Sahagún did not yield in his opposition to Commissary Ponce; on the contrary, at the head of his order and using all his influence in it, he led the hostilities. Surely a man of his age, ill, and the author of a gigantic work which he could more or less consider lost and to which he had consecrated a lifetime, would not do this without very powerful reasons and convictions so deep that they carried the true meaning of his entire existence.

Let us summarize and specify what we can infer from this new documentation. Sahagún's constant attitude throughout the seraphic conflict of 1584–87 cannot be attributed to senile weakness or to any intent to deceive, but rather to deeply rooted convictions. His attitude remains consonant with the policies followed by many great figures of the sixteenth century in the Franciscan order of Mexico. With a few exceptions, the great majority of the seraphic missionaries of New Spain in the sixteenth century belonged to the spiritual reformist breed originating in San Gabriel. In diverse ways and with varying degrees of success they tried to apply its ideas. Like Fray Martín de Valencia, like Motolinía, like Mendieta, Sahagún dreamed of an autonomous native Mexico under the strong authority of a substantially independent viceroy, structured and ruled by friars desirous of founding a New Church based on the pre-Constantine model—all of this probably with millenarian and apocalyptic ambitions. The refusal of Fray Gerónimo de Mendieta, Motolinía's disciple and the greatest exponent of this vision of Mexico, to intervene in the conflict is evidence of Mendieta's prudence. Very well connected in the Council of the Indies years before (he was a friend of the president, Juan de Ovando), he well knew the details of the brutal change in American policy begun by the council in 1575. Let us emphasize that Sahagún had been the most visible victim of this change in policy.

Some day perhaps it will be useful to relate the ethnographic investigation on the native world of America to the millenarian projects. For now, the fact is that in opposing Father Ponce with the support of his order and of the viceroy, Sahagún was defending the direction of the accomplishments of the College of Tlatelolco and the evangelizing work of his foremost coreligionists—perhaps with a bitter dawning comprehension of the reason for the confiscation of his ethnographic work. It is strange, in fact, that the beginning of this conflict in 1585 coincided with the renewal of Sahagún's ethnographic efforts, shaped into the "Calendario," "Arte Adivinatoria," and so on. The fact that in a paragraph of the "Arte Adivinatoria" (which we shall treat further below) Sahagún spoke against the supposed ethnographic naïveté of "one of the first twelve" in reference to the Mexican calendar is of no importance here; furthermore, as we shall see, it can be explained. What is important to us is the fact that the Franciscan returned to the papers left to him after the confiscation, to rescue those he believed to be most fundamental.

A thematic analysis of the fragments written around 1584–85 will be essential to understanding the situation. However, to understand as best we can what Sahagún was after, we must bear in mind the coincidence between this late ethnographic work and his firm, persistent attitude in the conflict that placed him and his order in opposition to the commissary general from Spain.

THE PARTIAL RESCUE OF THE CONFISCATED ETHNOGRAPHIC WORK. THE RELIGIOUS SUBJECTS CHOSEN IN *1585* AND THEIR MEANING.

Very little of the rescued material exists; very little of that has been studied. The texts themselves have not yet received proper editing and criticism. Therefore, let us first summarize the state of the question. From García Icazbalceta (1954: 368–87) we know that after 1584 (that is to say after the Gregorian calendar correction made in Mexico in that year) Sahagún began the partial reconstruction of his work with such notes, memoirs, and transcripts as he had left and with the help of several loyal copyists, such as Martín Jacobita or Agustín de la Fuente. It was a partial reconstruction because of the impossibility of completely reviving the *General History*. It was also a selective reconstruction, obviously dedicated to retaining what was urgent in Fray Bernardino's opinion. Two fragments of this reconstruction are left to us: the "Calendario Mexicano, Latino y Castellano" and the "Arte Adivinatoria"; as a fruit of this effort and in the same period, one should add the new version of Book 12 or "Libro de la Conquista" and the "Vocabulario Trilingüe."

For information on the locations and characteristics of the manuscripts, see García Icazbalceta (1954), Jiménez Moreno (in Sahagún 1938:1), and Nicolau D'Olwer (1952:8:112–24). Nothing subsequent seems to have greatly changed what was established by these three studies. According to them the texts had diverse fates.

Sahagún's personal copy of the new "Libro de la Conquista" ended up, as far as we know, in the Librería Laietana of Barcelona, which offered it for 15,000 pesetas in 1935 to the National Museum of Mexico (Jiménez Moreno in Sahagún 1938). According to previously mentioned bibliographical studies, other copies still exist. The "Vocabulario Trilingüe" that Torquemada says he owned might be identified with Manuscript No. 1478 of the Ayer Collection (Newberry Library, Chicago), although given its elementary character this may be only a draft copy of the "Vocabulario." Finally the unique copy of the "Calendario" and the "Arte Adivinatoria," contemporary with Sahagún but not made by him or his secretaries, is in the National Library of Mexico (Manuscript No. 1628 bis, Folios 96–112 for the "Calendario" and Folios 116–42 for the "Arte Adivinatoria"). Here again we refer to García Icazbalceta, Jiménez Moreno, and Nicolau D'Olwer for the characteristics and history of the manuscripts.

The last manuscript, which is in our opinion of the greatest interest and with which we will work here in a photographic copy, has never received proper critical publication. The only edition of the "Calendario" is that of Juan B. Iguíniz (1918). García Icazbalceta published the prologue, the dedication to the reader, and the first chapter of the "Arte Adivinatoria" (García Icazbalceta 1954:382–87). He analyzed the most obvious internal characteristics of both texts and correctly noted that these fragments were obviously part of a lost work, more extensive and ordered differently from the *History* that we know. I infer that they might be fragments of a complete new reconstruction of the *History*— or an attempt at one—begun by the Franciscan in 1585, exhibiting different viewpoints from those that governed the texts confiscated in 1577–78 (García Icazbalceta 1954:371).

It is regrettable that another very detailed study of these fragments, made by Paso y Troncoso in 1886, has not been published. It is preserved in the National Museum of Anthropology and History of Mexico (Chapultepec, Historic Archive, Collection Papeles Sueltos, 2d Series,

180

Leg. No. 88, Doc. No. 3, 36 manuscript pages, dated Mexico, May 12, 1886 and entitled *Fragmentos del Padre Sahagún, 1585*). According to Paso y Troncoso, the "Calendario" must be only a fragment of a fuller text by Sahagún, now lost. Four manuscript copies of that text must have existed. Fray Martin de León used one in his *Camino del Cielo* (León: 1611) without acknowledging the Sahagúnian origin of the text, as is also noted by García Icazbalceta. The second was used by Torquemada. The third was in the possession of Ixtlilxochitl at the beginning of the seventeenth century and according to Paso y Troncoso would later have passed through the hands of Sigüenza, Boturini, Veytia, León y Gama, and finally Aubin. This one, it seems to me, could be the original of the seventeenth-century copy preserved in the National Library at Paris (Manuscript No. 65–71, Folios 113–22), which corresponds with variations to Book 2, Chapters 1–19 of the Spanish text of the *History*. The fourth, taken from the former library of the Jesuits in Mexico, the work of a curious Jesuit of the sixteenth century, is identified with the sole extant manuscript, that of the National Library of Mexico.

We shall now examine the studies of the "Calendario" and of the "Arte" by Paso y Troncoso, as well as considering a "Relación de los edificios del gran templo de México" attributable to Sahagún and standing as appendix to his Book 2, a copy of which is in the Library of the Royal Academy of History in Madrid.

Like Icazbalceta, and using the identical method, Paso y Troncoso proceeded to a preliminary internal analysis of the texts of the "Calendario" and the "Arte," noting their peculiarities: to wit, the differences between this text of 1585 and the calendar included in Book 2 of the *History*, exemplified in the fact that the "Calendario" of 1585 followed the Christian months, starting the year with the eleventh day of the month of Tititl, that is, January 1; the arbitrary division of the *nemontemi* among five different months; and other peculiarities. The idiosyncracies of the "Arte" are also noted: the "recent invention" of the Tonalamatl, "discovered" by Sahagún; coincidences between the second chapter of the "Arte" and the first chapter of Book 4 of the *History*, and the continuation of these coincidences between chapters up to Chapter 32 of the "Arte," corresponding to Chapter 31 of Book 4 of the *History*; and so on. As we can see, the approximation to the texts of 1585 was already important and permitted serious conclusions. We shall try to follow this in part from the angle that interests us, using the photographic copy of the manuscript from the National Library of Mexico.

"Calendario Mexicano, Latino y Castellano"

The reading of the "Calendario" reveals the following preoccupations on the part of Sahagún during the time of its composition. First, he wanted to achieve and make public a native calendar perfectly adjusted to the Christian model, for immediate use even with the most recent innovations, since the Gregorian calendar correction is made in it. This slightly forced adjustment has the direct objective of the rapid location of the pre-Hispanic Mexican holidays in the course of the year:

> . . . and by these means it will be easily known on what days of our months theirs started and what feasts they made then, as is pointed out and noted throughout this Calendar (Sahagún 1585b: Prologue).

In the same way the *nemontemi*, "empty or unlucky days of which the Mexicans told many superstitions" (ibid.), are to be displaced and dispersed in order to erase their memory and their religious content:

> . . . to remove all these superstitions [they have] been swallowed up into the months of the Mexican language, by putting in five interpolated months of twenty-one days; and in this way all the days of the year fit in the calendar of the Mexican language (ibid.).

The "Calendario" will thus begin with the Christian January 1 and the Mexican 11 Tititl:

> Seventeenth month of the Mexicans, named *Tititl*, in which they celebrated a feast called *Ilamatecuhtli*, and by another name *Tonan*, and by another *Cozcamiauh* (ibid.).

The correspondence will be maintained throughout the entire calendar containing the Mexican months, Atlacahualo, Toçoztontli, Toxcatl, Tecuhilhuitontli, and Panquetzaliztli having twenty-one days and the other months twenty. Let us remark in passing that in the manuscript Tititl also has twenty-one days, which makes one extra day, due to an oversight either by the copyist or by Sahagún. The first column shows the principal Christian feasts and notable dates, and the central column details precisely the pre-Hispanic Mexican feasts and their rituals.

Finally, in the three pages that follow the presentation of the calendar, dedicated "to the reader," Sahagún gives the reasons for this arrangement, explaining some of the details of the syncretistic confusion organized for the natives, and warning:

> It is very necessary that all the ministers of this Indian work and conversion should have this Calendar, for even though at the beginning when those who first came to it declared and affirmed that idolatry was totally destroyed, and assuming that such were the case, yet the evils and especially the things of idolatry sprout again and spread through secret caves; and having this Calendar they will be able to know whether there are any idolatries still alive and for this reason not only is the Calendar necessary for the ministers and preachers of this new Church, but also it is indispensable to have the *Arte* of the divining sciences used by these natives; and I have the intention of putting it into Spanish together with this Calendar for the same reason as mentioned above, if Our Lord provides the opportunity for it (Sahagún 1585b:folio 105).

"Arte Adivinatoria"

As expressed by Sahagún in the above paragraph of the "Calendario," it is important that the "Arte Adivinitoria" was written after the "Calendario," has its origin in a Nahuatl text, and represents a moment of reflection subsequent to the elaboration of the "Calendario." These points are responsible for the exasperated and polemical tone of his prologue, which has always been a puzzle and which must correspond to the occurrences of the seraphic conflict already under way in 1582. Its purpose is the same as that of the "Calendario," to which it is intimately linked in the author's mind, the two texts being complementary parts of a single whole. But in the "Arte" the objective takes on an obsessive character, and the reasons expressed in the prologue reveal bitterness in the face of awareness of failure as well as the urgency of a desperate attempt to save a long-cherished project.

The whole text of the "Arte" gives evidence of these emotions. Let us note in the second folio of the prologue the reproach made against the first twelve seraphic evangelists, guilty through lack of prudence of not having understood the syncretistic tradition of the Mexican religion and its broad and amalgamating hospitality toward foreign beliefs and myths.

Observe in Folios 3 and 4 of the prologue the exasperation Sahagún confesses in grasping blindly at the nonsensical idea, almost certainly not his own, that the bases and origin of the Tonalamatl were a recent invention of the Mexican natives subsequent to the conquest, the work of rebellious priests and lords trying to maintain pre-Hispanic ritual secretly in the very teeth of the missionaries. This implausible fantasy of Sahagún's reveals a great deal. We must also reappraise the attack against "the first friars, *especially one*," accused of praising in words and writing the demoniacal tonalamatl through lack of perspicacity and knowledge, when in fact this particular first friar was one of Sahagún's most respected teachers and guides. Also worth noting is Sahagún's recollection of Fray Rodrigo de Sequera on the resemblance between the fate of the Moriscos of Granada and that which threatened the Mexican Indians—"their irremediable destruction." Finally there is the insistence on the fundamental importance of the ethnographic and linguistic preparation of missionaries faced with the lively persistence of pre-Hispanic beliefs more than sixty years after the beginning of missionary work.

CONCLUSION

It is fitting, then, to suggest a new explanation of all these seemingly strange elements within Sahagún's work. It may be helpful to relate them to the spiritual background of the Franciscan epoch in New Spain.

First of all we must emphasize once more the fact that the subject matter chosen by Fray Bernardino in 1584–85 is narrow and exclusive. He has paid attention only to the rescue and reelaboration of research on the most notable and spectacular aspects of the pre-Hispanic religion. Of course this selection can be related to Sahagún's perennial interest in a conversion of the natives based upon their own most intimate ethnographic and linguistic reality. Unlike those who were satisfied with an ecclesiastic structure based on a clearly metropolitan model and the superficial submission of the natives to the external ritual forms of Catholicism, Sahagún pleads for a profound undertaking of enormous scope, an undertaking based on the elaborate utilization of Mexican cultural patterns. The adjustment and adaptation of the native calendar to Christian use proceeds from the same will and the same spirit as the translation and arrangement of the sacred Nahuatl texts. We have already seen that on one occasion Sahagún and Fray Alonso de Molina fought for this purpose with the support of Sequera, faced by the adverse and restrictive opinions of the Inquisition in this area (Baudot 1969). Even up to the last days of his life, Fray Bernardino tried to change the ideology of the Indian by using the Indian's own cultural and subjective reality and originality. This is the hallmark of the rest of the Franciscan ethnographers in sixteenth-century Mexico.

The thematic selection of the materials of the "Calendario" and the "Arte Adivinatoria" demonstrates another obsession, a more and more insistent fear of demons, clearly evidenced by Sahagún's denunciation of the ritual use of the "flying pole" (Sahagún, 1585a: Prologue) and by his fantastic version of the origin of the tonalamatl.

Why did this preoccupation become so acute in 1585? Clearly it was because the pre-Hispanic religious beliefs had remained alive even to that time and because time pressed if one hoped to build a New Kingdom with any possibility of success.

In the seraphic perspectives of San Gabriel the foundation of the New Church bypassed an earlier, intangible question: the integral and complete conversion of the gentiles. The extirpation of the pre-Hispanic religion was a *sine qua non* for the construction of a millenarian, non-Hispanicized, autonomous Mexico. Unlike the "first twelve" who, carried along by the prophetic enthusiasm of beginners, believed they would be able to skip some stages, Sahagún knew through his experience as an investigator that he had to do more than simply baptize Indians by millions, as Motolinía had done in the first half of the century. He also knew that the project would demand more time than that foreseen by the "first twelve." Already in 1585 he was beginning to worry that it would take too long.

The persistence of idolatry was a bad sign, one which after sixty years of evangelic labor could definitely compromise the spiritual bases of millenarian ideals. Other adverse signs also emerged; their conjunction with the demonstrated strength of idolatry was alarming. The prospect in 1585 could not have been more desolate, given Sahagún's vision of Mexico.

His life's work had been confiscated without further explanation, and his advocates, such as Sequera—also the defender of Molina and of this whole seraphic movement—had ceased to exercise any influence in the

Council of the Indies, of which Juan de Ovando was no longer president. Much had been expected from the College of Tlatelolco in the formation of a native clergy, but the college was now no more than a shadow of what it had been. Sahagún was also faced with the hostility of the colonial administrative machine and of the Spanish settlers, whose influence was growing rapidly. Furthermore, epidemics and hunger had decimated the Mexican population; should the population continue to diminish at this rate the kingdom of the dream could not be achieved. In fact, the demographic catastrophe, calculated by Cook and Borah (1960), was such a threat that Sahagún, living in its presence, could not fail to be aware of it. This is what made him aware of the similarity between the Mexicans' situation and that of the Moriscos of Granada and made him fear that the former confronted a similar destiny. Meanwhile, the Spaniards increased and settled in.

Finally, Sahagún felt that he was witnessing the end of the heroic and enthusiastic times of the first evangelization. Everywhere the secular clergy (and after 1572 the Jesuits) were gaining positions. The attempt to impose the tithe on the Indians in 1558 had already proved the strength of the desire to build in New Spain a traditional, peninsular, European church, antagonistic to any attempt at preapocalyptic renovation (Baudot 1965). And from then on the diminishing importance of the evangelizing friars was a painful fact. The appearance in 1584 of Father Ponce as head of the order and commissary general named by the metropolis was the decisive sign of the imminent and definitive victory of the metropolitan ecclesiastic model in the face of the seraphic hopes of the older missionaries of New Spain. Finally, therefore, the conflict emerged into the open. Now we see why, in his urgent last-minute rescue of what were to him the most useful elements of his ethnographic work, Sahagún insisted so vehemently on the persistence of idolatrous beliefs and rites: he was trying to prove that the friar evangelists who were intimately associated with the authentic native reality of Mexico were still indispensable, were in fact more necessary than ever. He maintained that the epoch for archbishops, secular clergy, canons, and Father Ponce had not arrived, that they were out of place and out of context.

Hence, Sahagún's exasperation and his attempt at the end of his life to place the blame for the palpable failure of the seraphic hope. Who could be responsible for the facts and events which announced at the very least an irremediable setback, at most a complete failure of the apocalyptic achievement? Obviously there were only two possible culprits. The Devil, first, because the whole enterprise was directed against his empire in the hopes of its final obliteration. But also the first promoters of this hope, the "first twelve," who inculcated the consciousness of its possibility and imminence without realizing the time and difficulties involved and without providing adequate arms to carry it through. In the last analysis they were fathers of disillusionment and disappointment.

It was possible to curse the Devil, since he was the enemy whose cunning and deceit were to be discovered in the most recondite areas of human activity, such as playing godfather to belated inventions of the tonalamatl. He was even more dangerous when one fought to expel him from the portion of the inhabited world in which he appeared to have established his lordship.

The human initiators of the evangelizing enterprise could also be reproached, even though they were older brothers, if all the perceptible signs more and more urgently predicted a short-term failure that would destroy the exalting dreams that they themselves had propagated and represented as imminent during the first half of the century.

Between 1585 and 1590 Sahagún was a stubborn old man. He weighed the balance of his life and his work and implacably deduced their consequences—all with admirable logic and without denying a single point of the convictions and hopes he had cherished in 1529 when he reached the New World. Until we discover new documentation, which might induce us to imagine otherwise, Sahagún's last years show us how one of the first myths of America began to die.

8

The Sahagún Texts as a Source of Sociological Information

EDWARD E. CALNEK
University of Rochester

Despite their unique importance for the study of Aztec society, the Sahagún texts (described in Chapter 1 of this book) manifest peculiarities of emphasis and data selection which, if not given explicit recognition, severely limit their value as a source of sociological data. The *General History of the Things of New Spain* may have been encyclopedic in intent, but in fact it reflects the social perspective of only a small minority of the indigenous population. Neither Sahagún nor his Indian collaborators were entirely dispassionate commentators on pre-Spanish social institutions and systems of belief. Sahagún's millenarian ideals, as described by Georges Baudot in chapter 7, unquestionably influenced the direction of his researches, as did his close personal identification with the Catholic intelligentsia of the late Renaissance. His informants, by his own testimony, were for the most part selected from the native elites, and the data they provided reflect an upper-class viewpoint. The sources for the material collected at Tepepulco were "ten or twelve leading elders"—a choice of informants that may have been suitable, given Sahagún's limited objectives at the time, but which can hardly be regarded as *representative* of the population as a whole. The information collected in Tenochtitlan-Tlaltelolco was heavily based on the testimony of "leading merchants" and members of the highest strata of the Aztec nobility.

None of this detracts from the authenticity of the material presented in the *General History*. It does raise serious questions relating to the influence of "informant bias" in the selection, interpretation, and organization of ethnographic data. The strength of Sahagún's work derives primarily from the fact that it is a firsthand description of pre-Spanish customs, beliefs, and social organization, dictated by men who had reached maturity prior to the Spanish invasion. This does not guarantee that it is an entirely objective account. Any discussion of the *pilli* (noble) class by members of the nobility is likely to be well informed. But we must surely view what noblemen say about the condition of peasant farmers or the urban masses with a certain skepticism.

The influence of informant bias extends far beyond the expression of personal sentiments; it accounts at least in part for systematic omissions and for the lack of interest in large groups not represented among Sahagún's informants. Book 8, for example, deals almost exclusively with the interests and activities of the inner circle of high-ranking noblemen and royal princes (*tlazopipiltin*) who were active within the highest echelons of the governmental system; it says relatively little about the situation of the thousands of *pipiltin* who had little direct connection with the imperial court (see below). Eight of the fourteen chapters of the Florentine Codex which discuss *pochtecayotl* or "merchantship" deal with the expensive feasts and rituals by means of which the wealthiest merchants converted mercantile profits into a higher status (Sahagún 1950–69:Book 9:Chapters 7–14; the book and chapter references are for the most part valid for the Tolosa and Madrid manuscripts as well). The degree to which the same world view may or may not have been representative for merchants who were only moderately prosperous or even poor is entirely conjectural.

The situation of the urban masses of Tenochtitlan-Tlaltelolco emerges only in scattered and fragmentary references. The hand-to-mouth existence of the very poor, for example, is described in connection with the feast called Uei Tecuilhuitl, when the ruler distributed foodstuffs

> because verily there was much hunger; when dried maize was costly, then there was much want, [and] it was hard to gain a livelihood; [and] many then were our dead (Sahagún 1950–69:2:Ch. 27, p. 93).

A description of the good and bad fortunes linked to the day 1 Ocelot includes the remark that female "embroiderers lived in great vice and became terrible whores"—a sharply caustic reference which does not, it should be noted, say anything about wages or working conditions, and does not inform us who the patrons for off-hours vice may have been (Sahagún 1950–69:4:Ch. 2, p. 7). This very short text provides more than a simple instance of upper-class hypocrisy; it offers one of a small number of clues suggesting the existence of textile workshops operated on the basis of wage labor. Although the point cannot be pursued here, we may observe that this piece of information, if it can be corroborated by other sources, is an economic datum of great interest and importance in its own right, and should provoke a thorough reexamination of the economic basis of urban life at Tenochtitlan. The same inference can be taken from the wording of the passage cited above, which deals with food distributions: "there was much hunger; when dried maize was *costly* . . . [and] it was hard to *gain a livelihood*" (emphasis added). We are not told that dried maize was in short supply, although Uei Tecuilhuitl fell toward the end of the agricultural year, but that it was expensive. It is the price of maize that counts, and we must conclude that this was subject to seasonal fluctuations in relation to supply and demand on the market. That there was no absolute maize shortage is indicated by the claim, possibly exaggerated, that the *petlacalco*, or imperial storehouse, contained "more than two thousand [measures of] grains of dried maize—a store of twenty years for the city," in addition to bins holding "dried beans, chía, amaranth seeds, wrinkled chía, salt jars, coarse salt, baskets of chilis, baskets of squash seeds, and large squash seeds" (Sahagún 1950–69:8:Ch. 14, p. 44).

The condition of the masses stands in sharp contrast to that of the merchant as he "spread out his possessions, his goods," in order to show that he could afford to feast the leading merchants and the nobility

(Sahagún 1950–69:9:Ch. 7, p. 33). It is not our task to issue judgments on these and similar matters, but the social historian must plainly utilize such scraps of information for his own purposes. The fact that Sahagún's informants were real people sometimes enables us to grasp something of the real bitterness of class antagonisms—whether they involve rich and poor, or simply the asymmetrical distribution of political authority. Thus, the wealthy merchant who, at one moment, offered tobacco, food, and other gifts to "the commanding general. . . . the *atempanecatl*; all the lords, and the eagle warrior guides, or the noblemen" (Sahagún 1950–69:9:Ch. 7, p. 34), on other days went about "abasing" himself, in humble clothing, lest his life and possessions fall prey to the cupidity of the *pipiltin* who "in envy, falsely, by means of false testimony, with imagined deeds, condemned the disguised merchants, in order to slay the innocent, so that . . . the Otomí warriors, the war leaders, might be sustained" (Ibid.:Ch. 6, pp. 31–32). Even here, nonetheless, we are told not that the leading merchants were indiscriminately attacked by the lords and warriors, but only that they risked their lives and wealth if they violated norms of behavior prescribed for them by the ruling class.

It must be emphasized that the authenticity of Sahagún's material is not seriously involved in the discussion to this point. On the contrary, it would be impossible to utilize the bits and pieces of data relating to the situation of the lower classes if we could not trust their validity. Problems of this type appear to be inherent in Sahagún's restricted use of the informant method, and they arise quite independently of the validity or nonvalidity of the informational content of the *General History*. We are merely stating that our objectives are not precisely the same as those which motivated Sahagún's work, and that, for our purposes, it is essential to recognize and compensate for the multiple effects of informant bias in the description of pre-Hispanic social organization.

A somewhat different type of problem arises in connection with the meaning of terms such as *pilli, macehual, calpulli*, and numerous others that refer to social status or particular corporate groups. Sahagún's informants commonly employ such words as simple vocabulary items, on the assumption that their language will be understood. A good many terms of this type, however, are untranslatable, except insofar as the entire social matrix within which they are imbedded can be understood. The English word "nobleman" provides a rough equivalent to the Nahuatl *pilli*, but European and Aztec conceptions of nobility differed in important respects. The European aristocracy was based on hereditary succession to titled statuses (count, marquis, duke, and so on) and was closely connected with legal domain over both men and territorial estates. The status of *pilli*, on the other hand, was open only to offspring and descendants of kings, but was transmitted through males and females without any definite connection to hereditary succession to offices or titles of high rank. Such offices and titles, of course, influenced the ranking of individual *pipiltin*, but did not function as a criterion for membership within the dynastic group. The structural implications of this system are complex, and are discussed in greater detail elsewhere (Calnek 1969). The essential point, however, is that the word must be defined by outlining rules of membership, on the one hand, and by describing the rights, prerogatives, and obligations inherent in noble status, on the other. Whether the *pipiltin* were also a social class within the modern meaning of the term is still another question, and is discussed at length in the last part of this chapter.

The word *macehual* ("commoner") presents similar difficulties. That it was not a class term is clear from the fact that it was applied indiscriminately to merchants, artisans, peasant farmers, and all other free citizens who lacked noble pedigrees. Although a relatively simple two-class system may have existed in rural states where the *macehualtin* were, for the most part, peasant farmers, this was not true in Tenochtitlan, where the great diversity of economic interests and positions fostered by the growing importance of trade and craft manufacture resulted in much more complex class formations. The word *macehual*, in this context, means "a subject," and little more. There was, in the first place, an exceptionally sharp differentiation between urban and rural components within the Aztec state (see Calnek 1972a; 1972b). The urban populace consisted overwhelmingly of full-time nonagricultural occupational specialists. The agrarian population, on the other hand, was made up largely of administrators and tenant farmers who received rights of cultivation in estates held by public officials or private owners in return for the payment of rents (Calnek 1973). The tenants, in turn, included free peasants (*macehualtin*), serfs (*mayeque* or *tlalmaitin*) who were bound

193

to the land, and slaves (*tlacotin*) bound to the service of a particular master. Since all tenants, regardless of their legal status, worked the land on what amounted to a share-cropping basis, it may be more reasonable to regard them as comprising an incipient class, rather than as members of the three distinct classes suggested by the terminology given above. In any case, their economic position differed substantially from that of the urban population, and this is sufficient to place them in an entirely different category for analytic purposes. It must be emphasized that the concept of hierarchical ranking possesses only a limited value when considering class differentiation among the *macehualtin*. Merchants and master craftsmen doubtless outranked any peasant farmer, but rank order would be completely irrelevant in comparing the positions of peasants and, for example, domestic servants or *tlamemes* (porters).

At the present time, our investigations are not sufficiently advanced to offer any concrete formulations with respect to the problem of class organization within the city. Merchants usually owned their own stocks-in-trade; the master craftsmen owned their tools, workshops, and raw materials. Before concluding that either or both ought to be regarded as a true social class, however, it would be necessary to obtain a great many more quantitative data than are now available, and to work out the implications of the guildlike structure of the calpulli system. This being the case, the problem of translation and definition must be held in abeyance pending the results of future research.

That Sahagún himself was at least partially aware of the difficulties inherent in the language employed by his informants is suggested by the three column format of the "Memoriales con Escolios" (Sahagún 1905–8:6:177ff.), in which the third column contains explanatory glosses for lexical items occurring in the Nahuatl text of the second column. In the first column there is, in addition to a brief summary translation of the Nahuatl text, occasional reference to customary usages underlying certain words and expressions, as in the description of the "good uncle" (p. 203) where we are told that "these natives had the practice of leaving him in charge of their children, of their estates, of their wives, and the whole house." This is not, strictly speaking, a definition of "uncle" (*tlatli*), but nonetheless it defines a key aspect of the relationship between uncles and their nephews and nieces.

This annotating procedure, unfortunately, was applied to only a small

194

part of the *General History,* and in the majority of cases the reader himself must supply essential definitions and contextual data—if he is in a position to do so. The potential value of the *General History* as a source of valid sociological data, therefore, depends on our ability to reorganize and rework the Sahagún materials, and to relate them to information derived from other colonial period chronicles and archival texts.

In the remainder of this chapter I will illustrate these points with two cases in which it has been possible to clarify important problems by either reanalyzing information contained in the Sahagún texts, or by supplying background information from other sources. The first example is an analysis of the kinship system denoted by the word *tlacamecayotl,* based on material contained in the first chapter of Book 10. The second example is an analysis of the historical development of the *pipiltin* as a ruling class, based primarily on evidence which is not given in the Sahagún texts, but which must necessarily influence our reading and interpretation of references to the nobility in the *General History.*

KINSHIP THROUGH TLACAMECAYOTL

The analysis of Mesoamerican kinship systems has been a favorite topic for anthropologists—primarily because of the influence of theoretical studies published by Morgan (1877) and A. Bandelier (1877, 1878, 1880). Both insisted that Aztec social organization was based on kinship institutions, and had not yet "advanced" to the evolutionary stage characterized by centralized state systems. Although this view has been largely abandoned by modern investigators (see Carrasco 1971: 349), a strong interest in kinship systems per se has survived into modern time. So far as central Mexico is concerned, however, little is known other than that "the kinship terminology of classical Nahuatl is of a bilateral type," and that there are instances in which patrilineality seems to be important (Carrasco 1971: 370-71). There has been a strong tendency to link studies of kinship and marriage to the problem of calpulli organization (see, for example, Monzón 1949). Owing to the paucity of relevant historical documentation, however, discussions of this point have been heavily theoretical rather than empirical. In the case of Tenochtitlan-Tlatelolco, detailed information relating to marriages exists only for the *pipiltin*. Its relevance to the population at large is wholly undemonstrated at the present time.

Sahagún's discussion of *tlacamecayotl* or "the succession of kinship," (Sahagún 1905–8:6:199) holds, or at least ought to hold, unusual interest for students of Aztec kinship systems. It is, in fact, the only known text which takes the concept of *tlacamecayotl* (lit. "a line [rope] of men, a lineage") as its major theme. Unfortunately, the greater part of the chapter (Sahagún 1950–69:10:Ch. 1) tells us nothing about the meaning of *tlacamecayotl*—except that it is somehow related to descent —but concentrates instead on personal qualities supposedly associated with good and bad kinsmen, as designated by a particular term. The good father, for example, is "diligent, solicitous, compassionate, sympathetic" and so on; the bad father is "lazy, incompassionate, negligent, unreliable . . . unfeeling, neglectful of duty, untrustworthy; a shirker, a loafer, a sullen worker" (Ibid.:pp. 1–2). We receive, in short, a list of descriptive adjectives instead of a discussion of kinship. This doubtless accounts for the relative lack of interest in the chapter on the part of Mesoamericanists. On closer inspection, nonetheless, we discover a good deal of vital information about what the Aztecs meant when they spoke about *tlacamecayotl*.

TABLE 15
AZTEC KINSHIP TERMS
OCCURRING IN THE FIRST CHAPTER OF BOOK 10
(Sahagún 1950–69; 1905–8:6:177ff.)

Nahuatl[1]	English	Gloss (relating to kinship)
1. Tatli	Father	"Source of lineage, the beginning of lineage."
2. Nantli	Mother	
3. Pilli[2]/Conetl[3]	Child	The glosses include various Nahuatl terms distinguishing "the legitimate child" from "the secret child, the bastard"; a female child (ichpuchtli); "small boy of noble descent" (oquichpiltontli) and "small girl [of noble descent]" (eivapiltontli); and the following terms specifying the order of birth for daughters: tepi or tiacapan, teicu, tlaco, and xoco.

Nahuatl[1]	English	Gloss (relating to kinship)
4. Tlatli	Uncle	"Provider for those who are orphaned, the entrusted one, the tutor, the manager." See also the discussion of the "good uncle" cited in text, which suggests that a father's brother was the preferred stepfather, and that the orphan might be someone who was fatherless rather than parentless. Archival sources, however, include instances where the same role was played by a mother's brother, and in some instances, a maternal or paternal aunt.
5. Auitl	Aunt	
6. Machtli[2]/ Pilotl[3]	Nephew or niece	"[He is] an orphan—parentless—who serves in another's house."
7. Culli	Grandfather	
8. Citli	Grandmother	
9. Achtontli	Great-grandfather	
10. Ueltiuhtli	Great-grandmother	"She is the founder, the beginner [of her lineage]."
11. Mintontli	Great-great-grand-parent	"The originator of good progeny. He started, began, sowed . . . he produced off-shoots."
12. Ixuiuhtli	Grandchild	"A noble descendant, one's descendant."

1. The Nahuatl terms as given in this text have been revised to agree with the form that would appear in a dictionary or *vocabulario*. Thus, *teaui*, "one's aunt," is recorded here in the form *auitl* meaning simply "aunt."
2. Form employed when a male is speaking.
3. Form employed when a female is speaking.

If the descriptive glosses, except those which deal explicitly with kin-ship or lineage, are ignored, it is still reasonable to suppose that the kin terms listed in this chapter at least denote relatives within the meaning of *tlacamecayotl*. To simplify this discussion, I have listed these, in their order of occurrence and with potentially useful material from the written glosses, in Table 15. Several features of the list are immediately evident. All terms, with the exception of uncle (*tlatli*), aunt (*auitl*), and nephew-niece (*machtli,* male speaking; *pilotl,* female speaking), refer to lineal rather than collateral relatives. The glosses associated with these terms specify, however, that they are relevant (to the content of the chapter) only where the parents, or at least the father, of an implied propositus (Ego) are dead. The uncle is "the provider for those who are orphaned"; the nephew-niece is "a parentless orphan who serves in another's house" (Ibid.:pp. 3–4). The obvious conclusion to be drawn is that the kinship terms in question are not intended to express collaterality, but rather to identify persons who may stand in lieu of one's own parents. Table 15 also contains duplicate terms for Ego's own children. The basic term for *child*, however, is clearly *pilli* or *conetl*, depending on the sex of the speaker; the remaining terms are secondary, and served to specify whether a particular child was male or female, legitimate or illegitimate, noble or commoner. (There were also special terms designating the birth order for daughters.) There is, on the other hand, only a single term—*ixuiuhtli*—meaning *grandchild*.

If we purify our list by omitting surrogate parents and secondary terms for one's own offspring, the result is a very simple chart of kin relationships (Figure 4) with the following important characteristics:

1) All terms are defined in relation to an assumed propositus (Ego).
2) There are no terms for siblings, cousins, or collaterals in any generation.
3) Ego's parents and ancestors are terminologically differentiated according to sex through the first three ascending generations.
4) A single term—*mintontli*—means a great-great-grandparent of either sex.
5) There are no terms for an ancestor more remote than great-great-grandparent.
6) Ego's own children and grandchildren are not differentiated by sex.

If we assume that Figure 4 incorporates the basic set of relationships meant by *tlacamecayotl*, then the following preliminary conclusions can be drawn:

1) Ego could use any combination of named male or female ancestors to show lineal descent from a particular person who would be called *mintontli*.
2) Ego must choose only one person in each ascending generation to establish descent from a named *mintontli*, unless an ancestral couple are both descendants of the same person, in which case he will

MINTONTLI

ACHTONTLI	UELTIUHTLI
CULLI	CITLI
TATLI	NANTLI

(EGO)

PILLI / CONETL

IXUIUHTLI

FIGURE 4. KINSHIP TERMS EMBODIED IN *TLACAMECAYOTL*.
(See Table 15 for definitions)

(Ego will trace genealogical relationships by selecting a male or female ancestor in each generation, to prove descent from a specific person (male or female) called Mintontli. If the linking ancestor is male (e.g., *culli*, "grandfather"), there will be no female called *citli*, "grandmother" in Ego's pedigree leading to a named Mintontli, and vice versa.)

be able to construct alternative pedigrees, leading to the same result.

3) All descendants through male or female links from any person (or couple) called *mintontli* occupy identical structural positions as members of the same cognatic stock, spanning a maximum of five generations, and including persons no more distantly related than third cousins.

4) Ego may, by exploiting the bifurcating nature of cognatic kinship, show that he is equally descended from a theoretical maximum of eight great-great-grandparents.

5) It is a matter of indifference whether the founding ancestor is male or female, except where the male has offspring by more than one woman.

The terminological differentiation of parents, grandparents, and great-grandparents according to sex suggests that pedigrees could include only named individuals. This condition would not hold for Ego's own descendants, and could not be applied—except under highly unusual conditions—to one's great-great-grandchildren, because they would not yet be born at the time of Ego's death.

If this interpretation is correct, *tlacamecayotl* expresses the relationship between members of the same cognatic descent group descended from the same *mintontli*, or at least provides a formula for the generation of such groups. The same formula could also have been used to construct personal kindreds consisting of all relatives up to third cousins descended from all persons called *mintontli* by a single propositus.

The question of whether stocks or kindreds or both played important roles in the social organization can, of course, be answered only on empirical, not on theoretical grounds. Although we cannot undertake a detailed discussion of the evidence here, we can note that there are references to, for example, laws holding a man's kinsmen "even to the fourth generation" jointly culpable with him for certain criminal acts (Las Casas 1958:2:262; "Conquistador Anónimo" 1941:33), and we can note the customary recognition of kinsmen "up to the third and fourth degree of kinship" by the Indian population of Tenochtitlan in the decades immediately following the conquest (see, for example, Anon. n.d.: 20(2,2):folio 67r). We cannot, as yet, determine from the available evidence whether our sources refer to stocks or kindreds. It may be that each individual was required to opt for affiliation to only one of the several stocks in which he might be able to claim membership on genealogical grounds (perhaps on the basis of residence in the same household or barrio), or that different types of membership were utilized for different purposes.

The interpretation of *tlacamecayotl* outlined here appears to be consistent with information available in other sources. There are, nonetheless, numerous ambiguities, relating primarily to its application, which remain to be resolved. In this case the Sahagún texts yield information of a type that has not yet been identified in any other source. Further analysis of actual case materials will be required before the role of kinship in the organization of Aztec society can be fully understood.

THE PILLI "CLASS"

References to the *pipiltin* occur frequently in the *General History*. That this group controlled virtually all significant political and administrative positions within the Aztec state at the time of the conquest would be obvious from simple contextual evidence if from nothing else. The actual size and internal structure of the group as a whole is not, characteristically, explicitly described. The long debate over the class position of the *pipiltin* stems largely from this fact. The issue has been greatly complicated by the wholly unjustified assumption that a system of tribal organization predominated throughout the Valley of Mexico (see Gibson 1964:9ff.). The early Aztecs, as noted by Carrasco (1971:349–50), are frequently described as "a kinship-based equalitarian society, whereas the later empire was a state organization." Monzón (1949), among others, denied that the Aztec nobility ever achieved the position of a true ruling class. Kirchoff (1954–55), Katz (1966), Caso (1963), and others have argued that the *pipiltin* became a ruling class only when they had achieved a kind of economic independence on the basis of privately owned agricultural estates, which were worked by tenant farmers, as discussed earlier in this chapter. Relatively little attention has been given to the demographic history of this group as a vital factor in its emergence as a true ruling class, nor have the implications of the political subjugation of both Tenochtitlan and Tlatelolco to Azcapotzalco prior to 1427 or 1428 been taken into consideration. The Aztec chronicles emphasize the powerful role played by a large popular assembly in the decision-making process throughout the preimperial period. They do not, on the other hand, give sufficient emphasis to the obvious dependency of the Tenochca and Tlaltelolca on the highly urbanized Tepaneca of Azcapotzalco. The popular assembly was hardly in a position to decide issues relating to war and peace. The Aztecs were obligated to support their overlords on the battlefield; their kings, for all practical purposes, must be regarded as agents for the Tepanec dynasty, with whom they were closely allied through marriage and descent by the early sixteenth century. In about 1426, Maxtla, then ruler of Azcapotzalco, was obliged to convince his own noblemen that Chimalpopoca of Tenochtitlan could not be regarded as one of themselves, because "on the father's side he was a child of the Mexicans, and would always incline to the father's side and not the mother's" (Durán 1951:1:65). This suggests more than a close alliance between two ruling dynasties, a virtual identity of interests, in fact, until the Aztecs—largely because they sided with the wrong faction in an intradynastic feud—were forced into an unwanted and unpremeditated rebellion (see Durán 1951:1:62ff.; Tezozómoc 1944:23ff.).

The issue, therefore, is not whether the Aztec nobility in itself constituted a ruling class. The historical evidence suggests instead that they were an extension of the Tepanec aristocracy, and that the process of autonomous development began only with the imperial period (that is, following 1428). The demographic antecedents of this process are of considerable interest in their own right.

So far as can be determined, the hereditary nobility of Tenochtitlan at the time of the conquest consisted solely or primarily of lineal descendants of the first king, Acamapichtli, who assumed the throne no earlier than 1367 and died in or before 1391 (Tezozómoc 1944:85–86; Berlin 1948:51–53). The word *pilli* means "a child" but also had the special meaning of "persons of royal blood." The position of ennobled commoners within this group is uncertain. The earliest Spanish writers called them *caballeros pardos,* and they may have been distinguished from the true nobility by the Nahuatl term *quauhpipiltin* or "eagle children," which alludes to the acquisition of noble status through valorous conduct on the battlefield (Carrasco 1971:354). There is a possibility that the *quauhpipiltin* commonly intermarried with the true nobility. Since *pilli* status could be conveyed through both males and females, their children would simply be *pipiltin* by virtue of the maternal link.

If the first *pipiltin* were children of Acamapichtli, the eldest would just have been reaching maturity at the time of his death; the second generation would have been reaching early adulthood beginning in about 1410. Despite a high rate of proliferation because of extensive polygyny, the total number of adult males could not have been very large at the time of the rebellion against Azcapotzalco. Although exact calculation is impossible, we can assume that Acamapichtli's biological descendants would have numbered in the tens of thousands by the early sixteenth century. Several otherwise puzzling historical developments become understandable when projected against this specific pattern of growth. We can, for example, immediately reject the claim made by the authors of the "Crónica 'X'" as translated by Durán (1951:1:75ff.) and Tezozómoc (1944: 3off.) that the military force engaged in the rebellion consisted almost entirely of *pipiltin.* The latter simply could not have been sufficiently numerous to have taken the field against that powerful city-state, to say nothing of contributing significantly to its ultimate defeat. The same situation would have persisted into the early decades of the imperial period, when the rate of increase among the *pipiltin* would have been insufficient to staff all significant positions within a vastly expanded politico-administrative system. What this situation does explain is the liberalization of the laws of succession to high office promulgated by Moctezuma Ilhuicamina (1440–67), so that the sons of secondary wives and concubines would compete on an equal basis with the children of high-ranking women (Durán 1951:1:241–42). Until the end of Ahuitzotl's reign (1502), commoners continued to hold powerful positions within the imperial court, and in some instances must have outranked hereditary noblemen by virtue of their offices. The so-called aristocratic reaction under Moctezuma Xocoyotzin (1502–20), however, included the forced retirement (and in some cases execution) of commoners from government office, down to the level of barrio headmen (Tezozómoc 1944:399ff.; Durán 1951:1:416ff.; Ixtlilxóchitl 1952:2:310). In addition to replacing commoners with members of the *pilli* group, the class position of the *pipiltin* appears to have been strengthened through legal enactments restricting upward mobility, and eliminating competition between the *pipiltin* and *quauhpipiltin* for the same offices and prerogatives. It is worth noting that these acts were undertaken by Moctezuma on his own initiative, and at a time when most titled noblemen of the highest rank were absent from the city during a military expedition. They reflect, therefore, a considerable strengthening of the monarchy, by restricting the decision-making functions of the class that was also the principal beneficiary of these reforms.

The Sahagún texts describe a situation that had existed for little more than a decade before the conquest, and there are no empirical grounds for concluding that an equilibrium had been achieved when the process was abruptly terminated by the Spanish invasion. That the nobility itself was very numerous and complexly differentiated is evident from the great proliferation of titles and statuses represented in the Sahagún texts (Book 8, *passim*; Book 10, Chapters 4 and 5) and in other sources, and from the tendency to make the offices of *calpixqui* (tax collector) and headman of rural estancias—both of which appear to have been filled primarily with noblemen—at least quasi-hereditary (see Calnek 1973). The tax or tribute system, in addition, had become highly bureaucratized (Calnek 1966). In the course of time *pipiltin* with strong vested interests in particular governmental departments might easily have formed self-perpetuating subgroups in a position to exercise a considerable influence on their own behalf.

It would seem, therefore, that the otherwise dry and matter-of-fact description of the political system as given in Book 8 of the Sahagún texts must be reevaluated in the light of this information as representing no more than a moment in a highly dynamic process of historical change. It is, of course, the best available description of the imperial court and its basic subagencies, but becomes a good deal more illuminating when it is recognized that it is only a partial description of the *pilli* class as a whole.

CONCLUSIONS

To summarize the points made in this paper, it must be emphasized that the Sahagún texts provide information of inestimable value, providing that they are read critically, with close attention to contextual backgrounds that must frequently be supplied from other sources, and within an explicitly diachronic as well as synchronic frame of reference. They describe selected aspects of Aztec social structure at a particular point in time, and from a predominantly upper-class point of view. Social institutions of major importance—most notably those which relate to the situation of less privileged groups—are sometimes represented only in chance remarks. A great many others have almost certainly been completely ignored. The lack of explicit definitions and descriptive material is a major deficiency of the Sahagún texts and appears to be inherent in the informant method as developed by Sahagún himself. Further progress in the study of Aztec social organization, therefore, requires close analysis of Sahagún's material, with emphasis on techniques for verification and amplification of its positive content, and an explicit recognition of its defects as well as virtues.

9

Sahagún's Work and the Medicine of the Ancient Nahuas: Possibilities for Study

ALFREDO LÓPEZ AUSTIN

Universidad Nacional
Autónoma de México

INTRODUCTION

Sahagún was above all an evangelist, dedicating his life to the conversion of infidels. But in the prologue of his *History*, where he explains his purpose in preparing this work, he compares his endeavor with that of a doctor. His work shows a consistent preoccupation with the health of the body along with that of the soul.

Sahagún elaborated no other subject so thoroughly in his *General History*; the only informants whose names he mentioned were the doctors, whose names appeared in two extensive lists. He acknowledged that the experienced doctors "cured publicly," contrary to the opinion of other reliable authors, among them Francisco Hernández (1959–67), who explicitly disdained the knowledge of the native specialists.

In the valuable material concerning medicine in the *General History*, we can distinguish the information arising spontaneously from answers the Franciscan obtained while asking about other subjects. Among these spontaneous data are references to the gods who protect medical practices and to the causes of different illnesses and misfortunes; to the transgressions causing the acquisition of certain ills; to therapeutic methods and rituals; to the classification of illnesses like gout, numbness, or sluggishness among the "cold" diseases and to the promises made to the gods of the wind, water, and mountains in order to be cured of them; to the actions of the gods visited upon those who drank pulque before the general offering, and the effects of these actions, such as paralysis of the face or of a limb and trembling of the face; to the preventive measures against the penetration of worms into the eyes; to the participation in social and religious life of the specialists in the art of curing or of bringing children into the world; to the magical measures taken to make children grow; to those sick from particular diseases who died and were offered to the gods; to the activities of the experts on the calendar of destinies who indicated the gods to whom the offerings of ritual paper should be directed; to the amulets that should be hung around the necks and wrists of children; to good and bad days for health; to the animals that were agents of the gods and announced disaster and death; to the consequences of minor transgressions like licking the grindstone or eating tamales that were stuck to the pot; to the supreme will of Titlacahuan as dispenser of fortune and disaster, health and illness, life and death—in short to an enormous amount of information that makes Sahagún's work one of the greatest monuments of historical literature.

The second kind of material, that which Sahagún sought out with the specific purpose of recording the medical knowledge and the therapeutic properties of different species in New Spain, includes two main categories, one on the illnesses of the human body, the other on medicines. Two more categories can be added: the facts Sahagún collected on the parts of the human body for the purpose of compiling a vocabulary; and the general information on flora, fauna, and minerals, containing valuable data on pharmacology. In this chapter I will examine these data in close detail.

STEPS IN THE ELABORATION OF THE TEXTS

Illnesses and Their Remedies

Sahagún's inquiry into illnesses and their remedies was early. In the Tepepulco documents are two brief texts that I have entitled "Illnesses of our body, I," (Figure 5A) and "Illnesses of our body, II," (Figure 5B) corresponding respectively to Folios 69 and 81. The first, originally entitled "On the Divers Illnesses That Are Produced in Our Body," is written in a clear and uniform handwriting with few corrections. It is a list of illnesses in which we can discern no clear order of mention on the part of either Sahagún or the informants. There exist ills that do not correspond to the Franciscan's medical concepts: *tlanatonahuiztli, yohualehecatl, necihuaquetzaliztli, tlalatonahuiztli,* and others (see below). After the name of the illness is that of the corresponding medicine, or an indication (in six of the fifty-six cases) that no remedy exists. The information consists of brief accounts of one or more of the necessary medicines, the part of the plant needed, and, in some of the many cases in which the prescription belongs to the vegetable world, the indication of whether the product is native to the locale and whether it grows everywhere or comes from a specific place and environment. In 10 percent of the cases there is mention of its preparation or administration.

The second text is very different; the writing is very bad, and the text is messy, with many blotches. Two-thirds of the descriptions of illnesses refer to preparation or administration of the medicines; in only one case is the place of origin of an herb mentioned. In spite of the fact that this text (again in contrast to the preceding one) does not have a heading specifying its placement in the work, it undoubtedly precedes the data later collected in Tlaltelolco, for a certain similarity of sequence is discernible.

Once in Tlaltelolco, Sahagún used the Tepepulco material as a foundation for the continuation of the investigation on a much larger scale. This was the pattern for the elaboration of all his work, but that relating to illnesses and remedies had a particularly complex history, which can be discovered both by the comparison of folios 163r–72v of the Madrid Codex of the Royal Academy of History with folios 97r–113v of Book 10

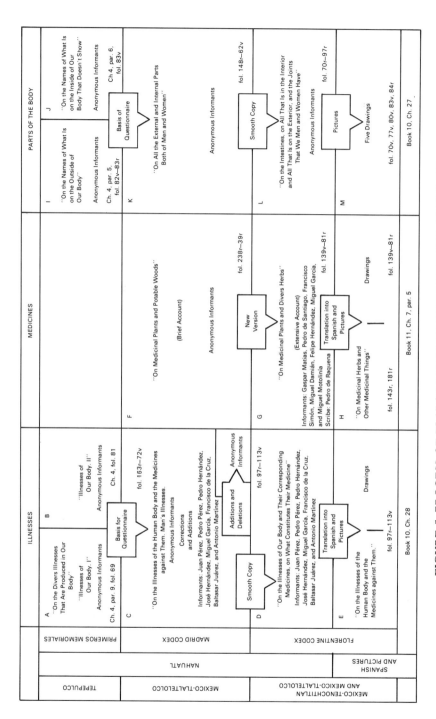

FIGURE 5. PROCESS OF ELABORATION OF THE PRINCIPAL TEXTS OF SAHAGÚN ON MEDICINE.

of the Florentine Codex and by the erasures and corrections in the Madrid Codex. A summary of this history, whose erasures I specify in the translation I have made into Spanish (López Austin 1969b), affirms that the Acolhua original served one or more Mexican doctors in drawing up the first five paragraphs of the six that made up "On the Illnesses of the Human Body and on the Medicines against Them. Man's Illnesses," Chapter 28 of Book 10 (Figure 5C), with several corrections and additions made at the moment of preparation. Later Doctors Juan Pérez, Pedro Pérez, Pedro Hernández, José Hernández, Miguel García, Francisco de la Cruz, Baltasar Juárez, and Antonio Martínez revised and corrected the text, added the last paragraph, and included their names. The differences in opinion indicate that the first part was not written by exactly the same people as the second. The Madrid version was recopied into the Florentine Codex with the usual changes or additions in the headings of the paragraphs and chapters. Also added in some twenty words at the end of the fifth paragraph was an account of infections, wounds, and cuts.

Twenty-seven illustrations of patients and doctors were added to the text of the Florentine Codex. The drawings are very simple, but some benefit can be obtained from a detailed study of them. Several instruments which appear minute in the drawings can be mentioned; they show how to administer medicaments against ocular and hemorrhoidal problems. There is also a glyph giving us to understand that the fever caused by tooth infections was considered aquatic, in a system of classification that I believe to have been the basis for the modern folk taxonomy of "cold" and "hot" diseases.

From the section of the Florentine Codex entitled "On the Illnesses of Our Body and Their Corresponding Medicines, on What Constitutes Their Medicine" (Figure 5D) was translated into Spanish what we know from the *General History* as "On the Illnesses of the Human Body and the Medicines against Them" (Figure 5E). But although in the manuscripts of the Florentine Codex and of the *General History* the preparation of the definitive version continued, in the Madrid Codex someone (who from his differing opinions may be supposed not to have belonged to the group of doctors who left us their names) corrected the text, eliminated important parts, and added to it, aided by the same scribe used by the previous group. It may even be that the work of incorporating the material was done by various people, for in Folio 163r there is a notation in a very different hand.

Sahagún's purpose in collecting the material probably derived from his confidence in the native doctors and in their knowledge. Sufficient proof of this confidence is the recording of their names and the request that they intervene in a work which could have been considered already finished. One must remember, too, that whatever did not serve therapeutic ends was blocked out of the original data. The deleted material was linked to magical and religious ideas. In Tlaltelolco a whole series of headings was not repeated: *necihuaquetzaliztli*, a form of death sent by Huitzilopochtli and Quilaztli to the women they wanted as escorts during the solar course; *netlahuitequiztli*, the death used for the same purpose by the aquatic gods; *tlalatonahuiztli, yohualatonahuiztli,* and *yohualehecatl*, sicknesses that may be supposed (and the problem deserves careful study) to be connected to spirit entities originating from the dead or to aquatic and terrestrial gods. A man broad-minded enough to bequeath us such valuable information on the native religion would not have been frightened by these ideas; they had to be eliminated if the purpose of Chapter 28 of Book 10 was its utility in the search for health.

On Medicines

The history of this type of text begins later. It was not started in Acolhuan country but rather in Mexico, in Book 11 of the *General History*, dedicated to animals, vegetables, and minerals. The original version had as its title "On Medicinal Plants and Potable Woods," and it is found in folios 238r–39r of the Madrid Codex of the Royal Academy of History (Figure 5F). Initially numbered Chapter 15, later numbered paragraph 5 of Chapter 7, it is but a small part of the extensive chapter on herbs. It is obviously in two parts, the first written on a broad, full scale, the names of the plants constituting the headings of the lines and making up both the heading and the text in the last three sections; the second a sketch or plan, filling in the spaces marked by the headings with brief accounts of the plants listed. The informants who dictated the broad plan and those who dictated the sketchy one were not the same, for the latter left fifteen of the fifty-nine sections blank, and disagreed over whether *chichi-*

pilli was a medicine. The remaining sections indicated the illnesses against which the medicine was useful, the great majority explaining its preparation or administration. In thirteen cases the part of the plant to be used is specified, and in eleven something about its appearance.

From this meager beginning it was necessary to move on to a more complete investigation. The task was entrusted to seven doctors from Tlaltelolco who inscribed their names on the document. They seem to have used the previous list as a basis for their work, although they did not follow it strictly. They doubled the number of plants and added the names of stones, animal products, and something on steam baths, considerably augmenting the information in each section. The resulting data were recorded in the Florentine Codex under the title "On Medicinal Plants and Divers Herbs" in the original text (Figure 5G) and under "On Medicinal Herbs and Other Medicinal Things" in the Spanish version, in folios 139v–81r of Book 11 (Figure 5H). The names, cosigned in both the Nahuatl and Spanish columns were: Gaspar Matías, Pedro de Santiago, Francisco Simón, Miguel Damián, Felipe Hernández, Miguel García, and Miguel Motolinía, and as scribe Pedro de Raquena (whom I have identified with the kind assistance of Howard F. Cline). The information replies to a questionnaire which can be reconstructed as follows:

1. What kind of plant is it?
2. What does it look like?
3. What are its useful parts?
4. Against what illnesses are they useful?
5. How is the medicine prepared?
6. How is it administered?
7. Where is it found?

These questions were frequently answered. In addition there is information about diet in about 17 percent of the cases, and in a smaller percentage there is complementary information of some interest. The greatest attention is paid to the botanical characteristics of the species. As throughout the work, the manuscript of the Florentine Codex is enriched with drawings, very important ones in this section since they are a magnificent means of scientific identification. The Spanish version is incomplete, for the first thirty-four plants are missing, and in the editions of the *General History* seven more have been omitted.

The close attention Sahagún paid to the data and the fact that he solicited the participation of professionals in medicine again suggest that he was interested in the topic because he expected it to be therapeutically useful.

On the Parts of the Human Body

Fray Bernardino begins worrying about the names of the parts of the body in Tepepulco. Two very brief texts, "On the Names of What Is on the Outside of Our Body" (Figure 5I) and "On the Names of What Is On the Inside of Our Body That Doesn't Show" (Figure 5J) constitute respectively paragraphs 5 and 6 of Chapter 4 in the "Primeros Memoriales" and are found in folios 82v–83v. They are simple lists of sixty-eight body parts, most being accompanied by one to six words, mainly verbs, whose purpose is the enrichment of the Nahuatl vocabulary planned by Sahagún.

In Tlaltelolco the Franciscan collected enough material to form a whole chapter (Chapter 27 of Book 10 of the Florentine Codex), and he had terms for everything from the names for the skin to those related to excrement. In each case the associated words are abundant, very often synonyms, which would have constituted valuable material for the aforementioned vocabulary. This text, which in folios 148r–162r of the Madrid Codex goes under the title "On All the External and Internal Parts, Both of Men and Women" (Figure 5K), is passed on into clean copy in folios 70r–97r of Book 10 of the Florentine Codex, where it is called "On the Intestines, on All That Is in the Interior and All That Is on the Exterior, and the Joints That We Men and Women Have" (Figure 5L). It has a few unimportant drawings (Figure 5M).

There was no point in translating materials like these into Spanish. In the *General History* Sahagún made a notation indicating their replacement by a noteworthy account of pre-Hispanic education and the education given by the missionaries.

The Information on Medicinal Species in Book 11

Paragraph 5 of Chapter 7 in Book 11, which treats the medicinal species and to which we have already referred, attained such magnitude, independence, and importance that it can well be considered a booklet inserted into an already complex book, from which it differs greatly. Even discounting the paragraph in question, Book 11 is still an important source of information about native medicine. For the most part—with the exception of paragraph 1 of Chapter 12, referring to intoxicating plants—the information is very scattered, and the characteristics of the paragraphs in which it is found are highly variable. Because of the diverse origins of these texts and of those of the medical informants, the species to which they allude are often also mentioned in other parts of the book, and the data are complementary.

The book on flora, fauna, and minerals has no direct antecedents in Tepepulco. It was initiated in Tlaltelolco and also contains very important illustrations.

POSSIBILITIES FOR STUDY OF THE TEXTS

A consideration of the possibilities for study of these texts should necessarily begin with due acknowledgment of fundamental previous works. It is not possible in this brief exposition to mention all of even the most outstanding works, but the following should be recalled: the works on the identification of species and anatomy by Rafael Martín del Campo (1938-40; 1959); the translation into German by August Freiherr von Gall (1940); the collaboration in botanical identification of George S. Diumenti and Aaron Margulis for the translations of Dibble and Anderson (Sahagún 1950-69); and in a special place, because of their quality and magnitude, the studies of Arthur J. O. Anderson and Charles E. Dibble themselves, including the complete English translation of the Florentine Codex—in which the parts relating to medicine are translated and annotated with singular erudition—and the articles the two authors have written separately on medicine in general, pharmacology, and anatomy (Anderson 1961; Dibble 1959; Rogers & Anderson 1965; 1966).

Those who prepare future studies will have various translations to deal with. That of Dibble and Anderson into English (Sahagún 1950-69), von Gall's into German (1940), and mine into Spanish (López Austin 1969a; 1971b; 1972) can be the bases for research to be carried out by specialists in various branches of scientific knowledge, either individually or in teams. This interdisciplinary collaboration is not only desirable but indispensable. We historians, and particularly Nahuatl translators, must often have recourse to doctors and botanists. When our work of translation is concluded, the roles will be reversed, and we shall be the assistants in the investigation.

Sahagún's work offers to contemporary and future investigators an extensive range of possibilities for study. It would be very pretentious to try to point out all the possibilities, many of which will be discovered by specialists in the course of investigation. I want to limit the contents of this exposition to a few ideas that have come up in the process of translation, and a few examples.

The European Influence

The native medicine recorded by Sahagún is a product not only of pre-Hispanic ideas, but also of an incipient confluence of native and Spanish concepts and techniques. One of the first desirable steps in research is the specification of this cultural process. In another work I have pointed out the use of lint packing for deep wounds, a procedure with a possible distant origin in the classic Mediterranean world, and the use of metal instruments like the syringe, of greater efficiency than the native ones made of clay. There are prescriptions which call for wine or wheat, and some which forbid the meat of animals imported by the Spanish. Germán Somolinos D'Ardois has suggested to me the possibility that Galen was the source of the physiological concept of the liver as the "pot of blood" (*teztecon*), as it appears in "The Internal Parts of the Body" in the "Primeros Memoriales" (and not in Book 10). It should also be noted that in the remarks accompanying the parts of the body it is said that our brains reason and warn, and that with the celestial part—the head—we remember and think. This concept was foreign to the natives, who made the heart the organ of consciousness.

The Human Body

The data referring to the human body were not collected for the purpose of recording the native concepts, but in order to create an extensive anatomical vocabulary. The possibilities of investigation, however, are not limited to simple vocabulary, as evidenced by the work of Rogers and Anderson (1965; 1966) with other Nahuatl vocabularies, comparing the inventory of the terms referring to the different parts of the body with the ancient vocabularies of Scandinavian, English, Norwegian, and High German.

The topic can be approached through etymological study. Not only the names of the parts of the human body but also those of illnesses can give an idea of the way an organ was supposed to function. *Cuitlatexcalhuaquiztli,* which means *constipation,* is literally translated as "dryness of the excremental oven." The texts studied say that our stomach purifies the food and cleans it, so we can imagine a digestive process in which the food descends to the stomach, where, by means of heat, the nutritious content is separated from what will make up the excrement, and we can infer that an excess of heat causes defecatory difficulties. Other ideas on physiological processes and anatomical conformations may be deduced from information relating to illnesses and therapeutics, such as the supposed organic connection permitting an enema to wash the interior of the kidneys and remove parasitic worms, or the supposition that a purge can evacuate the phlegms causing pressure on the heart.

Morbidity

In spite of the great concern at the time for knowledge about endemic diseases, shown in the questionnaire that was the background for the *Relaciones Geográficas* (Paso y Troncoso 1905–6), there are not many direct references to the presence and incidence of specific illnesses in Sahagún's documents. Some relevant material may nonetheless be obtained, not from the lists of illnesses but from the lists of remedies, since it is logical to suppose that the number of medicines recommended for each illness was in direct relation with the attention given to it by the natives, and the attention with its frequency. For example, in the Madrid Codex, out of sixty ailments mentioned, nine are problems of childbirth fever and as many more of other kinds of fever. Mentioned four times each are abscesses, the inability to eat, infant problems, eye problems, and "aquatic" or intermittent fevers. Twice mentioned are mange, being struck by lightning, and gout; the rest of the diseases are listed once each. In the Florentine Codex, of more than three hundred and sixty mentions of diseases, forty-five are of fever in general, three of white fever, three of head fever, eight of "aquatic" or intermittent fevers, and three of other types of fevers. There are twelve mentions of relapses, five of shortness of breath, five of extreme consumption, six of blistered body, five of rotten body, nine of body swelling. There are eleven of anal hemorrhage, four of diarrhea with blood, three of bloody stools, ten of swollen abdomen, fourteen of diarrhea, four of constipation, one of pus in the abdomen, two of noise in the intestines, one of worms in the abdomen, one of acidity, one of *aminaliztli* or the ills produced by water, one of stomach ache, one of hemorrhoids, four of cysts, nine of damages caused by sexual excesses or coital problems, eleven of illnesses of the penis, three of diseases of the groin, and one of normal sexual desires that must be calmed in the widower. There are twenty-two mentions of urinary problems, nine of gout, one of numbness, four of nerve diseases, one of swollen feet. There is one mention of the inability to conceive because of vaginal problems, three of delivery problems, four of childbirth fever, four of the purification of maternal milk, and one of the sickness of a child as a consequence of his mother's new pregnancy (*chipilez*). There are seven mentions of cough, six of back or chest ailments, five of nasal hemorrhages, two of phlegms, one of rotten lungs. There are more than eight apparent cases of illnesses produced by supernatural beings, and ten mentions of eye problems. In short, the total account would be very long and, if made by one who lacked the necessary medical knowledge, of little significance. Hence I believe it is better to leave the recounting in the hands of specialists, who will be able to relate the resulting figures to the very particular problems of a population situated on a lake and presumably burdened with sanitary difficulties.

Etiology

This is undoubtedly one of the most interesting points. The origin of illness is complex, including and often intertwining two types of causes: those that we would call natural—excesses, accidents, deficiencies, exposure to sudden temperature changes, contagions, and the like— and those caused by the intervention of nonhuman beings or of human beings with more than normal powers. For example, a native could think that his rheumatic problems came from the supreme will of Titlacahuan, from the punishment sent by the Tlaloque for not having performed a certain rite, from direct attack by a being who inhabited a certain spring, and from prolonged chilling in cold water; the native would not consider it all as a confluence of diverse causes but as a complex. This complexity, which is obvious not only in other sources on pre-Hispanic Mexico but also in Sahagún's work, is not evident in the texts with which we are presently concerned. These texts were unquestionably influenced by the firm decision and censorship of Sahagún and by the caution of the native doctors, whose contact with the missionaries enabled them to see what matters were best omitted. As a result, illnesses that were totally related to magical or religious concepts were eliminated from the lists, and only the "natural" etiology remained, usually by elimination of the rest, or sometimes by a tacit substitution influenced by the conquerors.

Thus there remained those documents that attributed lip blisters to heat, wind, or cold, or tooth decay to eating hot things (especially if cold things were eaten afterward), and to the presence of decomposed food, especially meat. An eye disease originated from the presence of a parasitic worm. There are other diseases whose causes must have seemed strange to the Europeans of the time: stuttering or overly childish speech were said to be caused by persistence in nursing in spite of the advanced age of a child, and serious sexual problems were thought to be caused by erotic dream visions (perhaps those not accompanied by discharge), by fright during copulation, and in a woman by having sexual relations or lifting heavy things immediately after giving birth. Breech births are attributed in Book 11 to nonabstention from coitus immediately before delivery, a pathogeny which is not described in that book but rather in the advice to pregnant women in the speeches of Book 6.

We must take into account that much can be obtained from information implicit in the language. It is said of many illnesses, particularly fevers, that they establish themselves in or inhabit certain parts of the organism: one causing blisters on the tongue, called *nenepilchacayoli-huiztli* ("formation of rings on the tongue"), is so localized: *"totonqui tocamac nemi,"* "the fever lives in our mouth." The same can be said of verbs used in reference to certain diseases known from their origin or their effects to be caused by divine beings. In speaking of the effects of air (and in this case air cannot be understood as simply the natural fluid or its current) the verb *quiza*, "go out," is used, preceded by *-pan* with a possessive prefix. The possessive refers to the patient, and the person of the verb to the agent. Exactly the same thing occurs in other books of the Florentine Codex, for example in Book 1, Chapter 10 and in Book 4, Chapter 22, where we find a description of the paralysis caused by the celestial goddesses, escorts to the sun. In both of the above-mentioned places the expression *"ipan oquizque in cihuapipiltin,"* "the noble women came upon him," is used to refer to the moment of the unpleasant meeting. Another very obscure expression is the verb *pehua*, "begin," used to indicate the presence of an illness with a similar origin. It appears not only in the texts we are now examining but also in Book 4, Chapter 22: ". . . *auh intla aca opeuh mococoa,*" "and if one began to get sick." Dibble and Anderson translate this as "when someone begins to get sick," and I have given the same translation. I suspect, however, that we have not fully understood the phrase. Another verb used in similar cases is *piqui*, which also merits study. Another that has been studied is the verb *ehua* preceded by *-tech* with a possessive prefix. Its apparent meaning is "intrusion," but the problem remains.

Illness

Many have argued for the absence of a theory of medicine in the Mesoamerican world. Nevertheless it is obvious that like all aspects of the culture—and the aspect of a culture corresponding to the limits of life, death, health, disease, and suffering is one of the most important—medicine was immersed in a scheme of classification of everything that exists. This classification provided the elementary principles of knowledge, tailoring the techniques to the problems. Superior and inferior, cold and hot, the four directions, the possibilities of temporal and spatial intervention by each divinity, the lucky and unlucky days were all applicable to this subject matter.

I do not believe it necessary to reconsider here the origin of the hot-cold concept in native medicine (see López Austin 1971b). Nevertheless it is worth pointing out that "cold" medicines and their effects are mentioned often. One plant is said to be cold and to counteract heat; another forces heat out because it is cold; another mitigates the effects of a purge because it is cold; another is used for the same reason against inflammation of the eyes; another is spoken of kindly because it helps the digestion: it cools the heat (which must be presumed harmful if excessive) and with it one does not feel the heat of the steam bath. It is said that the cold nature of the *coaxihuitl* (ident.?) lowers the blood of one who has twisted his neck, so the heart will not be damaged. And *cococ tlacotl* (ident.?) is said to be a cold root. Contrary to what is supposed by those who affirm that the distinction between hot and cold is a degeneration of the Old World concept of the four elements, no reference is made to the opposition of wet and dry.

The possible correspondence between different types of phlegms and fevers and the four cardinal points constitutes an interesting problem. Like the directions, phlegms are identified with colors, in which the natives discerned a relationship to illnesses and their seriousness. White, yellow, and green phlegms and pus are frequently mentioned in the texts referring to medicines. This four-part division is also made at the end of the anatomical list in Book 10. A different division appears in the first list of the "Primeros Memoriales," for the Acolhuan informants named phlegm, blood phlegm, white phlegm, and yellow phlegm. A dark green fever and a white one are mentioned by color. White is a strong fever, but it is not apparent, since it locates itself in the interior, not on the surface, of the body. It swells from below and causes rotting. The dark green fever also lodges itself in the interior of the body, but it manifests itself more conspicuously, blackening two or three zones of the skin. Will two other complementary fevers be discovered? It would be interesting to compare Sahagún's data with Hernando Ruiz de Alarcón's (1953).

Research can uncover interesting ideas about pathogeny. The connection between fever and the density of urine, one of the relationships most frequently mentioned, is worth investigating. One of the principal concepts is that of the placement of the illness in the interior of the body, whence the effects sprout to the surface. Before this emergence a difference in temperature may exist between the damaged and the healthy zones, which produces an undesirable sensation of great coldness in the nerves. The emergence may be spontaneous in the form of blistering of the lips, inflammation of the face and eyes, or the presence of spots on the face, this last being a result of rupture of the internal organs, hemorrhoids, infections, or cysts. When the movement toward the exterior is not spontaneous, it is induced by means of medicines, for it is easier to attack the "mature" illness by applying the medicines from the exterior, directly on the skin. Another serious problem is the accumulation of phlegms, white, green, and yellow, which penetrate the nerves, head, and chest. These phlegms produce pressure on the heart, fever, pulsations of the temple, and muscular and nervous trembling. The pressure on the heart proceeds from one side, injures the viscera (the organs of thought), and produces a loss of consciousness.

These are only examples. A careful reading of the texts awakens doubts, suggests answers, and invites investigation, which should be guided by the premise that knowledge follows a logical tendency to divide and classify, to take the world as a complex but orderly whole. The interrelation of findings on the functioning of the human body, on the nature of illnesses, and on the processes of their development will permit the explanation of the native concept of therapeutic processes.

Therapeutics

One frequently encounters in Sahagún's texts clear references to the reasons for the choice of certain types of remedies. He mentions, for example, that there are medicines applicable to all kinds of numbness, that bitter products are indicated for infections, and that any purge is medicine for weakness. It is affirmed that the heat of the sweat bath softens the hardened muscles and nerves of those who have been ill or beaten. It is believed that a sudorific causes a fever to exit through the skin, and that some medicines cool the damaged organs and thus reduce swelling. Bruises caused by a contusion are dangerous because beaten blood becomes corrupt and turns into an illness that provokes the drying out of the patient, the swelling of the abdomen, spitting blood, and constant coughing; thus the blood must immediately be made to flow throughout the body to prevent stagnation. The therapeutic medicine is obvious: bleeding to make the blood flow. On other occasions the effect of the remedy is described in very mechanical terms, as in the case of one that pushes the phlegms oppressing the heart until they exit through the anus. It is said of other medicines that they speed the process of the illness, motivating a maturation so that the disease can be more easily attacked, making the illness appear on the surface where it can be treated directly.

Other therapeutic measures are not so obvious. Among them is the very important one studied by Dibble, who proved not only that what was sought was the elimination of internal heat by means of the evacuation of the intestines and bladder, but also that the indicated medicines were actually very effective purges and diuretics. In another example, it is said that pus, yellow phlegm, and thick blood, which are said to be produced by "the male sickness," are expelled through the anus or urethra, and one is given to understand that with the expulsion of these products, the illness disappears.

There is undoubtedly an important reason why certain diseases—those related to the world of cold and water, such as swelling of the abdomen, gout, the evil effect of lightning, that of "air," perversity, *atonahuiztli* or "water fever," and others—should be attacked with censers, and why *yiauhtli* (*Tagetes lucida*), *picietl* (*Nicotiana rustica*), *teunanacatl* (*Panaeolus campanulatus v. sphinctrinus*), *peyotl* (*Lophaphora williamsii*), *toloa* (*Datura* sp.), and *ololiuhqui* (*Ipomea sidaefolia, Rivea corymbosa, Datura metaloides*)—all narcotics (in addition to *ehecapatli* (ident.?), which I do not recall as having this property)—should be prescribed as remedies.

Measures like the protection of an injured head by wrapping it so the harmful air will not penetrate have persisted until the present and belong to the "evil air" complex. It is interesting to see the degree of personification associated with an illness that can be weakened and dispelled by the odor of a plant hung around a child's neck. The diversity of maladies for which ocelot meat is used (possession by supernatural beings, madness, water fever, perversity, and the illness indicated by the verb *piqui*) suggests that they all form part of a category that can be studied through the common medicaments.

It is curious to note an element in the therapeutics that is also very significant in modern native magic: the time. For a cough with purulent phlegm, it is necessary that the *chichihualcuahuitl* (ident.?) be heated by the sun precisely at dawn, and for white excrement or bloody stools, the lime should be moistened in the afternoon.

The therapeutics contains in addition a conspicuous list of diets and prohibitions. The patient with a cough will have to eat turkey, rabbit, quail, pigeon, venison, and fried tortillas, and will drink a little wine and pulque, boiled chile water, and atole with honey or chile; he will not, however, be able to take cold water, cacao, fruit, or water pulque. He will be forbidden to face the cold and to drink much water, but it will be recommended that he take steam baths. One who has a turkey cataract should not look at white things. If categories of foods and prohibitions were obtained, no doubt a categorization of the illness could also be found through the counteractions used to reach equilibrium. This would probably lead to results parallel to those obtained from investigations of the modern native world, in which "cold" or "hot" medicines, foods, and drinks are recommended for the illnesses with opposite natures.

This configuration leads us back to the topic of colors, which, just as in modern Mexico, seem to have had great importance in ancient times. Red saltpeter is recommended in Sahagún's texts against the ocular excrescence called *ixhuahuacihuiztli*, and red medicines in general should be used against the white films and clouds that form in the eye. But the use of dark medicines is more salient: soot, *tlilpotonqui* (*Eryngium beecheyanium*), *tlaliyac* (copperas), *nacazcolotl* (*Caesalpinia coriacea v. coriaria*), *matlalli* (blue), black *axin* (an unguent), *palli* (black clay), and many others are used against body swelling, gout, aquatic fever, blisters, head eruptions, split ends, dandruff, diarrhea, white excrement, contusions and head injuries, chest aches, constipation, head fevers in children and old people (perhaps a particular type of fever), nits, tooth decay, and glaucoma. It is specifically stated that the parts of the body swollen by white fever are painted over and that the medicine bursts the tumors. Illnesses for which dark substances are not used are also important, because the diseases have a nature opposite to the previous group and are of the same nature as the medicines: *cocopaltic* (a tree resin) and soot are used against diarrhea, but the soot is eliminated when the patient's excrement or saliva are bloody. (There is an exception, however, concerning the application of soot in cases of bloody excrement: *cozcacuauhxihuitl* [*Perezia moschata*], *cuauhyayahual* [ident.?], resin, and soot are recommended for those who have been beaten, but if they have fever the resin and soot are eliminated.)

If we pass from the grouping of illnesses to that of therapeutic measures, we can see that certain diseases that are cured with dark substances are also cured with censers. The same kind of relation exists between bleeding and puncture, which are applied for headaches (if the censing is not enough), aquatic fever of the teeth, tooth decay, nits, abscesses, and swellings.

Many such equivalences could yet be indicated, but I believe these suffice. The only pertinent thing to add is that nowadays the dark colors belong to the domain of heat and the light ones to that of cold. This structure should be taken into consideration when a further investigation is made.

In other cases particular medicaments are used for simpler reasons. If we examine the list of ailments for which urine was used, the urine appears to have served as a disinfectant. Rubber was used to cure excoriations of the skin and irritations of the mucous membranes, and maguey was used in many forms to close up the tissues when there was continuing suppuration.

Pharmacology

Interest in the study and identification of medicinal plants used by the ancient Nahuas has developed not only for research on the native concepts, but also from the requirements of research in modern pharmacology. The botanical descriptions from Sahagún's texts, the drawings of the plants, and the study that can be made of the etymology of their names, will doubtless aid in taxonomy, the initial step in the research. Useful as Sahagún's texts are, they should be considered as complementary to other works, such as Francisco Hernández's, which is far superior in botanical description. The traditions of those who still use the ancient herbals and who conserve the Nahuatl names of plants should also be taken into account in the process of classification.

CONCLUSION

From among the many possibilities for the study of Sahagún's texts on medical subjects, I have pointed out several tracks and examples of topics for investigation, some imagined and others discovered in my work as a translator. I offer them without providing solutions because I am the first to admit that this is a task for specialists in matters in which I am inexperienced. The preceding pages have been suggestions and nothing more, hence bibliographical references are largely omitted. Anyone wanting to follow this path will need to review the material as a specialist.

10
The Nahuatlization of Christianity

CHARLES E. DIBBLE
University of Utah

Fray Bernardino de Sahagún compiled the drafts and copies of his *History* during the years 1547–85. During much the same period he was simultaneously engaged in preparing "Postillas" and "Doctrinas" for the effective conversion and indoctrination of the natives. Although he justified his *History* as an instrument to gauge the thoroughness of conversion, he seems nevertheless to have compartmentalized his labors. Other than the prologues and appendices of the *History* there is little evidence of cross-reference between his two labors. As one reads the Madrid manuscripts one discovers little or no reference to Christianity; as one reads his "Doctrina" (Sahagún 1579b) or his "Postilla" (Sahagún 1579a) there is little direct reference to the content of his *History*.

This characteristic separation of his two activities suggests a general question: When and to what degree were the pre-Hispanic metaphors of Nahuatl utilized in the presentation of Christianity to the natives?

The historical antecedents to this problem can be listed:

1. The Spanish conquest brought two languages, two cultures, and two religions into instant and continuous contact.
2. The Christian victory meant that Christianity was to be implanted in New Spain.
3. The decision was made that Nahuatl was to be the language of conversion in preference to Spanish; that Nahuatl was to take precedence over other native languages and become the "general language of the Indians." In the words of Philip II, "The knowledge of the general language of the Indians is the most necessary means for the explanation and teaching of the Christian doctrine and for the curates and priests to administer the sacraments to them" (Ricard 1947:137).
4. During the period 1536–40 the first group of native scholars was trained at the College of Holy Cross at Tlaltelolco. They were Christians by education and indoctrination, trilingual by training.

All of this means that by 1540 the decision had been made to use Nahuatl as the language of conversion. By this date Sahagún had been instrumental in training a group of native scribes and grammarians whom he and his colleagues could and did utilize for two related but separate goals. One was to gather information about native culture and religion to guard against the emergence of heresy in Christian teaching. This led to the *History* of Sahagún as well as the writings of Olmos, Motolinía, and others. The second goal was to translate Christian doctrine and ritual into Nahuatl with the aid of the native helpers.

Problems began to emerge as the fathers became increasingly familiar with aboriginal language and belief. Sahagún is very clear on this problem in his prologue to the "Arte Adivinatoria," dated 1585, wherein he laments that the first fathers considered the conversion to Christianity as achieved, and that it was only when he and others had become familiar with native language and belief that the superficiality of converson became apparent (Sahagún 1585a).

A delicate problem arose early, which, although there were partisan views, tended to end in compromise. How were Christian names and concepts unknown to the natives to be rendered? Should a Nahuatl equivalent be given for *Espíritu Santo, ángel, alma?* Was *God* to be rendered as *teotl?* Sahagún tended to favor the use of the Spanish term. *The Mother of God* was to be rendered *Dios Ynantzin*, rather than

Tonantzin, which was the name of an Aztec goddess: "The proper name of the Mother of God Holy Mary is not *Tonantzin,* but *dios ynantzin;* this satanic invention appears in order to palliate idolatry in the face of the error of this name of *Tonantzin*" (Sahagún 1950–69:Book 11:Folio 234v). The criticism of an excessive trend in this direction was that it would make Christian teachings superficial and unassimilated in native mentality.

The opposing view, of necessity, came later, as it required a delicate understanding of Nahuatl and native mentality, a mastery of the many metaphors. Those who urged the Nahuatl equivalent for such terms argued that it made Christianity more intelligible to the native, whereas those who opposed it argued that it tended to maintain idolatrous and pagan concepts.

A line of research that would give us a greater understanding of what might be termed the Nahuatlization of Christianity would be the chronological consideration of Christian texts in Nahuatl—a consideration of how and when Nahuatl literary style and Nahuatl metaphors appear in the texts. As a pilot attempt, let us examine a few texts.

First let us consider the "Sermonario" and "Santoral" compiled by Sahagún in 1540 with the help of his native students (Sahagún 1540a, 1540b). The Nahuatl text is in the hand of a native scribe, with additions in Sahagún's hand. In a prologue Sahagún states that they were composed rather than translated, although the text is doctrinal with frequent biblical references. As one reads the text the message is Christian, yet Nahuatl literary style is ever apparent. The sermons move in the direction of, but do not achieve, the florid quality of Nahuatl as found in the *Huehuetlatolli* and Book 6 of the *History.* The literary device known as parallelism—the repetition of two synonyms or similar phrases—is frequent: "*ic cenca yecteneualo, ic cenca mauiztilo*"; "*in cenca qualcan, in cenca yeccan*" ("much praised, much esteemed"; "a very good place, a very favorable place"). A second literary device, termed *disfrasismo* by the late Father Garibay, tends to be metaphorical in meaning. There are fewer instances of *disfrasismo:* "*moquetzal, mochalchiuh*"; "*çoquititlan, cuitlatitlan tinemi*"; "*otacatl, machiotl onamechtlalili*" ("your precious feather, your precious greenstone"; "thou livest in the mud, in the excrement"; "he places the measure, the model before you").

We would not expect many metaphors to be recorded and clearly understood at this early date. According to our present knowledge, the best and most exhaustive sources of metaphorical Nahuatl are the *Huehuetlatolli* of Olmos and Book 6 of Sahagún's *History*, both dated 1547. Once these works were compiled, however, we can infer that they must have been widely circulated and frequently copied. This conjecture is based on the inclusion of sections of the Olmos *Huehuetlatolli* in a sixteenth-century *Miscelánea Sagrada*, which includes the writings of Fray Juan de Gaona (Gaona et al. 1538–60[?]: folios 233, 239).

The *Huehuetlatolli* of Olmos (Bautista 1600) is an excellent source for the assessing of Nahuatl literary style in Christian texts, because it consists of two parts: a series of sermons and exhortations of the native elders, and a lesser number of sermons explaining Christian doctrine. The first part, consisting of exhortations to children, youths, rulers, and so on, and their responses, is perhaps the most complete presentation of Nahuatl metaphors. The Aztecs conceived of their orations and prayers as the stringing of a strand of beads and the *Huehuetlatolli* is just that— a series of metaphors one after another.

In the sermons dealing with Christ, baptism, confirmation, and the like, the examples of parallelism are frequent; metaphors are not as frequent as in the native sermons, but they are numerous, more frequent than in Sahagún's 1540 manuscript. Some examples of parallelism and metaphors are:

> *in cuitlapilli, in atlapalli; in quauhtla in çacatla otimoquixtiaya; immixtitlan in ayauhtitlan; in ihiyotzin in itlahtoltzin in ipalne-mohuani Dios; ca oancommololoque oancommolpilique in itla-quentzin in itilmatzin in totemaquixticatzin Iesu christo; in tzitzimitl in Satanas.*

> the tail, the wing (the common people); he has brought thee forth from the forest, the grasslands; in the clouds, in the mist (myste-riously); the breath, the word of God, he by whom we live; for ye have put on, tied on the blessed cloak, the blessed cape of Our Savior, Jesus Christ; the demon, Satan.

It is perhaps indicative of a trend that the literary characteristics so well developed in native sermons, so apparent in the Christian sermons in the *Huehuetlatolli* of 1547, found favor at the end of the century. Fray Juan Bautista's 1600 edition of the Olmos *Huehuetlatolli* included ap-probations by Padre Juan de Tovar of the Jesuit order and Padre Francisco de Solís of the Franciscan order. Padre Francisco de Solís states: "And it seems to me that above and beyond the propriety and elegance of the language, it would be of great utility and advantage for the reformation of customs and good guidance of the natives and would hence result in service to God, that it be printed and published" (Bautista 1600).

A *tratado* written by Fray Juan de Gaona with the aid of his students to provide Christian dialogue between teacher and student follows the pattern of the *Huehuetlatolli* in its format (Gaona et al. 1538–60: Folios 75–100). Written between 1538 and 1560, the year of Gaona's death, it reveals remarkable restraint in the use of metaphorical Nahuatl. The limited use includes such phrases as: *"tlatotonyan, tlayamanyan"*; *"in mix, in moyollo"*; *"yuhquinma ycochca, yuhquinma yneuhca"* ("a warm place, a temperate place"; "thy eye, thy heart [thy understanding]"; "such is his supper, such is his breakfast [his sustenance]"). Considering his acknowledged mastery of Nahuatl literary style, as attested by Mendieta (1945:4:144), this limited use of metaphor must reflect an editorial stance on the part of Fray Gaona, the order, or both.

In 1564 Sahagún produced a manuscript which has come to be entitled: "El Libro perdido de las Pláticas o Coloquios de los Doce Primeros Misioneros de México" (Sahagún 1564a). It is now housed in the Vatican archives. Father Garibay clearly demonstrated that the Nahuatl text dates from 1564, not from the arrival of the twelve; that the Nahuatl text was inspired by notes written in Spanish in 1525 or 1526; that the Spanish version may well be that of Sahagún, but the Nahuatl text is in aboriginal literary style, "a Nahuatl edition of a book on the same theme" (Garibay 1953–54:2:237–46). In a preface Sahagún acknowledges the contribution of the natives: "which was amended and polished in this College of Holy Cross of Tlaltelolco this aforementioned year with the ablest and best instructed of the students in the Mexican language and in the Latin language that have been trained in this college to the present times. . . . It was likewise polished with four very adept elders instructed both in their language and in all their antiquities" (Sahagún 1927:1:10).

The Nahuatl text places all the metaphorical wealth of the *Huehuetlatolli* in the mouths of the fathers as they present Christian doctrine and an understanding of the Holy Church. Included are: *"in mauh, in motepeuh"; "in ihiiotzin, in itlatoltzin"; "in ipetlatzin, in icpaltzin"; "in tecuiotl, in tlatocayotl"* ("thy water, thy mountain [thy city]"; "his breath, his word [his discourse]"; "his reed mat, his reed seat [his reign]"; "the lordship, the rulership [the reign]"). One sentence in Chapter 5, describing Christ's reign on earth, is typical of the literary style:

> *Auh in oncan hin ytlatocachantzinco cenca miec tlamantli in necuiltonolli in netlamachtilli mopie in ilhuicacaiotl ytoptzin ypetlacaltzin yn povi in tloque navaque, vellaçotli tzaccaio, auh vel pielo.*

And there in his lordly mansion very many kinds of riches, of wealth are stored; the secrets of heaven which belong to God (the lord of the near, the nigh), very precious, enclosed, and well guarded.

In contrast with the "Coloquios" is the "Postilla," which Sahagún wrote in 1579 (Sahagún 1579a). In 1577 Sahagún had completed his translation of Book 6 from Nahuatl into Spanish, and the rich metaphorical style of the native sermons was fresh in his mind. Yet there is no indication that he incorporated the richness of metaphor contained in Book 6 (Sahagún 1950–69:6); rather, it compares in this regard to the 1540 manuscript (Sahagún 1540a,1540b). In fact, he yielded less to Nahuatl literary style than did Olmos in the Christian sermons of the *Huehuetlatolli.* Of the limited number of metaphors used by Sahagún three are cited: *"in maxca, in motlatqui"; "yqualantzin ytlaueltzin ipan techtlaça in Dios"; "yn netlamachtiliztli, yn necuiltonoliztli"* ("thy possession, thy property"; "God casts his rage, his wrath upon us"; "wealth, riches [or joy, happiness]").

Even more revealing, the "Postilla" included the Nahuatl text of Chapters 22 and 40 from Book 6. The page order of the manuscript has been altered in places, some sections are repeated, and the second person singular has been changed to second person plural. Judging from the material here cited, we conclude that Sahagún has included these chapters from Book 6 for the sole purpose of refuting both their content and their metaphorical style.

> *Yn yehuati in tetaoa in tenaoa ynic quinonotzaya yn ompa calaquizque calmecac quimilhuiaya*

yn axcan ma xoyauh in vmpa omitzamapouh in monantzin in motatzin in calmecac, in choquizcalli yn ixayocali, in tlaocolcali yn ompa mopitza momamali, in no oncã xotla, cueponi in tepilhua, in vncã cozcateuh, quetzalteuh, motemanilia in tote°, tloque nahuaque, in vncã moteicnoitilia yn ipalnemohuani, yn oncã quiça totecuiyoa in tetecuhti in tlatoque, in apia in tepepia yn ocã quiça in icpaltin in petlati, in oncã quimanilia, in onca quimopepenilia in tloque, nahuaque, in quauhpetlapa, yn ocelupetlapa.

Ynin tlatolli ynic quinnonotzaya in oquichpipiltotõti ynic quime-lehuiltiaya in vncã calmecac nemiliztli, auh ynin ca muchi yztla-catlatolli mochi teca necayahualiz: ca in iehuatl in titlacahua in quitecpanaz in quineltocaz in tlatocayotl ynin ca çan vel yzeltzin ytequitzin yn to°. dios ayac occe, auh yn quimilhuiaya in vncã xotla cueponi in tepilhuã in cozcateuh in quetzalteuh, etc. Ynin ca muchi yztlacatlatolli ca ça yehuatl in tlalticpacayotl in quitenehuiliaya

The fathers, the mothers so admonished them when they introduced them into the calmecac. They said to them:

"Now go where thy mother, thy father have dedicated thee with paper, to the calmecac, the house of weeping, the house of tears, the house of sadness, where the sons of noblemen are cast, are perforated; also where they bud, where they blossom; where like precious necklaces, like precious feathers they are placed by our lord, the lord of the near, of the nigh; where he by whom we live showeth compassion. Thence emerge our lords, the lords, the rulers, the guardians of the city; thence emerge those who assume the reed seat, the reed mat of authority, whom the lord of the near, of the nigh, setteth there, selecteth there; those who are of the order of eagles, those of the order of ocelots."[1]

These are the words whereby they admonished the young boys to encourage them for life there in the calmecac. But this is all false-hood, all mockery, for he whom we serve is to regulate, create the realm, this is the province of our Lord God alone, no one else. And when they said "there the sons of noblemen bud, blossom like precious necklaces, like precious feathers, etc.," this is all falsehood, for it is only the things of this world which they declared.

This example again illustrates Sahagún's predilection for maintaining a degree of independence between his *History* and his "Doctrina." The limited use of Nahuatl literary style in the "Postilla" is consistent with views he expressed elsewhere. In his prologues to his *History* and his "Arte Adivinatoria," he clearly identifies himself as a purist, ever careful to avoid terms which might serve to perpetuate the concepts of Satan. Perhaps he equated many of the metaphors with the *cantares* at the end of Book 2, which he recorded but failed to translate, stating:

> "It is a very old custom of our adversary the Devil to seek out hiding places for doing his business, in accordance to what is in the Holy Gospel, which says: "He who does evil abhors the light" (Sahagún 1956:1:255).

A final example illustrates how, in some instances, classical Nahuatl literary style was utilized in a Christian context. The example is taken from a sixteenth-century "Tratado y Manual de Doctrina Cristiana" in the Biblioteca de la Universidad Autónoma de San Luis Potosí (Sahagún n.d.b). A note says: "Anonymous (attributed by Wigberto Jiménez Moreno to Fray Bernardino de Sahagún)." Although written in a sixteenth-century hand, it appears to be a collection of several manuscripts, and Sahagún's authorship of the section cited might be questioned. A short fragment is cited and translated.

> Capitulo 1. Saludanse vn frayle de Sant. Fran.^{co} y vn natural llamado francisco.
> Francisco. *Ca nimitznotlapalhuico, nimitznociauhquechilico, notlaçotatzine: quen ticmomachiltia ymmonacayotzin: cuix huallehua yn içumal in iquallan yn itemox yn iehecauh, yn iteuh, yn iquauh, yn tloque nahuaque yn ipalnemohuani, totecuiyo Dios. Auh cuix quihuallaça yn tlacotl pitzahuac yn patlahuac tzitzicaztli yn acatl ahuacho yn teizcali yn tetzicuenolti mopantzinco.*

> Chapter 1. A Franciscan friar and a native called Francisco greet each other.
> Francisco: O my beloved Father, I welcome thee, I greet thee. How is thy health? Does perhaps the lord of the near, of the nigh, he by whom we live, our lord God, stir up his wrath, his castigation, his punishment? And does he perhaps cast upon thee the pointed stick, the broad nettle, the reed covered with dew which corrects one, reprimands one?

Apart from the occurrence of the word *God*, the whole section can be duplicated in a prayer to Tezcatlipoca in Book 6 and in sections of the *Huehuetlatolli*.

The examples cited suggest that a more thorough study will reveal that

The Nahuatlization of Christianity

Nahuatl literary style will appear gradually in the Christian texts, and only as it was mastered by the fathers. The texts will be seen to vary in their incorporation of Nahuatl metaphors. This variance will reflect the date of the text, the linguistic skill of the author, and his personal bias. It is further suggested that the use or nonuse, the influence or lack of influence, of the native grammarians may in many cases be discernible.

NOTE

1. The Nahuatl text of this paragraph varies little from the Florentine Codex. I have, therefore, followed our earlier translation. *See* Sahagún 1950–69: 6:214.

11

The Problematics of Sahagún: Certain Topics Needing Investigation

MIGUEL LEÓN-PORTILLA

Universidad Nacional Autónoma de México

Both the Nahuatl documentation, the fruit of Sahagún's research, and the greater part of his copious written production suffered from bad luck both during and for many years after his lifetime. The only work he lived to see published was the *Psalmodia Christiana y Sermonario de los Sanctos del Año, en lengua mexicana*, printed by Pedro Ocharte in 1583 (Sahagún 1583). The remainder of his papers not only were unpublished but were to end up scattered, in grave danger of being lost forever.

From the last third of the sixteenth century on, several investigators certainly benefited somewhat from Sahagún's works. Among them were Philip II's proto-physician, Doctor Francisco Hernández (1959–67), and the chroniclers Fray Gerónimo de Mendieta (1945), Juan Suárez de Peralta (1949), Diego Muñoz Camargo (1892), Fray Juan de Torquemada (1943–44) and Don Antonio de Herrera (1726–28). Later some of those who wrote about the native cultures of New Spain or who prepared bibliographical compilations on the subject mentioned Sahagún's works even though they were not personally familiar with them. Such was the case of the bibliographers León Pinelo (1629), Lucas Wadding (1906), Nicolás Antonio (1783–88), and Juan José de Eguiara y Eguren (1755), and of the historians Lorenzo Boturini (1746) and Francisco Javier Clavijero (1958). Nevertheless, although some remembered that Fray Bernardino had completed research and works of the greatest importance, by the mid-eighteenth century ideas on the nature of these works were very confused, and worse yet, their exact locations were unknown.

A belated discovery of the copy of the *General History of the Things of New Spain* preserved in the Franciscan convent of Tolosa in Navarre (Sahagún 1580) marked the beginning of investigation into the work of the illustrious Franciscan. Although this discovery had been noted in 1732 by Fray Juan de San Antonio (1732–33:1:214), nobody was interested in the manuscript except Eguiara y Eguren, who misunderstood the reference (1755:1, art. 608)—until Don Juan Bautista Muñoz borrowed it and took it to Madrid in 1783 with the idea of using it. From this manuscript, which would eventually come to rest in the Library of the Royal Academy of History, proceeded the later copies from which the first editions of the *General History* were made, well into the nineteenth century. These were brought out by Carlos María de Bustamante (Sahagún 1829; 1829–30; 1840), who made use of the copy that had belonged to Diego Panes; and also by Lord Kingsborough (1831–48:5,6), who included it in his *Antiquities of Mexico* on the basis of another copy belonging to Felipe Bauza, a Spanish refugee living in London.

This first kind of salvage was followed several decades later by the identification of Sahagún's important works by some Mexicanist scholars. Among the manuscripts they identified were those containing the Nahuatl documentation included in the Madrid Codices of the Royal Palace and the Royal Academy of History and the Florentine Codex in the Laurentian Library in Florence. The location of such important materials, as well as other discoveries in libraries and archives in Mexico, Spain, Italy, and the United States—of sermon books in the Mexican language attributed to Fray Bernardino, of other fragments of the *General History*, of vocabularies and tracts like the "Libro de los Colloquios" —gradually gave rise to a broad series of studies and publications relating to the life and work of Sahagún.

Topics Needing Investigation

The mere list of people who have investigated the subject from many different viewpoints is long. Thus among those who have applied themselves to the clarification of Sahagún's biography and of his copious production since the second half of the nineteenth century, we should mention: Bernardino Biondelli, Italian editor of the *Evangelarium epistolarium et lectionarium aztecum sive mexicanum* (*Aztec or Mexican Reader, Gospels, and Epistles*), a work attributed to the indefatigable Franciscan, first published with an ample preface and a vocabulary in Milan in 1858 (Sahagún 1858); Don José Fernando Ramírez (Ramírez 1903b:1–34), who presented in 1867 an important work on what he called "Mexican Codices of Fray Bernardino de Sahagún" to the Royal Academy of History; Alfredo Chavero, who made a study of the life of the Franciscan (1877); D. Jourdanet and Rémi Siméon, the editors of the French version of the *General History* that appeared in 1880; Joaquín García Icazbalceta, who made a fundamental contribution in his *Bibliografía mexicana del siglo XVI* in 1886 (1954:322–87), truly a point of departure for all subsequent investigation of Sahagún's work; and Daniel G. Brinton (1890), who, besides referring to Sahagún on various occasions, was the first to translate into a European language the twenty sacred hymns collected in Nahuatl by Fray Bernardino.

The works of Eduard Seler, who in 1890 began publishing the paleography of certain texts, such as those referring to goldsmithing, stonework, and feather working (Seler 1890), occupy a place of the highest importance in the study of Nahuatl documentation. Later the same renowned Americanist made other contributions to this same field (1908–9; 1902–23:2:961–1107), of which the most important, published posthumously, was the Nahuatl text and German translation of several chapters and even complete books of the Madrid and Florentine codices (Seler 1927). Also important are the works of the well-known investigator and editor of documentary materials, Don Francisco del Paso y Troncoso, to whom we owe the facsimile edition of the Madrid Codices published in Madrid between 1905 and 1908 (Sahagún 1905–8), as well as several studies describing the contents of these manuscripts (1896; 1903).

These investigators were later joined by many others who either treated diverse aspects of Sahagún's life and complex work or brought to light additional works or parts of them. Among these investigators we must mention Cayetano Rosell (1883), Antonio Peñafiel (1890), Wilhelm

Schmidt (1906), Herman Beyer (1922), Alfonso Toro (1924), José María Pou y Martí (1924), Walter Lehmann (1927), Fanny R. Bandelier (Sahagún 1932), Ignacio Alcócer (1938), Mauricio Magdalano (1943), Miguel Acosta Saignes (Sahagún 1946), Luis Villoro (1950:29–77), Luis Leal (1955), Donald Robertson (1959:167–78; 1966), Manuel Ballesteros Gaibrois (1964), and Georges Baudot (1969).

The contributions made by certain other specialists require separate consideration. A study that considerably enriched the information provided initially by García Icazbalceta is that of Wigberto Jiménez Moreno on "Fray Bernardino de Sahagún and His Work," included as an introduction to the new edition of the *General History of the Things of New Spain* prepared by Joaquín Ramírez Cabañas in four volumes (Sahagún 1938:1:xiii–lxxxi). And Lluis Nicolau D'Olwer (1952) brought out the most extensive biography of Sahagún to date.

To Leonhard Schultze Jena (1950; 1952) we owe the paleographic version and German translation of one part of the Madrid Codices, with various portions of the materials Sahagún used as the basis for Books 2, 3, 4, 5, 7, 8, and 9 of his *General History*. Although this work provides a less than complete understanding of the Nahuatl texts, it constitutes a contribution worthy of consideration. On the other hand, one must recognize the great achievement of Charles E. Dibble and Arthur J. O. Anderson in completing the paleographic version and translation into English of the twelve books of the Florentine Codex in a duly annotated edition (Sahagún 1950–69). They have also published other studies related to Sahagún's work (Anderson 1960; 1961; 1966; Dibble 1959; 1962; 1963; 1971).

We have intentionally left for the end of this enumeration the works carried out by Angel María Garribay K. and his group of disciples in the Instituto de Investigaciones Históricas of the National University of Mexico. Garibay has produced many works on this subject. On the one hand there are the translations of anthology type from some texts of the Madrid Codices (1940a; 1940b; 1943–44; 1945; 1948). On the other hand, his important work *Historia de la literatura náhuatl* (1953–54), includes not only the translation of some of Sahagún's texts but also a chapter entitled "Sahagún's Work as a Literary Monument," which analyzes Fray Bernardino's works from several viewpoints, particularly the literary one. We must also mention his edition of the *General His-*

tory of the Things of New Spain (Sahagún 1956), which includes introductions and notes for each book and translations of the Nahuatl text of
Book 12, the book of the conquest, and of the portions referring to the
costumes and insignia of the gods, the twenty sacred hymns, and the
texts telling about magicians and acrobats (Sahagún 1956: 4:81–314).

Among the other publications prepared by Garibay and his disciples,
we may mention the series now in the process of publication entitled
"Texts of Sahagun's Informants," of which four volumes have so far
appeared, by Angel María Garibay K. (1958; 1961), Miguel León-
Portilla (1958a), and Alfredo López Austin (1969a). The latter two investigators have also treated the subject of Sahagún's work and informants in other publications (León-Portilla 1960:15–21; 1965; 1966a;
1966b:8–15) López Austin 1963a; 1963b; 1965a; 1965b; 1967; 1971b).
We shall add that other students of the same group at the National
University of Mexico have also translated some of the documents collected by Sahagún: Thelma Sullivan (1963; 1965; 1966) and Victor
Manuel Castillo (1969).

The already long series of publications about the life and work of
Sahagún shows that a good deal has already been investigated in this field
in the last century. Nevertheless, as is true of the whole field of the history and historiography of ancient Mexico, we cannot be sure that all of
the documentation and the various known works of Sahagún are now
available in critical editions or that the enormous number of problems
related to them have been adequately solved. It is our purpose here to
enunciate succinctly some of the principal points in this problematics.
Our intention is to show various themes in which investigation is needed
as a preliminary step toward a more complete comprehension and utilization of these sources, of such fundamental interest for the study of
Mexico's pre-Hispanic past.

With selectivity in mind, we have chosen to present several problems
which up to now have been relatively overlooked or have been subject to
various sorts of controversy. We shall not dwell on all the questions that
have already received considerable attention, such as those referring to
the date of the beginning of the work and to the various modifications
Fray Bernardino introduced into his plans and outlines. On this subject
very valuable contributions have been made, such as the one already
mentioned by Wigberto Jiménez Moreno (Sahagún 1938).

In summary, we shall concentrate on the following points:

1. The necessity of an index or a descriptive bibliography of Sahagún's known manuscripts, both those that remain unpublished and those that have been published in various forms to date.
2. The question of the originality of Sahagún's enterprise. The possible influences in the conception of his work, in the methodology adopted, and in its elaboration.
3. The role played by the native informants and other of Sahagún's collaborators.
4. The origins and categories to which the native data collected by the Franciscan can be attributed.
5. Sahagún's intention in writing the *General History of the Things of New Spain* in Spanish and the relationship of this version to the information collected in Nahuatl.
6. The problems of the Spanish editions of the *General History* derived from the Tolosa manuscript or from copies of it.
7. Questions concerning the forms adopted to date in the translation of the Nahuatl texts collected by Fray Bernardino into European languages.

We now pass to a consideration of each of these points, turning first to the one we have mentioned as a preliminary question.

1. Need for an Index or Descriptive Bibliography of Sahagún's Manuscripts, Published and Unpublished

Although studies like those already cited by Ramírez, García Icazbalceta, Jiménez Moreno, Garibay, and Nicolau D'Olwer set forth abundant documentary and bibliographical references on this subject, there is no reconstruction of what can be called the Corpus Sahagunense that covers what we now know.

One consequence of the absence of such a critical and descriptive study of the Corpus Sahagunense is the fact that there is no edition of the *General History of the Things of New Spain* in which the variants contained in the oldest extant manuscripts of the *History* or parts of it are considered. Howard F. Cline pointed out in this connection some of the prologues omitted in the editions of the *General History*, all of them based originally on defective copies of the Tolosa or Royal Academy manuscripts (Cline 1971). García Icazbalceta (1954:376–87) notes the existence of an ancient copy of Book 4 of the *History* with an extensive prologue; this prologue has never been included or even mentioned in any edition of the *General History*. The manuscript in question is preserved in the same volume with the *Colección de Cantares Mexicanos* in the National Library of Mexico (see Moreno 1966:38–45).

There exist, furthermore, other texts by Fray Bernardino of which there is not even a precise description, let alone a critical edition. As an example I shall cite the one mentioned by García Icazbalceta entitled "Daily Exercises in the Mexican Language," which is numbered 1484 in the Ayer Collection of the Newberry Library in Chicago (Sahagún 1574a). Another document, cited by Chavero as having been part of his library, seems to be of still greater importance because of its relation to the contents of several portions of the Madrid Codices. In it there is a trace of the Franciscan's project of elaborating a trilingual vocabulary of Spanish, Latin, and Nahuatl. This manuscript is also found in the Ayer Collection (Sahagún 1585d).

We know for a fact that in the Ayer Collection, the National Library of Mexico, and the Vatican Library there exist several other documents belonging to the body of Sahagún's works which up to now either have not been taken into consideration or have not merited more than summary descriptions. This confirms, we believe, the necessity for elaborating the Corpus Sahagunense.

2. The Question of the Originality of the Enterprise of Sahagún. Possible Influences on the Conception of His Work, the Methodology Adopted, and Its Elaboration

It is well known that on several occasions Fray Bernardino altered the scheme of his investigation. Beginning with the editing of the outline "of all things that should be treated," he repeatedly reordered the materials he was collecting. Jiménez Moreno (Sahagún 1938:xl–l), treating the various stages in the elaboration of the *History*, identifies a Tepepulco Plan, 1558–60, "Primeros Memoriales"; a Tlaltelolco Plan, 1564–65, Madrid Codices; and a Mexico Plan, 1565–69.

Sahagún's alterations in the distribution of the texts constitute proof in themselves that, whatever the original influences that brought him to conceive his great work, he maintained considerable flexibility of spirit throughout its execution.

Angel María Garibay K., after searching for antecedents of Sahagún's enterprise in the works of classical antiquity, came to affirm that "all probability of direct influence favors Pliny's *Natural History*." Garibay stresses that Fray Bernardino, during his years as a student in Salamanca, had to have known the work of the celebrated Roman naturalist. He asserts that later, when Sahagún was a teacher in the College of Holy Cross at Tlatelolco, he could have consulted Pliny's writings again, since it is established that they were at his disposal in the library of the school. Garibay concludes, "It cannot be doubted that Sahagún, at the moment of writing such a work as this, must have read and studied the distribution of materials and the form of presentation of Pliny's descriptions and information" (Garibay 1953–54:2:68–71).

Garibay actually attempts a comparison between Sahagún's and Pliny's plans. In his judgment the plans are parallel, specifically in the parts concerning the world of nature—in other words between Book 11 of the final version of the *General History of the Things of New Spain* and the treatment of related subjects in Books 8–25, 33, 35, and 36 of Pliny's *Natural History*.

Donald Robertson has also established the existence of a definite relationship between the scheme of Sahagún's *General History* and the traditional organization of several medieval works of encyclopedic character, in which the presentation of subjects goes from the divine to the human to the natural in a hierarchical fashion (Robertson 1959:170–72). Specifically, Robertson compares the many books of the Florentine Codex with the structure of the work of Bartholomew Anglicus or de Glanville, *De Proprietatibus Rerum* (Robertson 1966:622–23, 627). Robertson himself admits nevertheless that there are several obvious differences in Sahagún's work, owing in his opinion to Sahagún's having introduced certain additions to his original plan. Among these additions are the *huehuetlatolli*, which constitute the subject matter of Book 6, and the account of the conquest in Book 12 (Robertson 1966:623).

Garibay also emphasizes another probable kind of influence traceable to the prior investigations by Fray Andrés de Olmos (Garibay 1953–54: 2:2–72). His example would explain Fray Bernardino's interest in collecting texts like the *huehuetlatolli*, the account of the conquest, or the twenty sacred hymns in Nahuatl.

What Garibay and Robertson point out indubitably sheds light on the probable sources that inspired Fray Bernardino. We believe, however, that it is also useful to ask about other kinds of possible influence—not just about the structure and distribution of subjects, but more specifically about the method used in what would today be called Sahagún's field-work. It has been said with reason that Fray Bernardino was the father of ethnological investigation in the New World; hence it seems impor-tant to inquire whether his method of direct interrogation was also influenced by somewhat similar procedures used by earlier investigators. We must emphasize the fact that Sahagún himself was fully conscious of the method he had adopted and described it in various places, even giving the names of some of his informants, such as the leading elder in Tepepulco, "whose name was Don Diego de Mendoza, an old man of great distinction and ability, very experienced in all civil, military, politi-cal and even idolatrous matters" (Sahagún 1956:1:105). We find simi-lar references to the informants on native medicine, whose names he likewise wanted to preserve (Sahagún 1956:3:326 and Madrid Codex of the Royal Academy, folio 172r–72v). In addition, Fray Bernardino sev-eral times listed the young trilingual natives who were also his col-laborators.

Also important is the matter of the questionnaires governing what the friar asked the different informants on each different subject. Both in-formants and questionnaires are obviously directly related to Sahagún's fieldwork. Here too we shall have to delve deeper into the question of possible influences. In addition, the successive modifications Sahagún introduced into his work should never be overlooked as a likely index to his thought, as they reflect everything he had been perceiving during his long experience. Needless to say, our attention is not to belittle the in-fluences Fray Bernardino received from others, but rather to arrive at an adequate evaluation of the originality of his great investigation.

3. The Role of the Native Informants and Fray Bernardino's Other Native Collaborators

Many viewpoints have been formulated on this point, and they differ substantially from one another, implicitly or explicitly. Even in the six-teenth century some supposed that the Nahuatl texts collected by the Franciscan constituted a work he himself had written in Nahuatl. This is the implication, for example, of the text of the well-known Royal Charter of Philip II, dated April 22, 1577, in which we read:

> From several letters which have been written to us from those provinces, we have learned that Fray Bernardino de Sahagún of the Order of St. Francis has composed a universal history of the most noted things of that New Spain, which is a very copious account of all the rites and ceremonies and idolatries that the Indians used in their infidelity, divided into twelve books and in the Mexican language . . . (García Icazbalceta 1941a:249).

Echoing the idea that Fray Bernardino "had composed in the Mexican language," Archbishop Pedro Moya de Contreras wrote in a letter to the king, March 30, 1578, about the matter of sending Sahagún's papers to Spain:

> The universal history of these natives . . . composed by Fray Bernardino de Sahagún . . . the author has told me that he has given it to the Viceroy together with all his original papers in Spanish and Mexican and with certain transcripts he had made.
> Your Majesty may appreciate the Mexican language of this priest, which is the most elegant and proper existing in these parts . . . and thus this priest's curiosity may be of great benefit, and this is apparent in that the Inquisition will be informed about their rites when it comes to know the faults of the Indians (Paso y Troncoso 1939–42:11:50).

On the other hand, Fray Bernardino complained that some of those who knew his many books—and particularly what became Book 6, with the texts of the *huehuetlatolli*—considered them fictions and lies, something which he could have fabricated. To refute such an opinion he did not hesitate to write:

> In this book it will be clearly seen that [in] what some rivals have affirmed, that everything written in these books before such and such and after such and such are fictions and lies, they speak in passion and as liars, because what is written in this book is beyond the capacity of mortal man to make up, nor could any living man invent the language in which it stands.
> And all the learned Indians would if asked affirm that this is the language proper to their forefathers . . . (Sahagún 1956:2:53).

In much later times, when some of the texts contained in the Madrid Codices and the Florentine Codex began to be published in a fragmentary way, they were almost always attributed in the title exclusively to Fray Bernardino. Such is the case, for example, in the posthumous publication by Eduard Seler published by Cecilia Seler-Sachs in collaboration with Walter Lehmann (Seler 1927) under the title *Einige Kapitel aus dem Geschichtswerk des P. Sahagún (Some Chapters from Father Sahagún's Historical Work)*.

In reaction against this mode of presentation, Garibay (1958; 1961), León-Portilla (1958a), and López Austin (1969a) have entitled their various publications of the texts included in the Madrid Codices "Texts of Sahagún's Native Informants."

This manner of presentation, designed to emphasize the ultimate origin of these texts, has been criticized by Robertson:

> Current writing by Canon Garibay and Dr. León-Portilla on the various texts of Sahagún tends to give credit for the writing of especially the early versions, the Primeros Memoriales and Códices Matritenses, to the "informantes de Sahagún." Although they should receive some credit, it gives the "research assistants" credit for the composition of the final work, something that is not done in current bibliographic practice where the names of assistants who aid authors or compilers of monumental works often do not even appear in the introduction or preface. What is overlooked by crediting the work to the informants of Sahagún is that he himself established the pattern of the work, established a true encyclopedia form, and that he by his questions elicited information through the answers of the informants to follow his pattern and to present material he thought worth presenting. In the beginning (Códices Matritenses) the role of the informants was in essence a passive role; the role of Sahagún was the active and dominant role, the role of editor and controlling mind of the whole enterprise—in short, the responsible author of the work (Robertson 1966:625, n. 26).

Robertson's statement clearly has some validity. We have tried to emphasize that certain texts—for example those which were spontaneous answers from the informants and in particular those, like the *huehuetlatolli* or the twenty sacred hymns, undeniably attributable to pre-Hispanic Nahuatl tradition—consisted of various thoroughly native expressions transmitted by the informants. To underline this fact is in no way to diminish Sahagún's credit for collecting and organizing such materials. In calling the statements "texts of Sahagún's native informants" we are not denying that Fray Bernardino directed the final integration of all these documents; as far as the *General History of the Things of New Spain* in Spanish is concerned, he was the author. Such texts are attributed to "the informants of Sahagún" in order to point out with precision the source from which the friar obtained the narratives, and also to emphasize his method in his fieldwork.

In order to deal more adequately with this question, which is related to the origin of the different types of Nahuatl texts Sahagún collected, let us move on to the next point in our discussion.

4. The Origins and Categories to Which the Native Texts Collected by the Franciscan Can Be Attributed

There has been little investigation of this matter to date, or so we believe. General statements have been made, with frequent reference to Fray Bernardino's own testimony that he obtained most of his material from his native informants, who also presented him on occasion with some of their ancient paintings. (See, for example, Jiménez Moreno in Sahagún 1938:1:xv–xvi, xli–xlvi; Garibay 1953:2:74–79).

Other investigators have begun to attend to a matter closely related to the question of the origin of Sahagún's native texts: the questionnaires used by the friar in his research. León-Portilla (1965:15–18) analyzes the Nahuatl text dealing with the Huaxtecans (Madrid Codices, Folio 187r–88r) and attempts to reconstruct the questionnaire used by the friar when inquiring about the somatic and cultural traits of this and other ethnic groups. López Austin (1969c) has dealt with the same theme in a broader way. He has focused on the forms of the questions that can be inferred from the informants' answers on the subjects that later formed the basis for a large part of the *General History of the Things of New Spain*.

Anyone familiar with the Nahuatl documentation and Sahagún's work in Spanish has noticed the presence in many places of answers, reelaborated in various degrees, to questions asked systematically, that is, according to questionnaires formulated by the Franciscan. Such a sequence is evident in the materials "on the gods worshipped by the natives of this land of New Spain" (Book 1), or in those on food and dress, especially of the nobles (Book 8). Even more easily detectable is the type of questionnaire adopted for matters of kinship, offices and

246

posts, the parts of the human body, illness, medicines, and nations, all subjects of Book 10. Robertson has presented the hypothesis of influence from classical authors, such as Bartholomew de Glanville, who used a similar mode of exposition (Robertson 1966:625), particularly on the questions the Franciscan must have posed in asking about the many offices and posts, searching for the images of what was considered good and bad. In Book 11, "on the properties of animals, birds, fish, trees, herbs, flowers, metals and stones, and on colors," it is also possible to reconstruct the questionnaires applied, as López Austin has shown in great detail (1969c:32–35).

All of these texts, which were answers given by the informants to Sahagún's sytematic questions, reflect native traditions in varying degrees, but they also reflect the friar's own mentality. This assertion gains even more force when we remember that such answers to questionnaires were later subject to varied reelaborations by Fray Bernardino and his collaborators, the former trilingual students of the College of Tlatelolco. Other texts in Nahuatl, however, are not answers to systematic questionnaires. These seem to fall into two categories.

The first comprises certain passages in which the informants appear to speak freely, without following any outline proposed by the Franciscan. In this category are several texts included in the so-called "Primeros Memoriales." To give two examples, I shall mention the tight account of all that belonged to the lords (Madrid Codex of the Royal Palace, Folios 60r–61r) and the spontaneous information—including genuine digressions—on the *tonalli* or destinies in several parts of the texts that later made up Book 4, "On Judicial Astrology or the Art of Divination."

The second category is made up of texts which seem to stem from ancient forms of pre-Hispanic oral tradition. Among these sections should be mentioned the twenty sacred hymns in Nahuatl (Book 2); the accounts of Huitzilopochtli and Quetzalcoatl (Book 3) and that of the creation of the fifth sun (Book 7), which seem to be relics of what we would call ancient poems classifiable as epics; the long series of the *huehuetlatolli* which form Book 6; and those passages which Sahagún specifically notes as displaying a "language proper to their forefathers" (Sahagún 1956:2:53). Finally, another example is the "Book of the Conquest," that is, Book 12 of the *General History*, about which it would be appropriate to raise a number of problems, including those relating to the two editions to which it was subject.

We can see that close attention to the problem of the origins and categories to which the native testimony obtained by Sahagún can be assigned reveals differences that must necessarily be noted. We have mentioned three distinct categories:

    a) Those that were the result of answers to systematic question-naires.
    b) Those due to the informants' spontaneous expression.
    c) The body of texts which were a relic of ancient traditions of pre-Hispanic origin.

What we have shown reveals that many problems in this area still require investigation. Only a detailed analysis of Sahagún's works in Nahuatl and Spanish will clarify this important question. On it will depend, in the last analysis, a deeper understanding of the Franciscan's enterprise and results.

5. Sahagún's Intention in Writing the General History of the Things of New Spain in Spanish and the Relation of This Work to the Information Collected in Nahuatl

Concerning this point questions like the following must of course be formulated:

Is the *General History* a translation in the strict sense of a good part of the material collected in Nahuatl?

Besides the prologues, introductions, and appendices that Fray Bernardino introduced into the *General History*, are there other elements of his own making, distinct from and even opposed to the data he had collected?

Was Sahagún's interpretation of certain of his informants' texts, as presented by him in the Spanish version of the *General History*, always the result of an adequate understanding of what the informants had said?

To what extent is the *General History* a sort of late and isolated compromise, in the light of Sahagún's original intention to offer in "three columns" the Nahuatl text, the Spanish translation, and the linguistic commentaries (Sahagún 1956:1:32)?

248

Why did the author decide in several cases not to consider certain Nahuatl texts, leaving what can be described as lacunae in his Spanish work?

Though some of these questions have received attention from several scholars, it cannot be said that they have been completely answered. Garibay has astutely written in this connection:

> As is natural the two works [the *General History* and the texts in Nahuatl] do not absolutely coincide. And they should not, since Sahagún is writing his book on its own, and not a mere translation of his documents. For this reason he omits, summarizes, amends. Sometimes, although it seems implausible, he errs in the translation of his texts in Nahuatl and he omits data or translates them badly. But at other times he adds information we might seek in vain in the text of his documents. It is understood that he obtains it from another source, perhaps oral, perhaps written, which may not fall under our eyes because we do not know its nature.
>
> Thus the two works are like touchstones to each other. In them the two ways of conceiving the world are interlaced. Sahagún remains influenced by the Indians even in his style. The Indians necessarily suffer his influence but retain both their own ways of seeing, thinking, and speaking, and their resonant, elegant, and expressive language ... (Garibay in Sahagún 1956:1:11–12).

We shall only add that not until all the texts collected in the codices of Madrid and Florence have been studied and translated will it be possible to make the analyses and comparisons required to answer more precisely questions like those we have formulated concerning the narratives in those sources and in the *General History of the Things of New Spain.*

6. The Problems of the Spanish Editions of the General History Derived from the Tolosa Manuscript or from Copies of It

As we have already noted, there does not yet exist an edition of Sahagun's text that takes into consideration all the complete and fragmentary manuscripts of it that are still extant. The editions of the *General History* (or parts of it) published to date (Sahagún 1829; 1829–30; 1831–48; 1840; 1880; 1890–95; 1905–8; 1932; 1938; 1943; 1946; 1956) are derived basically from copies of the manuscript of Tolosa, which is now preserved in the library of the Royal Academy of History. Only in some of the most recent editions we have mentioned (1938, with the introductory study by Jiménez Moreno; 1946 by Acosta Saignes; 1956 by Garibay) has the Spanish text of the Florentine Codex been considered in varying degrees, but never exhaustively.

Furthermore, so far as we know, the Tolosa manuscript has never been compared with other fragmentary manuscripts, such as the one kept in the Secret Archive of the Vatican, signed by Sahagún and dedicated to Pope Pius V, of parts of Books 1 and 2 (*Col. Miscellánea,* AA. Arm. XVIII, 1816); or the manuscript of Book 4 with an extensive prologue by Sahagún, unpublished to date, in the National Library of Mexico (Moreno 1966); or the text of the "Memorials in Spanish" included at the end of the Madrid Codex of the Royal Palace (folios 16or–17or and folios 88r–96r), in the custody of the Royal Academy of History. Howard F. Cline (1971), as noted above, has made several pertinent observations on the matters here in question. In the needed critical edition of the *General History* it will also be most important to make a series of comparisons, particularly with the Nahuatl texts of the Florentine Codex and that of the Madrid Codices. As an example of one case in which the importance of such comparisons is obvious, we may mention the chapter divisions made by Sahagún in relation to the text of Book 12, on the conquest.

References to the Nahuatl text will permit the identification of numerous aspects, hitherto only vaguely suggested, of the origin of the whole of Sahagún's work. In sum, we appeal to those professionally interested in the Opus Sahagunense: almost four centuries after the writing of the Spanish text it seems to be time to prepare a critical edition of it.

7. *Questions Concerning the Forms Adopted to Date in the Translation into European Languages of the Nahuatl Texts Collected by Fray Bernardino*

To conclude this enumeration of problems, we wish to focus our attention on the necessity of discussing some of the techniques and methods used by different investigators in preparing their translations of the Nahuatl documentation. We recognize, of course, that this is a question with so many implications that it could well be the theme for another symposium of specialists. In addition, the theme could undeniably be broadened to include the general problems of translation posed by other native Nahuatl texts and even by other Mesoamerican documents in different languages.

Restricting ourselves to the materials collected by Sahagún, we can formulate as examples several particular questions:

(a) Already in the *General History*, Fray Bernardino used a peculiar form of presentation for a considerable part of the data he had collected. As noted above, even though his work cannot always be considered a Spanish translation of the Nahuatl texts, it undeniably provides a kind of approximation to them. The first question to be proposed, then, relates to translation: How much independent judgment should the modern translator use in dealing with the contents of the Madrid and Florentine codices? We emphasize this problem even though it may seem obvious, because in some contemporary translations, at least in certain parts of the Nahuatl materials, one can perceive in the translators a fear of departing from what Sahagún wrote in Spanish.

(b) In this connection, too, it is useful to remember that Sahagún himself—maintaining various degrees of fidelity to the Nahuatl text— often simplified or abbreviated, omitting the many forms of repetition or parallelism so frequent in the Nahuatl. Some modern translators have occasionally followed a similar procedure. What Garibay has described as *disfrasismos*, which are so common in Nahuatl rhetoric, often disappear in modern translations, perhaps because the translators thought that the insistent repetition did not help—and did tire—the modern reader.

(c) It is particularly difficult to make adequate and concise translations of terms referring to specific pre-Hispanic institutions that have no equivalent in modern civilization. Innumerable examples could be adduced to illustrate this problem. Let us note a few:

Neyolmelahualiztli. This word was used to designate a sort of "confession" made to the goddess Tlazolteotl under special circumstances. In the *General History* Sahagún translated it simply as "confession"; Anderson and Dibble, following Sahagún, also use "confession" in English (Sahagún 1950–69:1:23). In analyzing the word from a philological standpoint we have taken into consideration the connotation of *yolotl,* which, in association with *ixtli,* is a designation of the human being (*in ixtli, in yolotl:* the face, the heart: the person). We have also noted several other texts where *yolotl* seems to mean the dynamic nucleus, the intrinsic motility of human beings. On the basis of such philological and linguistic comparisons, instead of using the complex Western term "confession" as an equivalent, we have preferred to translate the term as "action or rite of straightening someone's heart" (*ne-yol-melahualiztli*).

Other examples that pose similar problems are words like *macehualiztli, neixtlamachiliztli, cihuacoatl* (as a designation of a governmental office), *tlacochcalcatl, tlacatecatl, tepantlato, temacpalitoti,* and *calpulli.*

In cases of this sort many translators have elected to keep the translations adopted by Sahagún and other chroniclers of the sixteenth century. These Spanish terms constitute at best a mere approximation, but very often, by alluding to completely different institutions or categories, they blur our awareness of what was characteristic and native to the pre-Hispanic world. Even though one can resolve the problem with explanatory notes, we believe that many questions still deserve careful appraisal in this field.

(d) In other cases, when the native expression offers metaphors or symbols rich in connotation and typical of the Nahuatl language, the difficulty of translating them into a modern language has tempted some investigators simply to provide descriptions to elucidate the contents of the Nahuatl text. Thus the original metaphors are lost. Here, too, one can encounter problems like those mentioned above in part (c).

(e) There are other, more general questions, like those relating to the endless difficulties involved in the critical fixing or establishment of the text. Unfortunately we do not always find in the published translations the application of such philological and linguistic criteria as permit us to know how and why a certain reading has been reached in particularly difficult or unclear cases.

It is impossible here to continue listing the problems inherent in translating these texts into European languages, but we have allowed ourselves to give the following example, in which various approaches to the translation of a particular Nahuatl text may be seen. We have chosen a text in which the informants are talking about the ideal type of the celebrated *tlamatinime,* or wise men. For greater clarity, we offer on several successive lines (and in the classical manner of inter-linear translations), first, the text in Nahuatl, then Fray Bernardino's presentation in his *General History* (1956:3:116), then the version we have published (León-Portilla 1966a:65), followed by Anderson and Dibble's (Sahagún 1950–69:10:29), and finally Schultze Jena's (1952: 75). The Nahuatl text used is that of the Florentine Codex published by Anderson and Dibble (Sahagún 1950–69).

(Flor. Cod.)	In tlamatini, tlauilli, ocutl tomaoac, ocutl apocio,
(Gen. Hist.)	El sabio es como lumbre o hacha grande,
(León-P.)	El sabio: una luz, una tea, una gruesa tea que no ahuma,
(And.–Dib.)	The wiseman [is] exemplary,
(Schultze)	Der Weise ist eine Leuchte, eine Fackel, eine starke Fackel,

(Flor. Cod.)	tezcatl coiaoac, tezcatl necoc xapo,
(Gen. Hist.)	y espejo luciente y pulido de ambas partes,
(León-P.)	un espejo horadado, un espejo agujereado por ambos lados,
(And.–Dib.)	[no translation]
(Schultze)	ein klarer Spiegel, ein grosser Spiegel, beiderseits po-lierter Spiegel,

(Flor. Cod.)	tlile, tlapale, amuxoa, amoxe
(Gen. Hist.)	Y buen dechado de los otros, entendido
(León-P.)	Suya es la tinta negra y roja, de él son los códices, de él son los códices,
(And.–Dib.)	He possesses writings; he owns books,
(Schultze)	Er is in Besitz von Bilderschriften, hat Bücher, nenn sein eigen,

(Flor. Cod.)	tlilli, tlapalli, utli, teiacanqui, tlanelo
(Gen. Hist.)	y leído, también es como camino y guía para los otros.
(León-P.)	él mismo es escritura y sabiduría, es camino, guía veraz para otros,
(And.–Dib.)	He is the tradition, the road; a leader of men, a rower,
(Schultze)	Er is den Menschen ein Vorbild, er is der Weg, er ist der Führer, der antreibt,

(Flor. Cod.)	teuicani, tlauicani, tlaiacanqui.
(Gen. Hist.)	[no translation]
(León-P.)	conduce a las personas, a las cosas, es guía en los negocios humanos.

(And.–Dib.) a companion, a bearer of responsibility, a guide.
(Schultze) er ist ihr Begleiter, ist Leiter, der ihnen vorangeht.

This example clearly shows the different modes of translation of the Nahuatl text. Fray Bernardino gives a very abbreviated version. He keeps the fundamental ideas, but he eliminates many elements, among them several metaphors. For example, "*tlille, tlapalle, amuxoa, amoxe, tlilli, tlapalli*" is reduced in his version to "good example to others, wise and well read. . . ."

The purpose of our own version has been to reflect as much as possible the different shadings of the Nahuatl text. In one particular point this translation differs substantially from Sahagún's: "*tezcatl necoc xapo*" means to the Franciscan "mirror . . . polished on both sides." We have understood it as "mirror punctured on both sides." The reason for this interpretation is the consideration of the root *xapo*, "to open, puncture." At the same time we have paid attention to the parallelism implied in the preceding phrase, "*tezcatl coiaoac*," which we have translated as "perforated mirror." As an explanation of this, we refer to the *tlachialoni*, a type of scepter with a perforated mirror which formed part of the costume of several gods and which they used to look through. Describing the *tlachialoni* elsewhere, Sahagún himself notes, "It means seer or seeing instrument because he would look through it by the hole in the center" (Sahagún 1956:1:58). By applying this to the *tlamatini* and calling it a perforated mirror we have tried to affirm that he was himself a being dedicated to the observation of all things.

In Anderson and Dibble's translation of this text, all the metaphors of the first two lines have disappeared. The *tlamatini* is described as "*tlahuilli, ocutl tomaoac, ocutl apocio, tezcatl coyahuac, tezcatl necoc xapo*"; all this is converted to "the wiseman [is] exemplary." Here and in other parts of their translation of the Florentine Codex, the intention of these investigators often seems to have been to simplify the complicated expressions of Nahuatl thought (parallelisms, metaphors, and the like).

At various points Schultze Jena translates the Spanish version of the *General History* rather than the Nahuatl text. For example, where Sahagún says "*hacha grande*," Schultze writes "*starke Fackel*." The Nahuatl text says "*ocutl apocio*," "torch of pitch pine that does not smoke." Where Sahagún says *"espejo luciente,"* Schultze says *"ein klarer Spiegel."* The text in Nahuatl says *"tezcatl coyahuac,"* "perforated mirror." Further on we have another example of this: when Sahagún says *"buen dechado de los otros"* ("a good example to others"), Schultze says *"er ist den Menschen ein Vorbild."* The Nahuatl text, *"tlilli, tlalpalli,"* "black ink, red ink," does mean "example," but it also has other connotations.

We are far from thinking that the method we used in preparing our own translations is faultless. In fact, we are interested in treating some of the inevitable problems presented to anyone who tries to translate texts like those of the Madrid and Florentine codices. It is to be hoped that a symposium on the specific subject of the philological and linguistic problems inherent in the translation of texts in Nahuatl and other Mesoamerican languages may take place in the not too distant future.

In conclusion we shall say that, in focusing on the problems encountered in connection with Sahagún's work, our intention has been to revive the interest in other forms of investigation and to suggest that investigators take full advantage of the great wealth of information obtained by the Franciscan on the pre-Hispanic past of Mexico. Instead of reiterating what is already known, those of us who have occupied ourselves professionally with certain aspects or parts of the Opus Sahagunense should attempt to make new contributions on points like those that have been noted here.

References

ACOSTA, JOSEPH DE

1962 *Historia natural y moral de las Indias.* 2d ed. (Mexico City: Fondo de Cultura Económica).

ACOSTA SAIGNES, MIGUEL

1946 *See* Sahagún 1946

ALCÓBIZ, FRAY ANDRÉS DE

1543 "Estas son las leyes que tenían los indios de la Nueva España, Anáhuac o México," *Libro de oro y tesoro índico,* pp. 169–173. Manuscript in the García Icazbalceta Collection, University of Texas Library, Austin.

ALCÓCER, IGNACIO

1938 *See* Sahagún 1938:3:375–82

ANDERSON, ARTHUR J. O.

1960 "Sahagún's Nahuatl Texts as Indigenist Documents," *Estudios de Cultura Náhuatl* 2:31–42.

1961 "Medical Practices of the Aztecs," *El Palacio* 68 (no. 2):113–18.

1966 "Refranes en un santoral en mexicano," *Estudios de Cultura Náhuatl* 6:55–62.

——— AND CHARLES E. DIBBLE

1950 *See* Sahagún 1950–69
–69

——— AND SPENCER L. ROGERS

1965 *See* Rogers & Anderson 1965
1966 *See* Rogers & Anderson 1966

ANONYMOUS

n.d. "Archivo General de la Nación," *Tierras* 20 (2,2).

1553 Codex Tudela. Unprocessed photographic copy in Latin American Library, Tulane University, New Orleans. Original in Museo de las Américas, Madrid.

1554 "Hechicerías y sortilegios." Manuscript in Biblioteca Nacional, Mexico.

1562 "Libro de entradas y profesiones de novicios." Bancroft Library, University of
–84 California, Mexican MS 216, Berkeley.

1586 "Trial against Fray Pedro de San Sebastián et al., April." Archivo General de la Nación, Inquisición 120(12), Mexico.

1587 "Hearings on the Franciscan Order." Archivo General de Indias, Sección *Audiencia de México* 21, Seville.

1899 Codex Telleriano-Remensis. Mexican manuscript from the collection of Ch.-M. Le Tellier, ed. E. T. Hamy, Paris.

1900 Il Manoscritto Messicano Vaticano 3738 detto il Codice Ríos. Riprodotto in fotocromografia a spese di Sua Eccellenza il Duca di Loubat per cura della Biblioteca Vaticana. Rome.

1904 Codex Magliabecchiano. Post-Columbian Mexican manuscript, National Library of Florence, Duke of Loubat, Rome.

1935 *Tenayuca, estudio arqueológico,* (Mexico City: Museo Nacional de Arqueología, Historia y Etnografía).

1941   "Historia de los mexicanos por sus pinturas." Appendix I, *Nueva Colección de Documentos para la Historia de México* (Mexico City: Pomar-Zurita-Relaciones Antiguas, Editorial Salvador Chávez Hayhoe).

1966   "Tratado de hechicerías y sortilegios." Summary in *Boletín de la Biblioteca Nacional* 17(Nos. 1, 2).

ANTONIO, NICOLÁS
1783   *Bibliotheca hispana nova sive hispanorum scriptorum qui ab anno MD. ad*
–88   *MDCLXXXIV. floruere notitia.* 2 vols. (Madrid).

BALLESTEROS GAIBROIS, MANUEL
1948   "Un manuscrito mejicano desconocido," *Saitabí* 6(No. 26):63–68.
1964   *See* Sahagún 1964

BANDELIER, ADOLF E.
1877   "On the Art of War and Mode of Warfare of the Ancient Mexicans." In *Tenth Annual Report of the Peabody Museum of Archaeology and Ethnology,* pp. 95–161 (Salem, Mass.).

1878   "On the Distribution and Tenure of Lands, and the Customs with Respect to Inheritance, among the Ancient Mexicans." In *Eleventh Annual Report of the Peabody Museum of Archaeology and Ethnology,* pp. 385–448 (Salem, Mass.).

1880   "On the Social Organization and Mode of Government of the Ancient Mexicans." In *Twelfth Annual Report of the Peabody Museum of Archaeology and Ethnology,* vol. 2, pp. 557–699 (Cambridge, Mass.).

BANDELIER, FANNY R.
1932   *See* Sahagún 1932

BARLOW, R. H.
1948   "El Códice de Tlatelolco." In *Anales de Tlatelolco: Fuentes para la Historia de México,* pp. 105–28 (Mexico City: Antigua Librería Robredo).
1949   "The Extent of the Empire of the Culhua Mexica," *Ibero-Americana* 28:1–141.

BAUDOT, GEORGES
1964   "Le 'complot' franciscain contre la première Audience de Mexique," *Caravelle, Cahiers du Monde Hispanique et luso-brésilien* 2:15–34.
1965   "L'institution de la dîme pour les Indiens du Mexique. Remarques et Documents." In *Mélanges de la Casa de Velázquez,* Vol. 1, pp. 167–221 (Madrid & Paris: E. de Boccard).
1969   "Fray Rodrigo de Sequera, avocat du diable pour une histoire interdite." *Caravelle, Cahiers du monde hispanique et luso-brésilien* 12:47–82.
1972   "Apariciones diabólicas en un texto náhuatl de Fray Andrés de Olmos," *Estudios de Cultura Náhuatl* 10:349–57.

BAUTISTA, JUAN
1600   *Huehuetlatolli, o Pláticas de los Viejos* (Mexico City).

BERLIN, HEINRICH
1948   *Anales de Tlatelolco* (Mexico City: Antigua Librería Robredo).

BEVAN, BERNARD
1938   *History of Spanish Architecture* (London: Batsford).
1950   *Historia de la arquitectura española* (Barcelona: Editorial Juventud).

References

BEYER, HERMANN
1922   "El llamado 'Calendario Azteca' en la Historia del P. Sahagún," *Memorias de la Sociedad Científica Antonio Alzate* 40:669–74.

BIONDELLI, BERNARDINUS
1858   *See* Sahagún 1858

BOBAN, EUGENE
1891   *Documents pour servir à l'histoire du Mexique. Catalogue raisonnée de la Collection de M. E. Eugène Goupil (Ancienne Collection J. M. A. Aubin)*. 2 vols. (Paris: Ernest Leroux).

BOTURINI BENADUCCI, LORENZO
1746   *Idea de una nueva historia general de la América Septentrional* (Madrid: Juan de Zúñiga).

BRINTON, DANIEL G.
1890   *Rig-Veda americanus. Sacred songs of the ancient Mexicans with a gloss in Nahuatl*. Library of Aboriginal American Literature 8 (Philadelphia).

BUSTAMANTE, CARLOS MARÍA DE
1829   *See* Sahagún 1829
1829   *See* Sahagún 1829–30
–30
1840   *See* Sahagún 1840
1890   *See* Sahagún 1890–95
–95

CALNEK, EDWARD E.
1966   The Aztec Imperial Bureaucracy. Paper presented at Annual Meeting, American Anthropological Association, Pittsburgh.
1969   Dynastic Succession in Aztec Society. Paper read at Annual Meeting, American Society for Ethnohistory, Ithaca, New York.
1972a   "Settlement Pattern and Chinampa Agriculture at Tenochtitlan," *American Antiquity* 37:104–15.
1972b   "The Internal Structure of Cities in America. Pre-Columbian Cities: the Case of Tenochtitlan." In *Urbanización y proceso social en América* (Lima: Instituto de Estudios Peruanos).
1973   "The Organization of Urban Food Supply Systems: the Case of Tenochtitlan," *Revista de Indias*. In press.

CAROCHI, HORACIO
1892   "Arte de la lengua mexicana," *Anales del Museo Nacional* (Mexico).

CARRASCO, PEDRO
1971   "Social Organization of Ancient Mexico." In *Handbook of Middle American Indians*, ed. R. Wauchope, vol. 10, no. 1 (Austin: University of Texas Press).

CASO, ALFONSO
1936   "*La Religión de Los Aztecas*." In *Enciclopedia Illustrada, Mexicana* (Mexico).
1963   "Land Tenure among the Ancient Mexicans," *American Anthropologist* 65:863–78.

CASTILLO FARRERAS, VICTOR M.
1969   "Caminos del mundo náhuatl," *Estudios de Cultura Náhuatl* 8:175–88.

CERVANTES DE SALAZAR, FRANCISCO
1914 *Crónica de la Nueva España* (Madrid: Hispanic Society of America).
CHAVERO, ALFREDO
n.d. "Historia antigua y de la conquista." In *México a través de los siglos*, ed. Vicente Riva Palacio, vol. 1 (Mexico City: Publicaciones Herrerías).
1877 "Sahagún," *Boletín de la Sociedad de Geografía y Estadística de la República Mexicana*, Tercera Epoca 6.
1882 "Apuntes sobre bibliografía mexicana. Sahagún," *Boletín de la Sociedad de Geografía y Estadística de la República Mexicana*, Tercera Epoca 6:1–3, 5–42.
1948 "Sahagún," *Aportación Histórica*, 2d series (Mexico City: Vargas Rea).
CHIMALPAHÍN QUAUHTLEHUANITZIN,
DOMINGO FRANCISCO DE SAN ANTON MUÑÓN
1889 *Annales*. ed. Rémi Siméon (Paris: Maisonneuve et Ch. Leclerc).
CHUECA GOITIA, FERNANDO
1953 Arquitectura del siglo XVI. *Ars Hispaniae*, No. 11 (Madrid: Editorial Plus-Ultra).
CLARK, JAMES COOPER
1938 *The Mexican Manuscript Known as the Collection of Mendoza and Preserved in the Bodleian Library, Oxford* (London: Waterlow & Sons).
CLAVIJERO, FRANCISCO XAVIER
n.d. "Reglas de la lengua mexicana." Biblioteca dell'Archiginnasio, Mezzofanti MS xii–10, Bologna.
1958 *Historia Antigua de México*. 4 vols. (Mexico City: Editorial Porrúa).
CLINE, HOWARD F.
1970 "Notas sobre la historia de la conquista de Sahagún." In Bernardo García Martínez et al., *Historia y sociedad en el mundo de habla española*, pp. 121–40 (Mexico City: Colegio de Mexico).
1971 "Missing and variant prologues and dedications in Sahagún's *Historia General*: Texts and English translations," *Estudios de Cultura Náhuatl* 9:237–52.
CODEX
    Badianus: *See* Emmart 1940
    Borbonicus: *See* Hamy 1899
    Florentine: *See* Sahagún 1950–69
    Franciscan: *See* García Icazbalceta 1941a
    Madrid: *See* Sahagún 1905–8
    Magliabecchiano: *See* Nuttall 1903
    Mendoza: *See* Clark 1938
    Ríos: *See* Anon. 1900
    Telleriano Remensis: *See* Anon. 1899
    Tlatelolco: *See* Barlow 1948
    Tudela: *See* Anon. 1553
    Vaticanus A: *See* Anon. 1900
CONQUISTADOR ANÓNIMO
1941 *Relación de algunas cosas de la Nueva España y de la gran ciudad de Temestitan México* (Mexico City: Editorial América).
COOK, SHERBURNE F. & WOODROW BORAH
1960 "The Indian Population of Central Mexico, 1531–1610," *Ibero-Americana* 44.

References

CORTÉS, HERNÁN
1963   *Cartas de Relación* (Mexico City: Editorial Porrúa).

COSTUMBRES
        See Gómez de Orozco 1945

CUEVAS, MARIANO
1914   *Documentos inéditos del siglo XVI para la historia de México* (Mexico City: Museo Nacional de Arqueología, Historia y Etnología).
1922   *Historia de la iglesia en México.* 5 vols. (Tlalpam: Patricio Sanz).

DÍAZ DEL CASTILLO, BERNAL
1964   *Historia Verdadera la Conquista de la Nueva España* (Mexico City: Editorial Porrúa).

DIBBLE, CHARLES E.
1959   "Nahuatl Names for Body Parts," *Estudios de Cultura Náhuatl* 1:27–30.
1962   "Spanish Influence on the Náhuatl Texts of Sahagún's Historia," *Akten des 34en Internationalen Amerikanistenkongresses*:244–47.
1963   "Glifos fonéticos del Códice Florentino," *Estudios de Cultura Náhuatl* 4:55–60.
1971   "La olografía de fray Bernardino de Sahagún," *Estudios de Cultura Náhuatl* 9:231–36.
———— AND ARTHUR J. O. ANDERSON
1950   *See* Sahagún 1950–69
–69

DURÁN, DIEGO
1951   *Historia de las Indias de Nueva España y Islas de Tierra Firme.* 2 vols. (Mexico City: Atlas).

EGUIARA Y EGUREN, JUAN JOSÉ DE
1755   Bibliotheca Mexicana sive eruditorum historia virorum 1(A, B, C), Privately Printed, Mexico. University of Texas Latin America Library, Austin.

EMMART, EMILY WALCOTT
1940   *The Badianus Manuscript,* (Baltimore: Johns Hopkins University Press).

FLORENTINE CODEX
        See Sahagún 1950–69

FRANCO C., JOSÉ LUIS
1961   "Representaciones de la mariposa en Mesoamérica," *El México Antiguo* 60:195–244.

GAONA, JUAN DE, ET AL.
1538   "Miscelánea Sagrada." Biblioteca Nacional de México, MS 1477, Mexico.
–60

GARCÍA ICAZBALCETA, JOAQUÍN
1870   "Noticias del Autor y Tabla de Correspondencias." In Mendieta 1870:xvii–xlv.
1891   "Al Lector." In *Nueva Colección de Documentos* (Mexico City: Editorial Salvador Chávez Hayhoe).
1892a *Códice Mendieta.* 2 vols. (Mexico City: Editorial Salvador Chávez Hayhoe).
1892b *Nueva colección de documentos inéditos para la historia de México* (Mexico City: Díaz de León).
1941a *Códice Franciscano* (Mexico City: Editorial Salvador Chávez Hayhoe).

1941b *Nueva Colección de Documentos para La Historia de México* (Mexico City: Editorial Salvador Chávez Hayhoe).

1947 *Don Fray Juan de Zumárraga*. 4 vols. (Mexico City: Editorial Porrúa).

1954 *Bibliografía Mexicana del siglo xvi*. (Mexico City: Fondo de Cultura Económica).

GARCÍA PAYÓN, JOSÉ

1958 "Evolución histórica del Totonacapan." In *Miscelánea Paul Rivet*, pp. 443–53 (Mexico City: Universidad Nacional Autónoma de México).

1965 "Descripción del pueblo de Gueytlapan por el alcalde mayor Juan de Carrión." In *Cuadernos de la Facultad de Filosofía, Letras y Ciencias* 23 (Xalapa: Universidad Veracruzana).

1971 "Archaeology of Central Veracruz." In *Handbook of Middle American Indians*, ed. Robert Wauchope, vol. 2, pp. 505–42 (Austin: University of Texas Press).

GARIBAY K., ÁNGEL MARÍA

1940a *Llave del náhuatl* (Otumba).

1940b *Poesía indígena de la altiplanície*. Biblioteca del Estudiante Universitario 11 (Mexico City: Universidad Nacional Autónoma de México).

1943 Huehuetlatolli, Documento A, *Tlalocan* 1 (Nos. 1, 2).

1943 "Paralipópenos de Sahagún," *Tlalocan* 1:307–13; 2:167–74, 249–54.
–44

1945 *Épica náhuatl*. Biblioteca del Estudiante Universitario 51 (Mexico City: Universidad Nacional Autónoma de México).

1948 "Relación breve de las fiestas de los dioses," *Tlalocan* 2 (No. 4):289–320.

1952 "Versiones discutibles del texto náhuatl de Sahagún," *Tlalocan* 3 (No. 2).

1953 "Fray Bernardino de Sahagún. Relación de los textos que no aprovechó en su obra." In *Aportaciones a la Investigación Folklórica de México* (Mexico City: Sociedad Folklórica de México y Universidad Nacional Autónoma de México).

1953 *Historia de la literatura náhuatl*. 2 vols. (Mexico City: Editorial Porrúa).
–54

1956 *See* Sahagún 1956

1958 *Veinte himnos sacros de los nahuas*. Fuentes Indígenas de la Cultura Náhuatl. Informantes de Sahagún 2 (Mexico City: Universidad Nacional Autónoma de México).

1961 *Vida económica de Tenochtitlan*. Fuentes Indígenas de la Cultura Náhuatl. Textos de los Informantes Indígenas de Sahagún 3 (Mexico City: Universidad Nacional Autónoma de México).

1963 *Panorama literario de los pueblos nahuas* (Mexico City: Editorial Porrúa).

1964 *La Literatura de los aztecas*. (Mexico City, Joaquín Mortiz).

1965 *Teogonía e historia de los mexicanos: tres opúsculos del siglo XVI* (Mexico City: Editorial Porrúa).

1966 "Manuscritos en lengua náhuatl de la Biblioteca Nacional," *Boletín de la Biblioteca Nacional* 17 (Nos. 1, 2):5–19.

———— AND MIGUEL LEÓN-PORTILLA

1961 *See* León-Portilla & Angel María Garibay K., 1961

GIBSON, CHARLES

1964 *The Aztecs under Spanish Rule: a History of the Indians of the Valley of Mexico, 1519–1810* (Stanford: Stanford University Press).

References

GÓMEZ DE OROZCO, FEDERICO
1945   "Costumbres, fiestas, enterramientos y diversas formas de proceder de los indios de Nueva España," *Tlalocan* 2:37–63.

GONZÁLEZ, JUAN
1581   "Relación de Tetela, Papeles de Nueva España." In Paso y Troncoso 1905–8: 5:143–73.

HAGGARD, J. VILLASANA
1941   *Handbook for Translators of Spanish Historical Documents* (Oklahoma City: Semco Color Press).

HAMY, E. T., ED.
1899   *Codex Borbonicus, manuscrit mexicain de la Bibliothéque du Palais Bourbon* (Paris).

HERNÁNDEZ, FRANCISCO
1959   *Historia natural de Nueva España. In Obras Completas*, vols. 2, 3. (Mexico
-67   City: Universidad Nacional Autónoma de México).

HERRERA, ANTONIO DE
1726   *Historia general de los hechos de los castellanos.* (Madrid: Nicolás Rodríguez
-28   Franco).
1945   *Historia general de los hechos de los castellanos.* 5 vols. (Buenos Aires:
-47   Guarnía).

IGUÍNIZ, JUAN B.
1918   *See* Sahagún 1918

IXTLILXÓCHITL, FERNANDO DE ALVA
1952   *Obras Históricas,* ed. Alfredo Chavero. (Mexico City: Editora Nacional).

JIMÉNEZ MORENO, WIGBERTO
1938   *See* Sahagún, 1938:1:xiii–lxxxi

DE JONGHE, EDOUARD
1902   "Histoyre du Mechique," *Journal de la Société des Américanistes de Paris* 2:1–41.

JOURDANET, D. & RÉMI SIMÉON
1880   *See* Sahagún 1880

KATZ, FRIEDRICH
1966   *Situación social y económica de los aztecas durante los siglos XV y XVI* (Mexico City: Instituto de Investigaciones Históricas, Universidad Nacional Autónoma de México).

KELLY, ISABEL & ANGEL PALERM
1952   "The Tajín Totonac." In *Institute of Social Anthropology Publication 13* (Washington, D.C.: Smithsonian Institution).

KINGSBOROUGH, LORD
1831   *See* Sahagún 1831–48
-48

KIRCHOFF, PAUL
1954   "Land Tenure in Ancient Mexico," *Revista Mexicana de Estudios Antro-
-55   pológicos* 14:351–61.

KUBLER, GEORGE A.
1948   *Mexican Architecture of the Sixteenth Century*. 2 vols. (New Haven: Yale University Press).
1961   "On the Colonial Extinction of the Motifs of Pre-Columbian Art." In Samuel K. Lothrop et al., *Essays in Pre-Columbian Art and Archaeology*," pp. 14–34, 485–86 (Cambridge, Mass.: Harvard University Press).
1964   *Santos: An Exhibition of the Religious Folk Art of New Mexico* (Fort Worth, Texas: Amon Carter Museum of Western Art).
1966   "Indianismo y mestizaje como tradiciones americanas, medievales y clásicas," *Boletín del Centro de Investigaciones Historicas y Estéticas* 4:51–61.
———— AND CHARLES GIBSON
1951   "The Tovar Calendar," *Memoirs of the Connecticut Academy of Arts and Sciences* 11.
———— AND MARTIN SORIA
1959   *Art and Architecture in Spain and Portugal and Their American Dominions 1500 to 1800* (Baltimore: Penguin Books).
LANDA, DIEGO DE
1941   *Landa's Relacion de las Cosas de Yucatán*, ed. Alfred M. Tozzer (Cambridge, Mass.: Peabody Museum).
LAS CASAS, BARTOLOMÉ DE
1958   *Apologética historia*. Vols. 3–4 of *Obras Escogidas de Fray Bartolomé de las Casas* (Madrid: Biblioteca de Autores Españoles).
1967   *Apologética historia*, ed. Edmundo O'Gorman (Mexico City: Instituto de Investigaciones Históricas).
LEAL, LUIS
1955   "El Libro XII de Sahagún," *Historia Mexicana* 5(2:18):184–210.
LEHMANN, WALTER
1927   *Einige Kapitel aus dem Geschichtswerk des Fray Bernardino de Sahagun* (Stuttgart: Strecker & Schröder).
1949   *See Sahagún 1949*
LEÓN, MARTÍN DE
1611   *Camino del Cielo* (Mexico)
LEÓN PINELO, ANTONIO DE
1629   *Epítome de la Biblioteca Oriental i Occidental, Náutica i Geográfica* (Madrid).
LEÓN-PORTILLA, MIGUEL
1958a   *Ritos, sacerdotes y atavíos de los dioses*. Fuentes Indígenas de los Informantes de Sahagún 1(Mexico City: Universidad Nacional Autónoma de México).
1958b   *Siete ensayos sobre cultura náhuatl* (Mexico City: Universidad Nacional Autónoma de México).
1959   *Filosofía náhuatl* (Mexico City: Universidad Nacional Autónoma de México).
1960   "Sahagún y su investigación integral de la cultura náhuatl," *Nicaragua Indígena* 30:15–21.
1961   *Los antiguos mexicanos*. (Mexico City: Fondo de Cultura Económica).
1963   *Aztec Thought and Culture* (Norman: University of Oklahoma Press).
1965   "Los Huaxtecos, según los informantes de Sahagún," *Estudios de Cultura Náhuatl* 5:15–29.

References

1966a *La filosofía náhuatl, estudiada en sus fuentes.* 3d ed. (Mexico City: Universidad Nacional Autónoma de México).

1966b "Significado de la obra de fray Bernardino de Sahagún," *Estudios de Historia Novohispana* 1:13–28.

1969 "Ramírez de Fuenleal y las antigüedades mexicanas," *Estudios de Cultura Náhuatl* 8:9–50.

———— AND ÁNGEL MARÍA GARIBAY K.

1961 *Visión de los vencidos. Relaciones indígenas de la conquista.* Biblioteca del Estudiante Universitario 81 (Mexico City: Universidad Nacional Autónoma de México).

LÓPEZ, AUSTIN, ALFREDO

1963a El hacha nocturna," *Estudios de Cultura Náhuatl* 4:179–86.

1963b "La fiesta del fuego nuevo según el Códice florentino." In *Anuario de Historia* 3. Facultad de Filosofía y Letras, pp. 73–91 (Mexico City: Universidad Nacional Autónoma de México).

1965a "El templo mayor de México Tenochtitlán según los informantes indígenas," *Estudios de Cultura Náhuatl* 5:75–102.

1965b "Descripción de estupefacientes en el Códice florentino," *Revista de la Universidad de México* 19 (No. 5):17–19.

1967 "Juegos rituales aztecas." *Instituto de Investigaciones Históricas, Cuadernos, Série Documental* 5 (Mexico City: Universidad Nacional Autónoma de México).

1969a *Augurios y abusiones.* Fuentes Indígenas de la Cultura Náhuatl, Textos de los Informantes Indígenas de Sahagún 4 (Mexico City: Universidad Nacional Autónoma de México).

1969b De las enfermedades del cuerpo humano y de las medicinas contra ellas," *Estudios de Cultura Náhuatl* 9:51–122.

1969c "Estudio acerca del método de investigación de fray Bernardino de Sahagún, los cuestionarios" (Thesis for the Licentiate in History, Facultad de Filosofía y Letras, Universidad Nacional Autónoma de México, Mexico).

1971a "De las plantas medicinales y de otras cosas medicinales," *Estudios de Cultura Náhuatl* 9:125–230.

1971b *Textos de medicina náhuatl* (Mexico City: Secretaría de Educación Pública).

1972 Textos acerca de las partes del cuerpo humano y de las enfermedades y medicinas en los Primeros Memoriales de Sahagún," *Estudios de Cultura Náhuatl* 10:129–54.

LYELL, JAMES PATRICK RONALDSON

1926 *Early Book Illustration in Spain* (London: Grafton and Co.).

MADRID CODEX OF THE ROYAL ACADEMY OF HISTORY

See Sahagún 1905–8; 1964

MADRID CODEX OF THE ROYAL PALACE

See Sahagún 1905–8; 1964

MAGDALANO, MAURICIO

1943 See Sahagún 1943

MARAVALL, JOSÉ ANTONIO

1949 "La utopía político-religiosa de los franciscanos en Nueva España," *Estudios Americanos* 2:199–228.

MARTÍN DEL CAMPO, RAFAEL
1938 "Ensayo de interpretación del Libro Undécimo de la Historia General de las
-40 cosas de la Nueva España de Fray Bernardino de Sahagún," *Anales del Instituto de Biología* 9–11 (Mexico).
1959 "La anatomía entre los mexica," *Revista de la Sociedad Mexicana de Historia Natural* 17:145–67.

MEADE, JOAQUÍN
1950 "Fray Andrés de Olmos," *Memorias de la Academia Mexicana de la Historia* 9(No. 4):374–452.

MELGAREJO VIVANCO, JOSÉ LUIS
1966 "Los Calendarios de Zempoala." In *Cuadernos del Instituto de Antropología* 2 (Xalapa: Universidad Veracruzana).

MENDIETA, GERÓNIMO DE
1870 *Historia eclesiástica indiana* (Mexico City: Antigua Librería).
1945 *Historia eclesiástica indiana.* 4 vols. (Mexico City: Editorial Salvador Chávez Hayhoe).

MILLARES CARLO, AGUSTÍN
1929 *Paleografía Española.* 2 vols. (Barcelona: Editorial Labro).

MOLINA, ALONSO DE
1970 *Vocabulario en lengua castellana y mexicana y mexicana y castellana* (Mexico City: Editorial Porrúa).

MONZÓN, ARTURO
1949 *El calpulli en la organización social de los tenochca.* Publicaciones del Instituto de Historia, Primera Series 14 (Mexico: Instituto de Historia).

MORENO, ROBERTO
1966 "Manuscritos en lengua náhuatl de la Biblioteca Nacional de México," *Boletín de la Biblioteca Nacional* 17(Nos. 1, 2):21–210.

MORGAN, LEWIS HENRY
1877 *Ancient Society* (Chicago: C. H. Kerr).

MOTOLINÍA (TORIBIO DE BENAVENTE)
1941 *Historia de los indios de la Nueva España* (Mexico City: Editorial Salvador Chávez Hayhoe).

MUÑOZ CAMARGO, DIEGO
1892 *Historia de Tlaxcala* (Mexico City: Secretaría de Fomento).

NAVARRO, JOSÉ GABRIEL
1955 *Los Franciscanos en la conquista y colonización de América* (Madrid: Ediciones Cultura Hispánica).

NICHOLSON, H. B.
In press "Sahagún's Primeros Memoriales, Tepepulco, 1558–1561." In *Handbook of Middle American Indians*, Robert Wauchope ed. (Austin: University of Texas Press).

NICOLAU D'OLWER, LLUIS
1952 *Fray Bernardino de Sahagún (1499–1590).* Historiadores de América 9 (Mexico City: Instituto Panamericano de Geografía e Historia).
1973 "Fray Bernardino de Sahagún." In *Handbook of Middle American Indians*, ed. Robert Wauchope (Austin: University of Texas Press).

266

References

NUTTALL, ZELIA
1902   *Codex Nuttall: Facsimile of an Ancient Mexican Codex Belonging to Lord Zouche of Harynworth, England.* Introduction by Zelia Nuttall (Cambridge, Mass.: Peabody Museum).
1903   *The Book of Life of the Ancient Mexicans* (Berkeley: University of California).
1927   *See* Sahagún 1927

O'GORMAN, EDMUNDO
1972   "Cuatro Historiadores de Indias," *Sep-Setentas* 51 (Mexico: Secretaría de Educación Pública).

OLMOS, ANDRÉS DE
1547   "Arte de lengua mexicana." Copy in Latin American Library, Tulane University, New Orleans.
1552   "Tratado de Los Siete Pecados Capitales," *Sermones en Mexicano,* folios 312–87. Manuscript in Biblioteca Nacional, Mexico.
1875   *Grammaire de la langue náhuatl ou mexicaine,"* ed. Rémi Siméon (Paris).
1912   "Proceso seguido por Fray Andrés de Olmos en contra del cacique de Matlatlan." In *Publicaciones del Archivo General de la Nación* 3 (Mexico).

PAREDES, IGNACIO
1910   *Compendio del arte de la lengua mexicana del P. Horacio Carochi* (Mexico).

PASO Y TRONCOSO, FRANCISCO DEL
1886   "Fragmentos del Padre Sahagún, 1585." MS in Chapultepec, Archivo Histórico. Colección Papeles Sueltos, Segunda Série, Legajo No. 88, Documento No. 3, Mexico.
1896   "Etudes sur le codex mexicain du P. Sahagún conservé à la Bibliothèque Mediceo-Laurenziana de Florence," *Revista della Biblioteche e degli Archivi Firenze* 7:171–74.
1903   "Estudios sobre el códice mexicano del P. Sahagún," *Anales del Museo Nacional de México,* Segunda Epoca 1:1–34, Mexico.
1905   *Papeles de Nueva España* (Madrid).
–06
1905   *See* Sahagún 1905–08
–08
1939   (Ed.) *Epistolario de Nueva España.* 16 vols. (Mexico City: Antigua Librería
–42   Robredo).

PEÑAFIEL, ANTONIO
1885   *Nombres Geográficos de México* (Mexico City: Secretaría de Fomento).
1890   *Monumentos del arte mexicano antiguo.* 3 vols. (Berlin: A. Asher).
1897   *Nomenclatura Geográfica de México* (Mexico City: Secretaría de Fomento).
1901   "Huehuetlatolli." Part 3 of *Collección de documentos para la historia mexicana* (Mexico).

PHELAN, JOHN LEDDY
1956   *The Millennial Kingdom of the Franciscans in the New World. A Study of the Writings of Gerónimo de Mendieta (1525–1604)* (Berkeley and Los Angeles: University of California Press).

PILLING, JAMES C.
1895   "The Writings of Padre Andrés de Olmos in the Languages of Mexico," *American Anthropologist,* Old Series 8:43–60.

PINTURAS
    See Anon. 1941
POMAR, JUAN BAUTISTA
    n.d. *Relación de Tetzcoco* (Mexico City: Editorial Salvador Chávez Hayhoe).
PONCE, ALONSO
1873 *Viaje o relación breve y verdadera de algunas cosas de las muchas que sucedieron al Padre Fray Alonso Ponce.* 2 vols. Colección de Documentos Inéditos para le Historia de España 57, 58 (Madrid).
POU Y MARTÍ, JOSÉ MARIA
1924 *See* Sahagún 1924
RAMÍREZ, JOSE FERNANDO
1885 "Códices mexicanos de fray Bernardino de Sahagún," *Boletín de la Real Academia de la Historia* 6:85ff.
1903a "Apuntes de la cronología de Sahagún," *Anales del Museo Nacional*, Primera Epoca 7:137ff.
1903b "Códices mexicanos de fray Bernardino de Sahagún," *Anales del Museo Nacional*, Segunda Epoca 1:1–34.
RICARD, ROBERT
1947 *La conquista espiritual de México* (Mexico City: Editorial Jus & Editorial Polis).
ROBERTSON, DONALD
1959 *Mexican Manuscript Painting of the Early Colonial Period* (New Haven: Yale University Press).
1966 "The Sixteenth Century Mexican Encyclopedia of Fray Bernardino de Sahagún," *Cuadernos de Historia Mundial* 9(No. 3):617–28.
ROGERS, SPENCER L. & ARTHUR J. O. ANDERSON
1965 "El inventario anatómico sahaguntino," *Estudios de Cultura Náhuatl* 5:115–22.
1966 "La terminología anatómica de los mexicas precolombinos," *Actas y Memorias, XXXVI Congreso Internacional de Americanistas, España, 1964* 5:69–76.
ROSELL, CAYETANO
1883 "Historia universal de las cosas de la Nueva España por el M. R. P. Bernardino de Sahagún," *Boletín de la Real Academia de la Historia* 2:181ff.
RUIZ DE ALARCÓN, HERNANDO
1953 "Tratado de las supersticiones y costumbres gentílicas que oy viuen entre los indios naturales de esta Nueua España, escrito en México, año de 1629." In Jacinto de la Serna et al., *Tratado de las idolatrías*, vol. 2, pp. 17–130 (Mexico City: Ediciones Fuente Cultural).
SAHAGÚN, BERNARDINO DE
    (Note: Dates of unpublished manuscripts are assigned for easy reference only; many are likely to be revised in the light of works now in press.)
    Synonymous Titles:
    Cantares See Sahagún 1583
    "Doctrinas" *See* Sahagún 1579b

References

Evangelios y epístolas See Sahagún 1858
"Libro de los coloquios" *See* Sahagún 1564a
"Libro perdido de las pláticas o coloquios de los doce primeros misioneros de México" *See* Sahagún 1564a
"Modo y plática que los doce primeros padres tuvieron . . ." *See* Sahagún 1564a
"Sermones" *See* Sahagún 1540a

n.d.a "Relación de los edificios del gran templo de México." MS, Biblioteca de la Real Academia de la Historia, Madrid.

n.d.b "Tratado y manual de doctrina cristiana." MS, Biblioteca de la Universidad Autónoma de San Luis Potosí, San Luis Potosí.

1540a "Sermonario." Ayer MS 1485, Newberry Library, Chicago.

1540b "Santoral." Ayer MS 1485, Newberry Library, Chicago.

1560 "Primeros Memoriales" *See* Sahagún 1905–8:7

1561 "Memoriales Complementarios" *See* Sahagún 1905–8:6

1563 "Memoriales con Escolios" *See* Sahagún 1905–8:6,7

1564a "Coloquios y doctrina cristiana" (*See* Sahagún 1924; 1927; 1944; 1949). MS in Secret Archive of the Holy Office, Rome.

1564b "Memoriales en Tres Columnas" *See* Sahagún 1905–8:7, 8

1565a Madrid Codex of the Royal Academy of History. MS in Real Academia de la Historia, Madrid. (*See* Sahagún 1905–8:8)

1565b Madrid Codex of the Royal Palace. MS in Real Academia de la Historia, Madrid. (*See* Sahagún 1905–8)

1566 Book 4. MS in Biblioteca Nacional, Mexico.

1568 "Memoriales en Español" *See* Sahagún 1905–8:8: folios 160r–70r, 88r–96r

1570 "Breve Compendio." MS in Vatican Library, Rome. (*See* Sahagún 1942)

1574a "Ejercicios cotidianos en lengua mexicana." Ayer MS 1484, Newberry Library, Chicago.

1574b "Vida de San Bernardino." Whereabouts unknown.

1577 Florentine Codex. Mediceo-Laurenziana Library, Florence. (*See* Sahagún 1950–69)

1578 "Manual del cristiano." Whereabouts unknown.

1579a "Postillas." Ayer MS 1486, Newberry Library, Chicago.

1579b "Apéndice a la postilla o doctrina cristiana." Ayer MS 1486, Newberry Library, Chicago.

1580 "Manuscrito de Tolosa." MS in Real Academia de la Historia, Madrid.

1583 *Psalmodia Christiana y Sermonario de los sanctos del año, en lengua mexicana.* Pedro Ocharte, Mexico.

1585a "Arte adivinatoria." MS 1628 bis: folios 116–42, Biblioteca Nacional, Mexico.

1585b "Calendario mexicano, latino y castellano." MS 1628 bis: folios 96–112, Biblioteca Nacional, Mexico.

1585c "Libro de la Conquista." Librería Laietana, Barcelona (according to Jiménez Moreno in Sahagún 1938).

1585d "Vocabulario Trilingüe." Ayer MS 1478, Newberry Library, Chicago.

1586 "Letters to the King." Archivo General de Indias, Sección Audiencia de
–87 México 287, Seville.

17th c. "Calendario mexicano, latino y castellano" (*See* León 1611)

1793   Panes copy of Manuscrito de Tolosa (*See* Sahagún 1938). MS in Biblioteca Nacional, Mexico.

1820   Bauza copy of Manuscrito de Tolosa. MS in New York Public Library. (*See* Sahagún 1831–48)

1829   *Historia de la Conquista de México*, ed. Carlos María de Bustamante (Mexico City: Imprenta de Galván).

1829
–30   *Historia general de las cosas de Nueva España*, ed. Carlos María de Bustamante, 3 vols. (Mexico City: Imprenta del Ciudadano Alexandro Valdés).

1831
–48   *Antiquities of Mexico*, ed. Lord Kingsborough. 9 vols. (London).

1840   *La aparición de Nuestra Señora de Guadalupe de México comprobada*, ed. Carlos María Bustamante (Mexico).

1858   *Evangelarium, epistolarium et lectionarium aztecum sive mexicano nuper reperto*, ed. Bernardinus Biondelli (Milan).

1880   *Histoire générale des choses de la Nouvelle Espagne*, ed. D. Jourdanet & Rémi Siméon (Paris: G. Masson).

1890
–95   *Historia General de las cosas de Nueva España*, ed. Carlos María Bustamante. 4 vols. (Mexico City: Imprenta Litografía y Encuadernación de Ireneo Paz).

1905
–8   *Historia general de las cosas de Nueva España*, ed. Francisco del Paso y Troncoso. 4 vols. (Madrid: Fototipia de Hauser y Menet).

1918   "Calendario mexicano, latino y castellano, atribuidos a Fray Bernardino de Sahagún," ed. Juan B. Iguíniz, *Boletin de la Biblioteca Nacional* 12:189–272.

1924   "El libro perdido de las pláticas y coloquios de los doce primeros misioneros de México," ed. José María Pou y Martí, *Miscelánea Francesco Ehrle* 3:281–333. Vatican Library, Rome.

1927   "El libro perdido de las pláticas o coloquios de los doce primeros misioneros de México," *Revista Mexicana de Estudios Históricos* 1:101–41 and appendix.

1932   *A History of Ancient Mexico*, ed. Carlos María de Bustamante, trans. Fanny R. Bandelier (Nashville).

1938   *Historia general de las cosas de Nueva España*, ed. Joaquín Ramírez Cabañas; Wigberto Jiménez Moreno, preliminary note; studies by Nicolás León and Ignacio Alcócer, 5 vols. (Mexico City: Pedro Robredo).

1942   *Breve compendio de los ritos idolátricos de Nueva España*.

1943   *Suma indiana*, ed. Mauricio Magdaleno, Biblioteca del Estudiante Universitario 42 (Mexico City: Universidad Nacional Autónoma de México).

1944   *Coloquios y doctrina christiana con que los doce primeros frailes de San Francisco enviados por el papa Adriano Sexto y por el Emperador Carlos Quinto convirtieron a los indios de la Nueva España*, ed. Vargas Rea (Mexico City: Biblioteca Aportación Histórica).

1946   *Historia general de las cosas de Nueva España*, ed. Miguel Acosta Saignes. 3 vols. (Mexico City: Editorial Nueva España).

1949   "Coloquios y doctrina christiana." In *Sterbende Götter und christliche Heilsbotschaft*, ed. Walter Lehmann (Stuttgart).

1950
–69   *Florentine Codex, General History of the Things of New Spain*, ed. Arthur J. O. Anderson & Charles E. Dibble. 12 vols. (Santa Fe: School of American Research and University of Utah).

1954   "Arte adivinatoria," prologue, dedication, and chapter 1. See García Icazbalceta 1954:382–87.

References

1956 *Historia general de las cosas de Nueva España*, ed. Angel María Garibay K. 4 vols. (Mexico City: Editorial Porrúa).

1964 *Códices Matritenses de la Historia General de las Cosas de la Nueva España*, ed. Manuel Ballesteros Gaibrois. 2 vols. (Madrid: José Porrúa Turanzas).

SAN ANTONIO, JUAN DE

1732 *Bibliotheca universal franciscana*. 2 vols. (Madrid).
-33

SCHMIDT, WILHELM

1906 "Fray Bernardino de Sahagun O. Fn. M., Un breve compendio de los ritos ydolátricos que los yndios desta Nueva España usavan en el tiempo de su infidelidad," *Anthropos* 1:302-17.

SCHULTZE JENA, LEONHARD

1950 *Wahrsagerei, Himmelskunde und Kalender der alten Azteken*. Quellenwerke zur alten Geschichte Amerikas 4 (Stuttgart).

1952 *Gliederung des alt-aztekischen Volks in Familie, Stand und Beruf*. Quellenwerke zur alten Geschichte Amerikas 5 (Stuttgart).

1957 *Alt-aztekische Gesänge*. Quellenwerke zur alten Geschichte Amerikas 6 (Stuttgart).

SELER, EDUARD

1890 *L'orfèvrerie des anciens mexicains et leur art de travailler les pierres et de faire des ornements en plume* (Paris: Congrès International des Américanistes).

1902 *Gesammelte Abhandlungen zur Amerikanischen Sprach- und altertumskunde*.
-23 5 vols. (Berlin).

1908 "Costumes et attributs des divinités du Mexique, selon le P. Sahagún," *Jour-*
-09 *nal de la Société des Américanistes de Paris*, Nouvelle série: 5, 6.

1927 *Einige Kapitel aus dem Geschichtswerk des P. Sahagún* (Stuttgart).

SIMÉON, RÉMI

1885 *Dictionnaire de la langue nahuatl ou mexicaine* (Paris: Imprimerie Nationale).

———— AND D. JOURDANET

1880 *See* Sahagún 1880

SORIA, MARTIN

1959 *See* Kubler & Soria 1959

SOUSTELLE, JACQUES

1956 *La vida cotidiana de los aztecas en vísperas de la conquista* (Mexico City: Fondo de Cultura Económica).

SPENCE, LEWIS

1923 *The Gods of Mexico* (New York: Frederick A. Stokes).

STECK, FRANCISCO BORGIA

1944 *El Primer Colegio de América: Santa Cruz de Tlaltelolco* (Mexico City: Centro de Estudios Franciscanos).

1951 *Motolinía's History of the Indians of New Spain* (Washington, D.C.: American Franciscan History).

SUÁREZ DE PERALTA, JUAN

1878 *Noticias históricas de la Nueva España* (Madrid).

1949 *Tratado del descubrimiento de las Indias* (Mexico City: Secretaría de Educación Pública).

SULLIVAN, THELMA D.

1963 "Nahuatl Proverbs, Conundrums and Metaphors Collected by Sahagún," *Estudios de Cultura Náhuatl* 4:93–178.

1965 "A Prayer to Tlaloc," *Estudios de Cultura Náhuatl* 5:39–55.

1966 "Pregnancy, Childbirth and the Deification of the Women Who Died in Childbirth," *Estudios de Cultura Náhuatl* 6:63–96.

TEZOZÓMOC, FERNANDO ALVARADO

1944 *Crónica mexicana* (Mexico City: Editorial Leyenda).

THOMPSON, J. ERIC S.

1954 *The Rise and Fall of Maya Civilization* (Norman: University of Oklahoma Press).

TORO, ALFONSO

1924 "Importancia etnográfica y lingüística de las obras del padre fray Bernardino de Sahagún," *Anales del Museo Nacional de Arqueología, Historia y Etnografía*, Quarta Epoca 2:1–18.

TORQUEMADA, JUAN DE

1943 *Monarquía indiana.* 3 vols. Facsimile of 1723 edition (Mexico City: Editorial
–44   Salvador Chávez Hayhoe).

TOUSSAINT, MANUEL

1948 *Arte colonial en México* (Mexico City: Instituto de Investigaciones Estéticas, Universidad Nacional Autónoma de México).

1967 *Colonial Art in Mexico* (Austin: University of Texas Press).

TOVAR CALENDAR

See Kubler & Gibson 1951

TUDELA DE LA ORDEN

1948 "El códice mexicana postcortesiano del Museo de América de Madrid." In *Actes du XXXVIII Congrès Internationale des Américanistes*, pp. 549–56 (Paris).

VAILLANT, GEORGE C.

1960 *The Aztecs of Mexico* (Baltimore: Penguin Books).

VALERIANO, ANTONIO (?)

1961 *El Nican Mopohua.* Prologue by Enrique Torroella, S. J. (Mexico City: Buena Press).

VARGAS REA

1944 *See* Sahagún 1944

VÁSQUEZ VÁSQUEZ, ELENA

1965 *Distribución geográfica y organización de las órdenes religiosas en la Nueva España* (Mexico City: Instituto de Geografía, Universidad Nacional Autónoma de México).

VEYTIA, MARIANO

1944 *Historia antigua de Méjico* (Mexico).

VILLORO, LUIS

1950 *Los grandes momentos del indigenismo en México* (Mexico City: El Colegio de México).

References

VON GALL, AUGUST FREIHERR
1940   "Medizine Bücher (tici-amatl) der alten Azteken aus der ersten Zeit der Conquista," *Quellen und Studien zur Geschichte der Naturwissenschaften und der Medizine* 7(Nos. 4, 5):119–216.

WADDING, LUCAS
1906   *Biblioteca historico-bibliographica.* 4 vols. (Rome).

WILKERSON, S. JEFFREY K.
1971   "El Códice Tudela: una fuente etnográfica del siglo XVI," *Tlalocan* 6(No. 4):289–304.

ZURITA, ALONSO DE
1909   *Historia de la Nueva España*, Vol. 1. *Colección de libros y documentos referentes a la historia de América* (Madrid).

Index

275

Index

Index

Index

Index

Index

Index

Index

Saliva, 99, 222
Salt, 191
Saltpeter, 222
San Antonio, Juan de, 236
San Gabriel de Extremadura, 174, 178, 185
San Juan de Ulúa, 169
San Luis, Rodrigo de, 172, 174–76
San Sebastián, Pedro de, 166, 168–73, 175–76
Sanctions: Social, 32, 90; Supernatural, 121. *See also* Punishment
Santa Cruz, 64–65. *See also* Holy Cross, College of
Santiago, Pedro de, 208, 211
Santoral, 3, 227
Satan, 232
Schmidt, Wilhelm, 238
Scholasticism, 14, 44
Schultze Jena, Leonhard Sigismund, 12–13, 238, 253–54
Science. *See* Anthropology; Astronomy; Ethnography; Ethnology; Ethnoscience; Folklore; Geology; Linguistics; Mathematics; Medicine; Natural History; Taxonomy
Scribes, 7, 209, 226–27
Sculpture, 58, 99, 154
Secular clergy, 48–49
Seler, Eduard, 12, 237, 245
Seler-Sachs, Cecilia, 245
Sequera, Rodrigo de, 9, 184–85
Seraphic. *See* Franciscans
Serezeda, Pedro de, 22
Serf, 193
Sermones, 18
Sermonario, 3, 227
Sermons, 228, 230
Servant, 194
7 Flower. *See* Chiconxochitl
Seven Principal Sins, 29, 67
Seville, 153–54
Sex, 14, 43, 91, 124, 141, 216–17; Of speaker, 197–98. *See also* Adultery; Albur; Celibacy; Chastity; Concubinage; Homosexuality; Marriage; Prostitution; Virginity; Women
Shading, in art, 156–57, 163
Share-cropping, 194
Shaving, 138
Shell. *See* Conch

Shield, 47
Shortness of breath, 216
Sign, birth, 88, 96, 130–31
Sigüenza, 161
Siméon, Rémi, 66, 141, 237
Simón, Francisco, 208, 211
Singing, 91, 119, 161
Slaves, 92, 94, 140, 194. *See also* Tlacotin
Sluggishness, 206
Society. *See* Age; Class; Demography; Economics; Ethnicity; Kinship; Mobility; Politics; Religion; Sanctions; Sex; Status
Solís, Francisco de, 229
Sons, 91–92, 97, 102, 106, 122
Soria, Martín, 153
Soustelle, Jacques, 99
Spanish, 9, 208, 211–12; -ico suffix, 46; Idioms (*See* Discolo); Influence on art, 152; Influence on medicine, 214; Olmos's use of, 67, 73; Sahagún's use of, 7–8, 20, 119, 122, 142, 183, 226, 230, 246, 249
Speeches of the Elders. *See* Huehuetlatolli
Spence, Lewis, 42
Squash, 191
Star arrow, 135–36
State, 201
Status, social, 192
Steck, Francisco Borgia, 64
Stepfathers, 197
Stomach ache, 216
Stonecutting, 91, 158, 161, 163, 237
Stoning, death by, 44
Stools, 216, 221–22
Storehouse. *See* Petlacalco
Stuttering, 217
Style, 46, 59, 84–85, 98. *See also* Baroque decoration; Corinthian capitals; Decadence; Gothic architecture; Mudéjar; Nahuatl; Plateresque decoration; Renaissance; Tuscan capitals; Vulgarity
Suárez de Peralta, Juan, 235
Subsistence. *See* Cooking; Drink; Eating; Food
Succession, 91
Sulfates. *See* Copperas
Sullivan, Thelma, 12, 134, 239
Suma, 61–63, 70–72, 77
Sun, 135–36

Index